MOON RIVER AND ME

MOON RIVER AND ME

A MEMOIR

ANDY WILLIAMS

THORNDIKE
WINDSOR
PARAGON

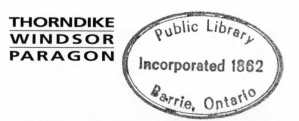

LIBRARY OF CONGRESS CATALOGING-IN-PUBLICATION DATA

Williams, Andy, 1930–
   Moon River and me : a memoir / By Andy Williams. — Large print ed.
     p. cm.
   ISBN-13: 978-1-4104-2057-2 (hardcover : alk. paper)
   ISBN-10: 1-4104-2057-4 (hardcover : alk. paper)
   1. Williams, Andy, 1930– 2. Singers — United States —
Biography. 3. Large type books. I. Title.
ML420.W542A3 2009b
782.42164092—dc22
   [B]
                                                        2009026114

BRITISH LIBRARY CATALOGUING-IN-PUBLICATION DATA AVAILABLE

Published in the U.S. in 2009 by arrangement with Viking, a member of Penguin Group (USA) Inc.

Published in the U.K. in 2010 by arrangement with The Orion Publishing Group Ltd.

U.K. Hardcover: 978 1 408 46024 5 (Windsor Large Print)

U.K. Softcover: 978 1 408 46025 2 (Paragon Large Print)

*I dedicate this book to my father,
Jay Emerson Williams,
who had the vision to see a future for me
as a singer, and the belief and the
relentless determination to make it happen.*

1

It was one of those sun-baked August days when, even at ten in the morning, the heat was rising in shimmering waves from the fields of ripening wheat and corn, making the water tank on the nearby hill waver like a desert mirage. The faintest breath of wind stirred the oak tree outside the window of a timeworn clapboard house perched on a cinder hill above the railroad tracks.

A woman, plump, dark-haired, and with a gentle smile, was at work in the kitchen, the air full of the enticing smell of baking bread. She was humming a tune to herself as she rolled out more dough, but she paused every couple of minutes, cocking her ear to listen. Then she heard it: the lonely distant whistle of a freight train. She dropped the rolling pin she was holding and took off her apron. She dusted the flour from her hands as she hurried out the door and down the hill toward the little station. The train was in sight now, slowing as it approached and trailing a plume of smoke against the cornflower blue of the sky.

The woman walked along the platform and past the tiny station building, its wooden walls plastered with sun-faded notices. She stopped at the side of the track by a timber frame with a projecting iron hook. As the train approached, a railman swung a canvas mailbag on an iron bar out of the mail car behind the engine. He looked up and blew a kiss to the woman. He was a handsome craggy-faced man in his early thirties wearing a railman's peaked cap stained by sweat and dust.

A cloud of steam billowed around her as the engine rumbled past, and there was a thud as the mailbag caught on the hook and swung there as the train moved on. The woman reached up and unhooked it, struggling a little with the weight as she lowered it to the ground. She stepped back and waited. There was a moment's pause, and then the sack began to wriggle and twist. An arm and then a tousled mop of hair appeared at the top of the sack, and a small boy fought his way out, emerging with the word "Surprise!"

Although we went through this ritual two or three times a week, my mom always managed a convincing look of surprise as I appeared. We both burst out laughing and turned to wave to my dad, still leaning out of the mail car and waving his hat as the train chugged on and rounded the bend. The plume of smoke and steam was still visible long after the train was lost to sight.

Hand in hand my mom and I walked back up the cinder hill to the house surrounded by the golden cornfields that stretched to the distant horizon under those vast midwestern skies.

I was born in that house on the hill on December 3, 1927, the youngest of four sons of Jay Emerson and Florence Williams. I was christened Howard Andrew Williams, but I was always known as Andy. I had three older brothers, Bob, Don, and Dick, and a sister, Janey, born the year after me. When I was six, my mom also gave birth to another child, Buddy.

My older brothers were contrasting characters. Bob was one of life's eternal pessimists, forever expecting the worst, and even when it didn't happen, he would soon convince himself that calamity had only been postponed, not averted. Don, the next oldest, was the polar opposite, a permanently sunny, optimistic character. No amount of obstacles or setbacks could wipe the smile from his face for long. Dick was the shy and sensitive one, happiest when off in a corner on his own, scribbling in a notebook or trying to compose a tune on our old and battered upright piano. I was shy, too, but hid it behind a veneer of cheek and self-confidence that only those who knew me really well could see through.

My mom's father, Andy Finley, also lived with us; I was named after him. In his working days he had driven "The Transfer," the horse-drawn bus that shuttled people between the Northwestern Railroad and the Illinois Central track a mile away on the other side of town. I remember him as a kindly figure with white hair and a thick white mustache. He died the morning after Buddy was born. As my mother said with a sigh, "I guess he just figured we needed the room."

We lived in Wall Lake in Sac County, Iowa, fifty miles northwest of Des Moines. It was one of those one-stoplight, one-horse midwestern towns that a motorist would pass through in the blink of an eye and probably not even notice, but if you were looking for a place that epitomized small-town America, Wall Lake would be as good as any. It was a great place to grow up. Everybody in town knew everybody else, and it was like living in a big extended family.

Despite its name, Wall Lake didn't have a lake of its own, but Blackhawk Lake was only a couple of miles to the west. Our one landmark was the steel water tower dominating the town, painted white and emblazoned with the words WALL LAKE in case anyone needed reminding about where he was. It looked down on a cluster of tree-shaded clapboard houses lining a handful of dusty streets. There were no paved roads in the town, just dirt and gravel, and none of the streets even had a name; it was that small a town. The population then was just 749, and that probably included the occupants of the cemetery. Small towns have their own way of keeping the population about the same year after year; every time a baby is born, someone leaves town.

We lived on the south side of Wall Lake, up the dirt road that ducked beneath a tangle of overhead telegraph wires and then a dogleg, left and right, before crossing the railroad tracks and climbing the hill. Across the road from our house was the hotel — the only one in town; it was built for railroad passengers in busier times and now struggled to survive — and next door to it were the café and the barber shop. Wall Lake was so small that even though we lived on the outskirts,

11

we were only half a block from the center of town. There was a standing joke that we were so desperate for entertainment, if word went around that someone was getting a shave or a haircut at the barbershop, we'd all turn out to watch.

Very little disturbed the sleepy calm of Wall Lake. The one thing that could be guaranteed to galvanize everyone into action was when a tornado roared through. They could appear at any time of year, but most came in May and June, usually in the late afternoon when the combination of heat and humidity seemed to trigger them. There was little advance warning. Sometimes the siren at the timber yard would wail, but most often it was just a sudden shout of "Twister!" yelled from one house to another.

Mom would drop whatever she was doing and holler to us to come running. Once I caught a brief glimpse of a dirt-black whirling column, like a charcoal smudge on paper, linking the earth and the bruised purple-gray of the sky, as it snaked through the cornfields toward us. Then Mom grabbed my arm, pulled me inside, and hustled us all down to the cellar. She paused on the top step to bolt the cellar door before following us down, as if this would somehow keep the tornado at bay. She didn't switch on the electric light down there, and we sat in near total darkness, broken only by the feeble daylight seeping through chinks in the wooden shutters that covered the coal chute.

As we waited for the twister to pass, I was a little frightened but excited, too, feeling the same electricity in the air that you get just before a summer storm. We sat in a row on the cold flagstone floor, our backs against the stack of logs for the stove and facing a wall lined with shelves of bottles and jars of preserves that began to clink against one another as the tornado winds started to shake the house.

The noise of the wind increased to a scream, banging the storm shutters and battering the walls, while debris hit the roof shingles with a machine-gun rattle. The tornado passed so close to the house that I heard a tortured squeal as a branch was torn from the oak tree outside. I kept my eyes tightly shut, dug my nails into my palms, and bit my lip to stop myself from crying out in fright.

Even when all was silent again, my mom made us wait a while longer and then went upstairs alone to check that we still had a roof and that the twister wasn't doubling back in its tracks. By the time we were allowed back upstairs, all fear was forgotten and our eyes were shining with excitement.

We rushed outside to trace the track of the tornado by the trail of flattened corn and damaged trees and buildings. Mom sent us to check that our neighbors were okay, and later we straggled back and held the ladder for Dad while he began repairing the storm damage and replacing the missing shingles.

Our house was Mom's family home, where she had been born and raised. It was built of white-painted clapboard and had a shingle roof and a covered stoop where we'd sit on hot days and warm summer evenings, shaded by a roof supported by three white pillars. The house was a plain, old-fashioned building; at first we didn't even have an inside bathroom, just an outhouse — a three-holer — a fifty-yard walk down the field toward the railroad siding where the steam trains took on water. It was called "The Y," I suppose because the railroad tracks formed that shape there. Whenever we needed to go to the outhouse, we'd say, "I'm just going to the Y." Even after we had an inside bathroom installed, my grandfather refused to have anything to do with such newfangled inventions, and in all kinds of weather he set off for the three-holer down the field with a determined expression on his face and an old newspaper in his hand.

There was a wood-burning cook stove in

the kitchen and an icebox on the shaded north-facing side of the house. There was no refrigeration then, and the icebox had to be refilled daily with a block of ice cut in winter from the frozen Blackhawk Lake and stored in a room off the main cellar, insulated by straw bales, for summer use. There was a parlor with a cedar chest, a couch, and two pictures on the wall — the only ones we had — but like a lot of families, the parlor was kept for "company," and we rarely used it. Family life centered in the kitchen.

We had a couple of acres of land where we kept a cow, two pigs, and a few chickens, and grew vegetables and a little corn to augment the family diet. When we got home from school, we'd do our chores and feed the animals. Then we'd play for hours on the rope swing hanging from the oak tree, play baseball in the field down the hill, using cow dung for bases, hunt for frogs in the ditch, or go fishing for catfish, croppies, walleyes, and bluegills in Blackhawk Lake.

On Sunday mornings we and everyone else in town would dress in our Sunday-best clothes and walk to church. There were several in town, but we attended the Presbyterian church on the main street, a white-painted clapboard building with the entrance reached by a flight of steps from the street. On hot summer days we would sometimes climb the stairs to the balcony in the tower, where we'd sit and talk after the service, cooled by the faint breeze.

We were an old-fashioned family: Dad went out to work, earned the money, and made the decisions, and Mom supported him in whatever he wanted to do. The only time I can recall her defying him was when she wanted to join the Eastern Star in Wall Lake, an organization for women whose husbands or fathers were Freemasons. When she told my dad, he just said, "You can forget about that, because I'm never going to be a Mason," but Grandpa Finley was listening to the conversation and said, "Well, we'll soon fix that," and went off and became a Mason so that his daughter could get her wish. She joined soon afterward, and a couple of years later she was installed as Worthy Matron of the Eastern Star, the leader of the organization. The Williams brothers sang "That Wonderful Mother of Mine" to her at the ceremony. I was five or six years old, and it was the first time we sang together in public. Perhaps that was the moment the thought first formed in my dad's mind that we could become professional singers. After we finished our number, our little sister, Janey, just two years old, toddled up to Mom with a basket of roses. It would have taken a far harder-hearted person than my mother not to cry after all that.

The monthly meetings of the Eastern Star were almost her only recreation. Otherwise she stayed home, cooked, cleaned, and raised the family, and she worked incredibly hard. In addition to her other chores, she milked the cow, collected the eggs, cold-packed meat, and canned fruit to see us through the winter. We had a bath every night, and despite our protests, she would scrub us with soap and a coarse flannel until we glowed. No children in Wall Lake were as well turned out as the Williams boys. Every night before she went to bed, Mom would line up five chairs — one each for her husband and sons — and put a washed, starched, and pressed shirt, neatly pressed trousers, clean socks, and polished shoes on each one. That was thirty-five shirts to wash, starch, and iron every week, and everything had to be done by hand, because there was no washing machine and no such thing as drip-dry shirts back then.

Mom and Dad had been sweethearts from the age of thirteen, and they were a loving and affectionate couple, always holding hands as they strolled down the hill into town together. I still treasure a picture of them when they were courting: My dad was decked out in a rented white tie and tails, with his dark hair slicked down, and my mom was beautiful in a borrowed ball gown and with a smile that was gentle, warm, and kind — all the qualities I knew and loved in her. My dad was also friendly and open, and popular with his neighbors, but if you studied the man captured in the family photographs, you'd also detect a touch of steel in his gaze and a faraway look, as if his eye was always fixed on some distant horizon.

My dad never spent money on himself; every spare cent he had was for his wife and family. One year I remember my brother Dick and I saving the few cents we earned from doing odd jobs and running errands for our neighbors to buy Dad a birthday present: a tiepin with a space where you could slide in the initials of the person who would be wearing it. It was such a secret that we didn't even tell Mom about it, and on the morning of his birthday we proudly presented Jay Emerson Williams with his new tiepin, complete with his initials in big, bold letters. My dad looked at it in silence for a few minutes. "Boys, it's lovely," he said, "and thank you so much for this present. However, I don't know how folks in Wall Lake are going to take my wearing a pin on my tie that says 'JEW' on it." I never did see him wear it.

My dad worked two or three jobs to support his family. In the evenings and weekends he sold insurance to try to bring in a little extra money. By day he was a mail clerk employed by the railroad company to sort the mail on the train and swing the sacks out at the little stations on the winding line that ran from Sioux City and Omaha all the way to Des Moines and Chicago. At each one the driver would slow the train to ten miles an hour or so, and when the mailbag had been dropped off, he'd give two blasts on the train whistle to signal the local postmaster that the mail was ready for collection. Because he worked on the mails for the railroad, Dad was given a telephone, the first one in Wall Lake, and I can still remember the wild excitement the first time it rang.

It wasn't quite the telephone system we have today. Everything went through an operator; ours was Myrna Winkelman. Nobody had a phone number; you just asked for the person by name, and Myrna put you through and then listened in herself. As a result, she was the source of all knowledge about what was going on in town. If you wanted to know where anyone was, you just asked Myrna, but you had to do so before nine in the eve-

19

ning when she finished work and the phone system shut down for the night. After that you were only allowed to make a call if there was a real emergency, such as a fire.

I grew up in the hungry 1930s when the Great Depression threw millions out of work, and overfarming, overgrazing, and a seven-year drought turned land to dust from Texas to the Canadian border. I can remember days when the wind blowing from the south carried a fog of choking black dust that blotted out the sun and left us gasping for breath. It settled on every surface and drifted like snow against walls and fences. There were two early summer days when it never got light as an endless dust storm raged around us, and over the next few days we heard on the radio that the winds had carried it right across the country, blanketing even the streets of Chicago, New York, Washington, D.C., and Boston with black dust.

With their crops dead, their soil stripped away, and their land worthless, millions of dispossessed farmers and sharecroppers abandoned their homes and began a long hungry trek in search of work. Even in Wall Lake we saw rickety trucks passing through, piled with the possessions of gaunt families in threadbare clothes. Every night Dad came home with tales of hobos dodging the railroad "bulls" in the freight yards and riding the boxcars from one coast to the other, seeking work or a new beginning.

Hollow-eyed figures also haunted the highways around us, some making for Des Moines and Chicago, others with their faces set to the west, heading for California. Their shoes — when they had any — were falling apart, and their clothes were so dust gray that they seemed to merge with the earth as they trudged slowly on. I can remember peeping from behind the shutters as they slowly shuffled past; it was like watching a parade of ghosts.

We were luckier than many in those long, hard years, but although we never were short of food, we were perennially short of money, and there was very rarely any to spare for new clothes. Mine were all hand-me-downs, but if our clothes were sometimes worn and threadbare, Mom made sure they were always clean. Any missing buttons were always replaced at once, and holes and tears were darned.

Our house in Wall Lake was always filled with music. Mom had the radio on from morning to night, tuned to a country music station, and she sang along as she did the washing, cooking, and ironing. I would

21

often join in with her in my piping little treble voice. One of my earliest memories was of sitting on the kitchen floor, nibbling on a just-baked cookie, and clapping my hands as Mom sang a country tune and did a little dance just to make me laugh.

Dad was also very musical; he had learned to play half a dozen instruments at school and had a good singing voice. In those pre-television days our entertainment was homegrown: sitting around the piano in the evenings and singing together. When I was little, I'd stretch out on the worn, warm floorboards with my head under the piano stool and watch my father's feet on the pedals; for some reason that fascinated me. Our standard repertory was hymns, because my parents and my two older brothers formed the Presbyterian church choir; it had not even had one until Dad volunteered himself and his family. They rehearsed at home, and when Dick saw his mom, dad, and older brothers singing, he wanted to join in.

I didn't want to be left out, either, and tried to sing along with them as they practiced. At first I got black looks and demands to "hush up, Andy. We're trying to practice here." I'd let my shoulders sag and my head hang, stick out my bottom lip, and make my slow, mournful exit from the room, hoping that my dad would call me back and let me take part. It didn't happen, but the next day I'd be back, singing along until I got kicked out again. I used to vary my tactics. Sometimes I'd join in from the start and keep going until I was told to hush up; other times I'd sit silent in a corner while they sang the first couple of hymns, and then I'd join in, singing as quietly as possible. If any of my brothers cast an eye in my direction, I'd snap my mouth shut tight as a clam and put on a look of injured innocence.

Finally, when I was seven, I wore my dad down. He interrupted choir practice and said, "Andy, sing this verse on your own for me." When I had finished, my dad — never lavish with praise in case we got swelled-headed — just grunted, gave a brief nod, and then said, "All right, why don't you come and sit over here and practice with us?" From then on I was a full-fledged choir member.

The very first time he heard his four sons harmonize together, my dad became a man with a dream and a mission in life, convinced that we had a future as professional singers. The Williams Brothers were formed on the spot with my dad as manager, impresario, agent, PR man, and factotum. From that moment on, just like the main character in *Death of a Salesman,* my dad — the Willy

Loman of Wall Lake — fulfilled his dreams through us.

We all loved singing at home, in school, at church, or anywhere, and Dad encouraged, trained, and nurtured us, forever pushing us to practice harder and longer. He wasn't really a clichéd, pushy "showbiz" parent, but I think he genuinely believed that singing might be a passport for us out of Wall Lake, Iowa, getting us out of the rut and giving us the chance to improve our lives in a manner that would never be open to us if we stayed where we were. And he was very cunning in some of the ways he went about keeping us in line with his vision.

Although Dad was our driving force, his idea of the right way to get us motivated had lasting effects. Time and again he would tell us, "You have to practice harder, because you're not as good as the others out there." It wouldn't have been so bad if he had said, "Come on. You're not as good as you think you are. You have the talent, but you still have to put in the work." The way he phrased it was a real body blow to our self-assurance. Whether as a result of this or not, my oldest brother, Bob, always had a negative outlook and never thought we were talented enough to perform professionally, and perhaps because I was the youngest, my

24

dad's comments seemed to affect me even more than the others. I really took them to heart. I don't hold this against my dad — he was doing what he thought was best — but it crippled my self-confidence. I worked as hard as I could, but I still didn't think I was good enough, and even now, seventy years later, despite all the success that has come my way, I still think I have to work harder because I'm not as good as the others out there.

I felt very proud the first Sunday that I followed my parents and brothers up onto the platform in the church as a member of the choir, even if it was composed only of members of my family. As I looked up, for the first time in my life I found myself facing an audience — the congregation — but they were people I had known all my life. The familiarity of the setting and the faces looking up at me meant that I didn't really feel any nerves at all. At the end of the service my dad gave me another of those curt nods of approval: I had passed the test.

The Williams Brothers' first professional performances were also pretty low-key. We sang at a church social and then at an Iowa Farmers' Association picnic, and didn't get paid for either of them. Our first paycheck came when we sang at the wedding of the daughter of one of the neighboring farmers. After we had serenaded her with "The Belle of the Ball" and "If You Were the Only Girl in the World," her father, teetering between smiles and tears as he gazed at his only daughter in her white wedding dress, allowed his emotions to overcome his normal prudence and pressed a $10 bill into Bob's hand, saying, "Here. Share this with your brothers."

My share turned out to be $1, which didn't seem a very fair division of the spoils to me, but since Bob was ten years older and very much stronger, it was pretty much take it or leave it, so I took it. It would be nice to think that the first dollar bill I ever earned was framed and hung on the wall as an inspiration, but in fact I spent it on sodas and candy in the café before I got home that afternoon.

One day in the spring of 1936 the sleepy familiar rhythm of our lives was broken when Dad announced that we had outgrown Wall Lake, and if we were ever going to amount to anything as professional singers, we had to move. He had applied to the railroad for a transfer to a new job in the big city, Des Moines, and he was certain we would soon be singing on the radio station there. Bob heard Dad out in silence and then said, "Are you out of your mind? We're not good enough to sing on the radio. It'll be a disaster."

Dad just told him, "You wait and see."

A week later I said a tearful good-bye to my school classmates and friends in Wall Lake. My best friend, George, the son of the hotel owner, came over to the house just before we left. "You will come back sometimes, won't you, Andy?" he said, his eyes shining with tears.

I was too choked to speak, and Mom answered for me: "Of course he will, George. You know Des Moines really isn't so far away."

After George had gone, a forlorn little figure trudging back across the dirt road, I took a last look around the house. I wanted to capture in my mind's eye a snapshot that I could always recall, but the furniture, our possessions, and our precious piano had been loaded onto a truck earlier that morning. Without them the house already seemed remote from me, a cold and empty shell, not the warm and happy home I had known.

Dad and Bob carried the battered family trunk between them while the rest of us straggled down the hill behind them, carrying a ramshackle collection of bags and boxes. We crossed the railroad tracks and lined up on the platform as the train that would take us to Des Moines rounded the shoulder of the hill. In my misery the train whistle sounded even more plaintive and desolate than usual.

We boarded the train, and as it pulled away from the platform, Dick and I pressed against the window for our last view of the little wooden house on the hill, the only home we had ever known. Then smoke and steam swirled around the railcar, and by the time it had cleared, our house and Wall Lake were lost to sight. It would be many years before I would see them again.

2

After the calm of Wall Lake, where more than one automobile an hour was considered a traffic jam, the noise and bustle of downtown Des Moines took some getting used to. I remember my first night in our new house in this strange city, lying awake listening to the hum of passing traffic and the clank and rattle of trains shunting boxcars in the railroad freight yards.

At first we lived in a rented house on Bratleboro Street, right across the road from Elmwood Elementary School, which Janey and I attended, and where I played the bass drum in the school band. We weren't living in the most fashionable part of town. When I went back to take a nostalgic look at the house on Bratleboro many years later, its windows had all been smashed and boarded up, and it looked as if it was being used as a drug den.

As soon as we arrived in Des Moines, Dad

— using a mixture of charm, bluster, and sheer dogged determination — talked his way into the manager's office at the largest radio station in the state — WHO, the Radio Voice of the Middle West — and arranged an audition for his sons. That wasn't an unusual way to try out for the radio in those days. There was no network of talent scouts, and it wasn't unheard of for unknowns to walk off the street and into the studio.

I was just eight years old, and when I first saw the imposing building with the station's WHO logo emblazoned on a huge neon sign, I was so frightened I could hardly speak, let alone sing. My brothers were just as terrified. Don said he thought he was going to turn to stone. Our nerves weren't helped by the knowledge that WHO had some big stars on its roster. We overlapped with Ronald Reagan, who was a sports reporter known as "Dutch" Reagan at WHO from 1933 to 1937 before going to Hollywood and making it in the movies. He spent most of his working days at WHO sitting in a tiny recording booth with a ticker tape and a baseball bat. At that time live commentaries of major-league baseball games were not allowed outside the clubs' home areas, and radio WHO, which wanted to broadcast the Chicago Cubs' games, had to use a little ingenuity to get around that rule. The ticker tape gave a running, pitch-by-pitch report on the big baseball game of the day, and Reagan would use it to do a commentary, complete with sound effects, as if he were really at the game. Over a recording of crowd noise he would say, "Here comes the pitch!" and then knock the bat on the edge of the desk to make it sound as if the batter hit it, or he would slap it into his hand next to the microphone as if the catcher had taken it. Then he'd shout, "Ball one!" or "Strike one!"

His most famous commentary feat, performed in 1934, was still being talked about at WHO when we arrived three years later. The wire went dead during a Cubs-versus-Cardinals game, leaving him with zero information for his commentary. As Reagan later related, "I had a ball on the way to the plate, and there was no way to call it back. There were several other stations broadcasting that game, and I knew I'd lose my audience if I told them we'd lost our telegraph connections, so I took a chance. I had [Billy] Jurges hit another foul. Then I had him foul one that only missed being a home run by a foot. I had him foul one back in the stands and took up some time describing the two lads that got in a fight over the ball. I kept

31

on having him foul balls until I was setting a record for a ballplayer hitting successive foul balls, and I was getting more than a little scared. Just then my operator started typing. When he passed me the paper, I started to giggle. It said 'Jurges popped out on the first ball pitched.'"

Our audition felt almost as nerve-racking as that and was made even more daunting because it was held in the studio, large enough to accommodate a small orchestra, from which the station's music and variety shows were broadcast. Only one light was switched on, leaving half the studio in darkness, and it smelled of stale sweat and cigarette smoke, making me feel even more out of place. I had never even seen a microphone before, let alone sung into one, and everything from the "deadness" of the soundproofed studio to the glass sound booth, to the impassive faces of the station manager, sound engineer, and secretary who had come in to watch was strange and a little daunting to me.

My brothers were equally ill at ease — as nervous as long-tailed cats in a room full of rockers, as they used to say in Wall Lake — and our nerves meant that we didn't perform as well as we could have. When we finished, there was a lengthy pause while the station manager, chomping on a wad of gum as slowly and rhythmically as a cow chewing its cud, deliberated for a few long minutes and then pronounced his verdict: "Your boys have got talent, Mr. Williams," he said, "no doubt about that, but they haven't got enough experience yet. Get them singing anywhere you can, whether it's for money or not, just to get some more experience. Then come back and see us again in six months' time, and I think we'll have something for you."

Dad couldn't hide his disappointment, but that only served to make him even more determined that next time nothing was going to stop us. For the next six months we rehearsed every day — before school, after school, in the evenings, and on weekends. Dad kept us rehearsing for up to six hours a day, and since we also spent six hours in school, pretty much the entire day was used up without doing anything else. Tired though he was, as soon as Dad came home from work, the first thing he did was sit down at the piano and say to us, "Right, boys, let's get started," and we'd get to work rehearsing the songs in our existing repertoire and trying out new ones and fresh arrangements.

Aunt Cornelia was already living in Des Moines when we moved there, and she took it upon herself to teach all of us to play the piano, but she was so kindhearted that she'd practically give us a gold star just for turning up. Without my father there to crack the whip, none of us practiced hard enough, though in later years Dick did become a very good pianist.

Dad also entered Dick and me in a talent competition on another radio station, KRNT. The first prize was a Silver King bicycle. Chromed and gleaming, it had been placed in the front window of the radio station to catch the eyes of passersby and promote the contest. Before we went in to take part, Dick and I spent long minutes with our noses pressed against the glass, taking in every detail of that beautiful bike. There were about a dozen other kids, mostly singers but also a poet, a guy who played the accordion, and, bizarrely, a ventriloquist, and a tap dancer. Dick and I were on next to last and sang "That Wonderful Mother of Mine." When the last act had finished, the three judges — the continuity announcer, the station manager, and the local Silver King salesman — put their heads together and then, after a tinny roll on a snare drum, the announcer read the results in reverse order. I didn't think we'd win and was only half-listening, gloomily imagining someone else riding off on that beautiful bicycle, when Dick's elbow hit me in the ribs. "We won! We won!"

We had to sing our winning song once more and were then presented with the bicycle. It was one of the most exciting moments of my life. We rode it home in triumph, squabbling every fifty yards over whose turn it was to get on, and we practically came to blows over who should be the one to ride it into our yard. In the end Dick solved that problem by stomping on the pedals and shooting off up the hill and in through our gate while I ran after him, red-faced and cursing.

As well as the constant rehearsals, we also sang at any venue that would have us, but one of our first professional engagements as a singing group in Des Moines was one we all wished had never been necessary. The fifth Williams brother, Buddy, was born the year before we left Wall Lake. Six years younger than me, he had blond curly hair and a very sweet nature, and he loved to hear us sing. But he was afflicted with spinal meningitis and had great difficulty walking.

He was already ill when we moved to Des Moines, and he deteriorated rapidly after that. Within a few months he was bedridden. Mom and Dad tried to hide the seriousness of Buddy's illness from us, but they couldn't disguise the somber face of the doctor when he visited, the looks that they exchanged, the tears that Mom hurriedly tried to wipe away when I walked into the room, and the muffled sobs I heard coming from their room late at night. Buddy's little face grew thinner and paler as the weeks went by, but whatever pain he was feeling, he never failed to greet us with a smile. When we sang for him, he would gurgle and laugh and bang his hand on the bedclothes in rhythm with the song.

One cold autumn day I came home from school to find the curtains drawn although it was still daylight outside. There seemed to be an unnatural stillness in the house, and I think I knew even before I saw my mother's face that Buddy was dying. When I went into his room, Mom and Dad were sitting at either side of the bed. Buddy lay between them, his eyes closed and his wasted little face the color of wax. His breathing was slow, wheezing, and irregular. I sat next to my mother and took her hand. She gave my hand an answering squeeze, but her eyes never left Buddy's face. One by one, Bob, Don, Dick, and Janey came in and sat down quietly, and together in silence Buddy's family watched his life ebb away. He died around nine o'clock that evening, still only two years old.

Nothing is bleaker than a child's funeral.

The day suited the occasion: raw and damp, with a biting wind blowing from the north. As the tiny casket was lowered into the wet black Iowa earth, it seemed ridiculously small, a cruel joke. How could Buddy's life, his heart, his brave smile, and his unquench-able spirit be contained by that pathetic little wooden box?

We stood in a row alongside the grave. Mom, eyes red-rimmed and with purple shadows beneath them revealing how little she had slept, leaned heavily on Dad's arm as the minister said the prayers. I felt a burning and entirely unreasonable resent-ment that this man, who had never even met Buddy, should be the last person to bid him farewell. Then, led by Mom and Dad, each of us in turn picked a small handful of earth from the mound at the graveside and tried to sprinkle it on that tiny casket, but each one fell as a lump on the wooden lid with a dull thud like a closing door.

Buddy's name was barely mentioned in our house for years after his death — the wounds were still too raw — but he was far from forgotten. I'd see Mom suddenly go still and silent, her expression masked, and I'd know that she was thinking of him. Dad would look up from his newspaper and then take her hand. They would sit in silence, staring into space, Mom's knuckles white as she gripped Dad's hand, like a shipwreck survivor clinging to a life raft. I don't think there was ever a day in the rest of her life when she didn't think of her lost son.

The loss of Buddy was tragic enough, but the cost of his funeral was more than we could afford. The surviving Williams brothers had to sing hymns in the funeral parlor in Des Moines every day after school and all day on Saturdays for weeks to pay off the debt my parents had incurred to give my little brother a decent burial. As the mourners filed in at the pillared entrance of the building, we would run around to the side entrance; then, hidden by a curtain, sang hymns for a succession of funerals. It was heartbreaking to see those endless lines of flower-laden caskets and mourners and to listen to the sobs of the grieving people, but, even worse, they were a daily reminder of our own recent and still painful loss. I have never liked singing at funerals since then and have only done so once.

Looking back, I find it hard to believe that there was not something else we could have done, some other way to earn the money to pay the debt, that would not have forced us to relive the same cycle of events, funeral after funeral, day after day. For everyone else at my school, the bell ringing to signal the end of the last lesson was the best moment of their day, but for the Williams brothers it was the worst, like a factory siren calling us to the work we hated. As my classmates whooped and hollered and ran off down the road, we began the slow walk, feet dragging, to the funeral parlor. I dreaded Saturdays in particular. The day seemed never-ending, and it felt as if we were being punished by some vengeful Old Testament God for allowing Buddy to die. On many of those awful Saturdays, listening to the sobs of the relatives of the dead on the other side of the curtains, I shed fresh tears of my own and then later cried myself to sleep in my bed.

We eventually sang our last hymn at the funeral parlor and cleared the family debt, but we were still so short of money that Mom and Dad took in lodgers to help pay the rent. The first two were work colleagues of Dad's, and a couple of basketball players from Drake University also lived with us for a while. Even with the rent they paid, there was still no money for luxuries such as new clothes, but when our old patched clothes or shoes had finally worn out and new ones became essential, Dad proved that even if he was short of money, he could be a shrewd negotiator. As Aunt Cornelia often remarked, he was always inventive: "If he couldn't go through the door, he'd go through the window instead."

One day he took us all to the Florsheim shoe store. He waited until we were all sitting in a row, each with a new pair of shoes on our feet, and then turned to the store owner and said, "Now, I really can't afford to buy these shoes, so what sort of deal can you do for me?" On this and on several other occasions he managed to barter an appearance by us to sing at a store or a local sales convention in exchange for the goods. He even paid off a long-overdue milk bill by persuading the milk company to have us sing at their annual picnic for their employees.

This time, as I sat in the shoe store listening to Dad haggling with the owner, I caught the eye of one of the other customers, a middle-aged woman who was looking at us with a mixture of pity and scorn. I dropped my gaze at once, blushing crimson to the roots of my hair. I felt embarrassed and ashamed that we should have to wheel and deal and practically beg to put clothes on our backs and food on the table, and I even resented my dad for putting us in that position.

Later, when I confided something of that feeling to Mom, she came as close as she ever came to hitting me. She shouted at me and dragged me into the hall, but then took a deep breath and said, "Listen, Andy, I know it's hard; it's hard for all of us. But don't you know that there's nothing we'd like more than to buy you the best clothes and shoes and everything else? But we just don't have the money. That's not your father's fault. God knows he works hard enough to try to make ends meet. And don't you think that he feels humiliated that he doesn't have the money and has to wheedle a deal out of a store owner who's probably down on his luck himself? It's not weakness that makes Dad bargain and horse-trade for what we need. It's a sign of his love for all of us that he's willing to do whatever it takes to ensure that his family is fed and clothed." She left me alone to think it over, and a few minutes later, ashamed of myself, I went back downstairs and gave Mom and Dad a hug and mumbled an apology.

We kept singing at any venue that would have us — church socials, weddings, parties, and picnics — and six months after our first audition, Dad marched us back into WHO, where we again sang for the producer and the station manager. When we had finished, there was a hurried consultation between them, and then the station manager, all smiles, told us that we were hired. "We're going to give you a fifteen-minute show every weekday morning," he said, "but you'll start Saturday with the Iowa Barn Dance Frolic. It goes out at seven in the evening, but be at the Shrine Auditorium at nine o'clock sharp for rehearsal."

We sat in reception drinking sodas — a treat in itself because we had been so short of money that trips to a drugstore, café, or diner were out of the question — while Dad thrashed out the details of our contract. I'll never forget the expression on his face as he turned to look at us, holding up the document that he had just signed on our behalf. His smile was broad enough to embrace everything: his pride in us and in himself for having the vision to see a different future for his boys, and the wit, grit, and determination to make it begin to happen. He had already achieved more than any of his family and friends had ever believed possible, but the look in his eyes said that while this was a moment to savor, it was not the endpoint; it was merely the first stop on a very long road.

Looking back now, I wonder if the pleasure I felt then was because of our success, or because I was witnessing my dad's joy at his vindication. There had been one or two in Wall Lake who thought that Jay Williams was getting a mite uppity and mocked his grandiose ideas about what his boys might achieve. They would not be sniggering into their sleeves now. We hurried home to tell Mom the news. She promptly burst into tears and then cried again when Dad produced the new hat he had bought for her on the way home, on the strength of the money that we would soon be earning. It was a token of the good times that were at last just around the corner.

The following Saturday morning we were wakened at six o'clock. We bolted our breakfast and hurried off to get ready for our first-ever radio program. The Shrine Auditorium, a huge building with twin copper domes on the corner of Tenth and Pleasant streets, had been built twenty years before. It was the biggest theater in the Midwest, seating over four thousand people. When I saw the size of the building, I felt a wave of panic. I tried to fight it down, telling myself that this was what we did all the time. It just happened that this time there would be a microphone, a live audience of a few thousand, and a radio audience of a million people. But that line of reasoning did me no good at all. I felt a bead of sweat trickling down my forehead and avoided catching my brothers' eyes. If they were as nervous as I was, we were doomed.

The auditorium was huge; the stalls seemed to go on forever, and there was a sweeping semicircular balcony above them. Prior to that moment I had never sung in any auditorium larger than the Presbyterian church in Wall Lake and the funeral parlor in Des Moines, and if ever there was a space guaranteed to give a nervous performer palpitations, this huge arena was it. The theater was packed to the rafters for the Iowa Barn Dance Frolic every Saturday night, and a radio audience also tuned in to hear the show's trademark mixture of old-fashioned popular songs, barbershop singing, novelty tunes, and country and hillbilly music. The show was almost as famous and as popular as the Grand Ole Opry from Nashville, but at nine in the morning our audience was smaller: a producer, an announcer, a pianist, and a couple of dozen elderly people who looked as if they had come in only to get warm. Gazing around the empty, echoing space, I could understand why some vaudeville performers had christened the Shrine "Death Moines."

We gave our music to the station's resident pianist, a frail-looking white-haired man

44

who gave piano lessons in his spare time, and then ran through our songs a couple of times. We had already rehearsed them at home so often that we could have sung them backward. The producer gave us a wink. "That's fine, boys," he said. "Be back here at six o'clock sharp, y'hear?" We had the rest of the day off, but I spent it in a state of steadily mounting panic. By six that evening, as we walked back to the Shrine, I was barely capable of speech, let alone song. The atmosphere inside was very different from the funereal silence of the morning rehearsal. The seats were all filled, and the place was buzzing. My nerves eased a fraction — the sheer electricity of the atmosphere was contagious — but it was still the scariest experience I'd ever had.

We stood backstage, exchanging nervous looks as the second hand of the clock ticked toward seven. Then the ON AIR light came on, and after the announcer read the sponsor's message, he introduced the hostess, an aging "sweetheart of the rodeo" in a rhinestone-studded top. Even offstage the sound of the applause and cheering was deafening. After the opening numbers, I heard these words through a mist of sheer panic: "Now, folks, we have a real special treat for you this evening — a bunch of boys all the way from

45

Wall Lake, Iowa, who are going to be singing for you this and every week on the Iowa Barn Dance Frolic. Ladies and gentlemen, boys and girls, here they are: the Williams Brothers Quartet." The band played a four-bar introduction, and we began to sing.

To my relief I found that my voice did not come out in a strangulated squeak, and within a few seconds I began to relax. It was all right. I could do this. I didn't like it, but I could do it. The applause at the end of the first song was warm and generous, and I relaxed even more as we did our second and then our last song. We then took our bows and hurried offstage, high as kites on a potent cocktail of adrenaline and sheer relief. Mom, Dad, and Janey were waiting in the wings. Mom hugged us, tears in her eyes, but Dad just gave us another of those curt nods of approval. "Not bad," he said, "not bad at all. But it could have been a lot better still." He did take us for a soda and an ice cream on the way home, suggesting to us that behind his stern exterior he was really bursting with pride.

We had Sunday off — apart from yet more rehearsals with Dad — and then on Monday morning hurried down to the WHO studios for the first of the fifteen-minute shows we would be doing every weekday. Only the producer, the announcer, and the same pianist were there (the accompanist already seemed like an old friend), and after the gut-wrenching tension of our first appearance at the Shrine, this show in a deserted studio was a breeze. We performed five songs, each one more drenched in sentiment than the last, ending with a hymn. Then it was over, and we were out in the cool air of the morning.

For the next four years the Williams Brothers Quartet appeared on the Iowa Barn Dance Frolic, live from the Shrine Auditorium, every Saturday night, and we also had our fifteen-minute show every weekday morning, always ending with a hymn. We were on-air from 8:00 to 8:15, and as soon as we had sung the last note, we hurried out of the studio. Bob had finished school just before we left Wall Lake — Dad said he was only waiting for him to graduate before moving — and he went off to his first job, as a masseur at the Des Moines YMCA. That occupation might cause a raised eyebrow or a knowing smile these days, but in those innocent times it was just a job.

While Bob went to work, Don, Dick, and I went to school. We had a special dispensation from the principal to turn up late every morning; the other kids had to be in school by 8:30, while we didn't arrive until 9:00. If that and our appearances on the radio bred a little resentment and envy among some of our schoolmates and got me in a few fights, it also brought admiring glances from some of the girls — and I'd have willingly swapped a few bruises for that. Not that there was much time for dating. Every night we spent a couple of hours rehearsing the songs we were going to sing the next day, and any homework or social activities had to be fitted in around that. We also sang hymns on another program on Sunday mornings and appeared as guests on a few other shows.

My schoolwork undoubtedly suffered because of the time I spent practicing and performing — a lot of the comments on my school report cards were of the "could do better" variety — but if my grades weren't the highest in the class, they weren't the worst, either. In any case the path Jay Williams had mapped out for his sons did not allow for irrelevant diversions such as a college education.

Dad decided that I had the best voice among us, so I sang the solos. We always did a lot of sentimental stuff, especially songs about mothers. Dad used to say in his more cynical moments, "If Jesus doesn't get them, Mother always will." I probably knew more "mother songs" than anybody alive. I sang hundreds of them, so many that in the end we ran out of new ones to sing.

As well as our radio show, we began to sing at other events. Dad got us a booking at the Elks Club in Des Moines, and we also appeared at summer fairs and private parties. I still remember being taken to sing "That Wonderful Mother of Mine" at a luncheon one day. When I had finished, one of the ladies at the party came over and said, "That was wonderful. Don't you just love to sing?"

I forced a smile and said, "Oh, yes, I love it," but the truth was that although I loved singing with my family around the piano at home, I hated appearing in public alone; it was that lack of self-confidence once more. I knew I could sing, but so could lots of other people. Average-looking, average-sounding, and more than averagely shy, I didn't think I was special in any way at all.

The Williams Brothers had become minor local celebrities in Des Moines — medium-sized fish in a fairly small pond — and I'd be lying if I said I didn't enjoy that. Given the material we were singing, though, most of our fans were women of a certain age rather than the teenage girls I had secretly dreamed would be hanging on my every word. Des

Moines was now almost as familiar to me as Wall Lake had been, but we were not destined to remain in our Iowa comfort zone for long because Dad was never going to be satisfied with that. He was eager to move on to bigger and better things, and in 1941, when I was thirteen, he recorded a demo disc of our morning show. It was a pretty cheap affair, done on a Wilcox Gay Recordio-gram, a recording machine you could use to make a record on compressed paper with a wax or shellac coating. It didn't have great recording quality — there were quite a few scratches and hisses — but it was good enough. There were one or two coin-operated devices, like photo booths, in big department stores, but we had one at home that Dad had bought. We used it all the time to record songs we heard on the radio; it was the way we got our new material.

One of the singing groups we recorded that way was the Merrymacs, the first group we had ever heard singing four-part close harmonies. Until then nearly all the singing groups were trios or barbershop quartets. As a result of hearing the Merrymacs, we also began to sing more arrangements that were modern and fewer hymns and mother songs.

As soon as he had made the demo disc of our

morning show, Dad told us that he was going to Chicago to get us on the *National Barn Dance* on WLS radio. Sponsored by Alka-Seltzer, and with a one-hour segment broadcast nationwide by NBC, it vied with the *Grand Ole Opry* to be the most popular country music program in the United States. Bob's immediate reaction was the same as it had been when Dad told us we were leaving Wall Lake: "Are you out of your mind? We're just country boys from Iowa. We're never going to get on the radio in a big city like Chicago." As usual, Dad ignored him, packed a suitcase, and caught the next train. He was away for several days.

When he arrived in Chicago, he went straight to WLS and began trying to get an appointment with the station manager, who didn't know Dad or the Williams Brothers from a bar of soap, so was always busy when Dad tried to see him. However, as Mom often said, Dad "never quit. By hook or by crook he would never quit." He just went to the WLS building every day and then waited and waited and waited. The manager still wouldn't see him, but one day Dad sat there until the manager went to lunch, and then he used his charm on the receptionist. Perhaps she felt sorry for him sitting there day after day, because he was able to talk his way into waiting in the empty office.

When the manager returned and demanded to know what Dad was doing there, he just said, "Oh, I have a record I want you to hear. As soon as you've listened to this record, I'll go." His persistence paid off. The manager listened to the demo disc and then hired us on the spot.

Dad returned home in triumph to announce that we were on the move again. Even though Mom and Aunt Cornelia both thought he had "lost his rockers," he quit his job with the railroad company in Des Moines and took much less well-paid work on the railroad in Chicago so that we could move there at once, changing schools and houses once more. It should have gotten easier; the more often we did it, the less strange and daunting a new home in a new city should have been, but I found it was the opposite. I didn't love our house in Des Moines as I had our home in Wall Lake — it was an unlovely place but at least familiar. I hated the thought of starting it all again: finding my way around a new city, getting through those first days at the new school where everyone stared at me as if I were from another planet, and then the school bully sauntering over just to let me know who was boss.

I had grown up in the era of the Great Depression and the dust bowl drought that had ravaged America, but perhaps I'd been too young to really comprehend what was happening around me because those great events had little effect on me. Money was tight, but Dad always had work and there was always food on the table. Now a new threat was emerging, and, older and more aware, I found myself pausing to listen to the increasingly ominous news bulletins on the radio. War had been raging in Europe since the fall of 1939, but at first it seemed as re-mote as the roll call of the far-off countries involved. Now it grew larger and more men-acing by the day, like the black clouds over the Iowa plains that warned of a tornado brewing.

I would hear Dad talking to the neighbors, some swearing that the United States would "never again get involved in another of those goddamn European wars," and others just as adamant that war was coming, "and it'll be worse than last time." Then on December 7, 1941, I and everyone else in America woke to the news that our safe, peaceful world had changed forever. Pearl Harbor had been at-tacked. The change to a war economy swept away the last traces of the Great Depression. Now factories were running twenty-four hours a day, and there was work for all who wanted it. The pace of everyday life seemed to increase almost overnight, and after years of making do and scraping by, people were suddenly spending money, dancing, and partying without apparent fear of tomorrow. Looking back now, it seems a bit like dancing on the deck of the *Titanic,* but perhaps it is always the same in wartime: People who know they may die tomorrow can be forgiven for taking what pleasures they can today.

3

If we thought Des Moines was the big city, Chicago was in an entirely different league. As our train clattered its way toward its center, the stockyards seemed to stretch for miles. A warren of rail tracks and sidings held trains from all over the Midwest, disgorging thousands of cattle that were prodded and herded into endless lines, moving toward the slaughterhouses and meat-packing plants like machine parts on conveyor belts of a vast assembly line. It made a lasting impression on me, and on those hot, humid summer days when the Windy City failed to live up to its name, it sometimes seemed as if the stench of blood and animal dung permeated the whole of Chicago.

The skyline of the city that invented skyscrapers was also very different and far grander than Des Moines, and if Al Capone and Prohibition were now just fading memories, the mob still ruled many of Chicago's meaner streets and even some of its broad boulevards. As we walked around, we would occasionally glimpse sharp-suited, swaggering figures emerging from their limousines and sauntering into one of Chicago's clubs or restaurants as their bodyguards fanned out around them.

We made our debut on the *National Barn Dance* that weekend; it was broadcast live from the Eighth Street Theatre and starred Clyde "Red" Foley. He was a huge star at the time, and I was in awe of him, though not so much that it stopped me from briefly dating his daughter, Shirley. I was only thirteen then, however, and it was all very innocent. We held hands and gave each other a shy peck on the cheek, but nothing more than that.

The move to Chicago signaled a big change in my brother Bob's life. His girlfriend from Wall Lake, Edna, had followed him to Des Moines and then to Chicago, and soon after we moved there, they were married. His three bachelor brothers sang at the wedding. Bob and Edna found an apartment a couple of streets away from where we were living in Oak Park west of the city. It was a nice house in a neighborhood that was more upscale than the low-rent districts where we'd lived in Des Moines, but not long afterward, Dad became very ill. He had had chest problems for years and blamed all the smoke he had inhaled on the railroad while working in the mail car just behind the engine. He now couldn't get his breath at all. Although Mom tried to hide the extent of her worries from us at the time, pretending that Dad just had "a touch of bronchitis," her face told a different story. She admitted later that she was afraid he was going to die. His recovery was slow, and he was off work for several months, so it was just as well that his sons were earning a few dollars by appearing on the radio.

I learned a lot from being around other performers, including how to breathe properly, through the diaphragm, which gives you much more power and control of your voice. Many pop singers don't use this technique and are still very successful, but if you're planning to be a professional singer, it can't hurt to learn how to do it right.

For the next year we did a weekday morning show on WLS and also sang on the *National Barn Dance* show live from the Eighth Street Theatre, but in 1942 we were forced to move again when our show was cancelled. The unions came in, and we were caught in the crossfire of a battle between the radio companies and the new American Federation of Radio Artists. AFRA had succeeded in forcing up the rates of pay for its members to unheard-of levels at the time (the union scale set by AFRA was three times our previous rate of pay), and the result was virtually to kill off live radio shows.

Until that time all radio stations featured live entertainers, but now most could no longer afford to have orchestras and singers. Many, including WLS Chicago, simply sacked all their live performers and began employing people to play records instead. The era of disc jockeys and record charts was born out of that conflict with AFRA. The first disc jockeys were often hopelessly bad — at the start, the station managers were responsible for spinning the records — and when one selection ended, there would often be a long silence, broken only by the hiss of the needle and the sound of the amateur disc jockey fumbling for the next record. They improved with practice, however, and there was no going back to the old era.

At least one radio station was still bucking the trend: WLW Cincinnati had the most powerful radio transmitters in the world. Like WHO in Des Moines and WLS in Chicago, it was a 50,000-watt station by day — the maximum permitted at the time — but for some reason at night it pumped out 500,000 watts. As a result, WLW Cincinnati could be heard all over the United States and throughout South America. It was so powerful that its signal reached Australia and New Zealand. It was said that you could even hear yourself coming back around the world the other way with a few seconds' time delay. Even if that was a myth, such power brought WLW a huge audience and, with it, the advertising revenue to be able to continue to pay live performers. They even kept a permanent orchestra on the staff. There were some big names there, too, including the Clooney sisters, Rosemary and Betty, and Doris Day.

A slot had become available on a morning show at WLW, replacing a singing group called the Smoothies. As soon as Dad heard about this, and despite the usual "Are you out of your mind?" outburst from Bob, we were heading for Cincinnati, moving house and changing schools yet again. Even in the brief intervals when Dad wasn't leading us to a fresh promised land in a completely new city, we were always moving house and changing districts. This frequently happened in the middle of the night, and because of the speed with which Dad hurried us away from some of our temporary homes, we formed the suspicion that he had fallen behind in the rent and was doing a "midnight flit." Every time we relocated, we left behind a trail of lost friends and sometimes one or two broken hearts, but we moved so often that it became increasingly hard to build new friendships. In the end I pretty much gave up trying. What was the point when Dad would just be hustling us off somewhere else in a few weeks or months? I made friends all over the world during my singing career, but I don't have a single friend from any of the half-dozen different schools I attended as a boy.

We had always been a tight-knit family, but the constant moves to new cities and the consequent lack of friends made us even more so, and I'm sure that was precisely what Dad wanted. He was so determined to ensure that nothing got in the way of his ambitions for the Williams Brothers that any outside interest which might jeopardize his plans was firmly vetoed. When he was in high school, Dad had been a good baseball and football player, and Bob was also a really fine athlete; he was the captain of the football, baseball, basketball, and track teams. He longed to be a football coach, but Dad wouldn't hear of it. He also stopped Don from playing football at Roosevelt High School in case he got to love it and started spending time at football practice when, in

Dad's opinion, he should have been rehearsing. When Dick wanted to take up the trumpet, that was also forbidden in case he joined a band instead of singing with his brothers. I got the picture and didn't even think of doing anything else.

Dad's obsession with turning us into singers even extended to cheating on our schoolwork. He actually paid an older girl at my school to come in and do my homework for me so that I wouldn't have any distractions from rehearsing when I was at home. While very grateful for the success that came my way, years later I came to resent the fact that I just barely got through high school and never went to college. "It's not important how well you do in school," my dad told me more than once, "because your career is going to be in music."

My brothers and I had also been deprived of the chance to be normal teens, playing softball, going to movies, and just hanging out with friends. Apart from singing, the only things we were allowed to do was to go bowling and play tennis, and then only because we did it as a family. Dad would also reinforce the message with regular pep talks. Like the Three Musketeers, we were told that in our family it was "all for one and one for all," and while we were practicing our songs, he would often say, "Let's do this one for Buddy." He certainly knew how to push those buttons.

Dad would probably have liked to keep girlfriends at bay as well, but he was less successful at that. Soon after we arrived in Cincinnati, I fell in love for the first time with a girl named Elaine Evans, an older woman: She was a senior in high school when I was a freshman. She had long dark hair and a way of looking at me, with a secret smile, that set my pulse racing. The first time we kissed I went home and studied myself in the bathroom mirror for many minutes, sure that such a life-changing moment must had left its mark on my appearance. We dated for the rest of that year. On weekends we'd go on hayrides, where a bunch of us would head off into the country on a cart covered in hay bales and stop for a picnic. There'd be a bit of kissing but nothing much more than that.

Elaine and I also used to sit for hours drinking sodas in Peggy's Grill, across from the school. I'd sing along to the Glenn Miller and Buddy Clark records on the jukebox and tell her, "I'm going to be a singer, and one day there'll be a record of mine on that jukebox. Then you'll have to pay a nickel to listen to what you're hearing for free now."

"Is that so?" she said. "Well, one day you'll have to pay a lot more than a nickel for what you're getting for free from me — so there!" She was my first real love, and I was crazy about her. But as often happens in high school romances, when she went away to college, it just fizzled out. I dated plenty of other girls in Cincinnati after that, but there were no others like Elaine.

Our house in Cincinnati was near the top of one of the seven hills on which, like Rome, the city was built, and my strongest memory now is of going down the hill and disappearing into the fog, as thick as London smog, that seemed to descend day after day in fall and winter. Every morning before school we'd walk down that hill into town and go to the studios in Crosley Square. The WLW building's tower, taller than any of the surrounding buildings, meant that the station's call sign was visible all over Cincinnati . . . whenever the fog lifted enough. We gathered around the microphone in the studio — the biggest we'd ever seen — with an announcer and a backing trio already in their places and the producer behind the thick glass of the sound booth in one corner.

When the studio clock ticked around to the hour, the producer gave us the 5-4-3-2-1 countdown on his fingers from the booth, the red light went on, and the announcer would say, "And now on WLW Cincinnati, it's time to shine with the Williams Brothers and Griffin Polish."

The jingle that my brothers and I performed at the beginning of every show started with four chimes: *Bong! Bong! Bong! Bong!* Then we'd sing.

It's time to shine,
So shine your shoes and you'll wear a smile.
Shine your shoes, and you'll be in style.
The sun shines east and the sun shines west,
Griffin Polish shines the best.
Some folks are not particular how they look around the feet,
But if they wore shoes upon their heads,
They'd make sure their shoes looked neat.
So keep your shoes shined all the time.
All the time is the time to shine.
When you hear this familiar chime — Bong! Bong! Bong! Bong! —
Everybody get set. It's time to shine.

Partly as a result of this sponsorship, our collective paycheck had now doubled to $400 a week. One hundred dollars went to Bob, who had his own apartment to pay for, leaving $300 for the rest of us. It was very good money in those days, enough to support the entire family, so Dad promptly quit his job to manage his boys fulltime. For the first time in our lives we had a little money to spare, and since Dad evidently didn't trust banks, he kept our cash under the carpet in the living room. There were $10 bills under one corner, fives under the next, and dollar bills under a third one. Having stowed the cash away, he turned to us and said, "The ones are for you, Andy, the fives are for Dick, and the tens are for Don. Just help yourselves when you need some money."

It was a very unusual way to pay us an allowance out of the money that we had earned, and we weren't entirely convinced that he was serious about our helping ourselves whenever we wanted. I waited a few days before I touched the money and then took just a single dollar. Nothing was said, so a few days later I took another, but I never took more than a couple of dollars at once. None of us ever cleared our pile of bills completely even though Dad never said anything more about the money and added more bills from time to time.

When we first moved into the house, one of the local grocery stores, hoping to get our regular business, sent around a box of groceries as a welcome-to-the-neighborhood gift. Unfortunately, it contained a case of beer, and since Mom and Dad were teetotalers and Mom had even "signed the pledge" as a teenager, not a drop of alcohol was ever allowed in our house. We kept the groceries but stood around and watched as Mom ceremonially took the tops off all the beer bottles and then, one by one, poured the contents down the sink. However, at least one of her sons failed to follow her teetotal example. Everyone in Cincinnati drank beer, and I was no exception; within a year of moving there I was even taking a bottle of beer to school in my lunch box every day, the start of my road to ruin.

In the two years we spent in the city, as well as appearing on our own radio show we guested on every other radio program on the station, including *The Boone County Jamboree,* the WLW equivalent of WLS's *National Barn Dance.* However, in January 1944, with the same blind faith and determination that had built our radio career, Dad announced that it was time to move on again. He was taking us out west to Los Angeles where, he was convinced, movie stardom awaited us.

There was no logical reason for this decision; he had simply persuaded himself that we would be perfect to play the Sullivan brothers in a forthcoming movie he had heard about. The Sullivans were a famous family who had all served together in the navy and died together when their ship was torpedoed by the Japanese. As a result, the government recommended that, to protect families from such a loss in the future, members of the same family not serve together on the same warship. The following facts proved no obstacle to Jay Williams's eternal optimism: that there were five Sullivan brothers and only four of us; that at fourteen I was much too young to play a man old enough to fight and die for his country; and that, in any event, the movie had probably already been cast and might even have been shot.

Bob's equally eternal pessimism was just as predictable. "The movies? Us? Okay, you were right about the moves to Des Moines, Chicago, and Cincinnati, but that was radio, not movies. We can sing, but we can't act and we can't dance, and, be honest, do we really look like movie stars?" He paused, trying to see if he was having the least effect on my father. "Dad, there is no way in the world we are going to make it as movie stars in Hollywood."

For once all the Williams brothers were in complete agreement. It was the nuttiest, most harebrained scheme Dad had ever come up with — and there were plenty to choose from. He remained adamant, however; he had made up his mind: We were going to Hollywood; end of discussion. So, like the Joad family in *The Grapes of Wrath,* we set off for California with a mixture of hope, desperation, resignation, and fear in our hearts. But Dad saw only blue skies, sunshine, and golden movie opportunities awaiting us.

Our only contact when we first got out there was an American Indian whom we had gotten to know when he was working as an announcer at WLS in Chicago. He was now living in a large house in South Pasadena, and the Williams family descended on him en masse, staying for a few weeks until we found a place to rent in Westwood. The house we rented had a big yard at the back containing a beautiful avocado tree. Unfortunately, none of us had even seen an avocado before, and the only use we found for those big, luscious ripe fruits was throwing them at one another. We lived in that house for a couple of years and then moved to a bigger place off Venice Boulevard, where we planted a vegetable garden — a victory garden, as they were called in wartime.

When I went to school, I took an instant dislike to one of my new classmates, a girl who was curly-haired and cute in a teeth-grindingly saccharine sort of way. She was apparently so in love with herself that she barely acknowledged the rest of us. If I had gone to the movies more often in Cincinnati, I'd have known at once who she was, but it took me a couple of days to realize that I was sharing a classroom with Shirley Temple. I didn't see much more of her after that because she was hardly ever at school, always away making a movie or in professional school.

I was really lonely when we first moved to California. I didn't know anyone, and, as usual, I didn't have any friends at school. We didn't even have the morning radio show anymore to give me a focus to my day. If school was bad enough, after school was even worse. Dad still didn't want his boys doing anything that would distract them from the career path he had mapped out, and while everyone else my age was out tossing a football around, hanging out at the beach, or going on dates, I was stuck at home feeling sorry for myself.

Things improved greatly when I went to University High School for my senior year. I made a couple of friends there, and we built a hot rod together. Dad definitely didn't approve of the idea, but for once he didn't intervene to stop me. It was a 1929 Ford Coupe. We took the fenders off, put a 1941 Mercury engine in it, added big tires on the back and motorcycle tires on the front, and chromed everything we could. I didn't know too much about cars, but the other guys did, so I helped out where I could. My principal contribution was actually coming up with the money to pay for it; they did the technical stuff like taking it apart and putting it back together again.

The finished product was fantastic, and I was living the California dream: cruising up and down in my hot rod and drawing admiring looks from the girls. I used to drive to Westwood Village, where there was a square with two movie theaters; everyone would hang out there and watch the cars going by. We went to drive-in movies, too, something we had never encountered before. On our first visit we didn't realize that you had to hook up the sound, and we all sat in baffled silence inside the car trying to figure out what the heck was happening on the screen and wondering why the sound was so lousy. You can take the boy out of Iowa, but you can't take Iowa out of the boy.

I soon figured out where we were going wrong with the sound, and I was back there a few nights later with my first California girlfriend, Nancy Duke. She lived on Mulholland Drive and was an extra in the movies and much older than me — thirty-seven to my seventeen — but she was a great-looking girl, and we found ways to bridge the age gap, so much so that I was soon taking part in that great all-American pastime: steaming up the car windows at the drive-in.

We all fell in love with California. Back then Los Angeles was a beautiful place, more like an overgrown country town than the sprawling collection of "suburbs in search of a city" that it has now become. The weather was sunny, and the air was clear, with none of the smog that now fills the basin between the mountains and the sea. There was only a single highway then, going from downtown L.A. to Pasadena, and there was literally nothing between Beverly Hills and the beach. Our house was opposite a nine-hole golf course and was surrounded by bean fields and open country.

If Los Angeles was very different back then, so was the music business. In the 1940s the record industry was pretty small, and almost no one there was actively looking for new recording talent. If you were discovered at all, it was almost entirely due to your own — or your father's — efforts.

For once Dad wasn't able to charm his

way past security and into the office of a top movie producer, but if the Hollywood studios' doors remained closed to him, he did soon find us some work, singing for the radio on the *Sweeney and March Show*. On this show, for the first and only time in our careers, our sister Janey sang with us. They had been using Doris Day as a singer but let her go, a decision that must have come back to haunt them many times. We were hired to replace her, and since we had always felt guilty that Janey wasn't getting the attention we were, we asked her if she wanted to join us. She said she'd give it a try and did the first show with us, but when we asked her afterward, "So, how did you like it?" she said, "I hated it, and I never want to do it again." She wouldn't budge, and that was the end of her showbiz career.

Doris Day was not yet twenty but was already divorced from her first husband — she had married when she was just sixteen years old — and was living with her son, Terry Melcher, in a trailer park two blocks from our house. She was a bubbly, vivacious girl and certainly didn't show too many signs of the "virginal girl next door" image that she was saddled with and grew to hate during her long movie and television career. She came from Cincinnati originally, and we knew her slightly from our time at WLW there. She didn't stay in the trailer park for long. She began singing with bandleader Les Brown and his Band of Renown, and in 1945 released the single "Sentimental Journey." Adopted as an anthem by returning GIs, it was an enormous hit, made her a star, and remained Doris's theme song throughout her career.

As well as our radio work, we were also singing at any venue that would have us, and we did many *Mail Call* programs: hour-long shows made for our servicemen overseas. Many Hollywood stars appeared on *Mail Call,* and it was through the show that we secured our own breakthrough: a recording session with the biggest star of them all, Bing Crosby. It is hard now to believe just how much Bing dominated the music industry at the time. At one point *Music Digest* estimated that his recordings accounted for more than half of the entire eighty thousand hours of recorded music played on the radio every week. Backed by the Notre Dame boys' choir, Bing had sung a number called "Swinging on a Star" in the movie *Going My Way.* He now wanted to put it out as a record, but the boys' choir was not available, so Bing's musical director, John Scott Trotter, was looking for another backing group. He heard us singing on *Mail Call* and promptly hired us to do the backing vocals for $25 apiece.

Bing Crosby was an idol to us, and it was an honor to be given the chance to sing with him, but we were so in awe of him that we were practically trembling, with our arms around one another, as we recorded the song. Bing had a reputation for being a lot less charming offstage than on it, but, if so, we never saw that side of him. He was always very kind and encouraging, both then and in later years.

Released in early 1944, "Swinging on a Star" became a huge hit. Our next big break did not come from that, however, but from some sessions that Dad had arranged for us at the Hollywood Canteen, entertaining servicemen home on leave. There we had one of those life-changing chance encounters that could never have been predicted by anyone — except possibly my dad. Louis B. Mayer's executive secretary, Ida Koverman, happened to be in the Hollywood Canteen one night when we were singing. She went back and told her boss about us, and within a week we were signed to a contract by MGM.

Once more Dad had been proved right, if not quite in the way he had anticipated. His relentless persistence, guile, and incurable optimism had paid off: His sons were going to be in the movies, just as he had predicted. He would have been forgiven for greeting us with an "I told you so," but instead he contented himself with a broad smile and a hug for each of us. Then, just in case we were getting complacent, he issued a stern reminder that all we had done so far was get a foot in the door, and the only way to become stars was "through sheer hard work, starting now." He then sat down at the piano and made us rehearse.

On our first morning at the studio, still half-expecting to be stopped by the security guards and sent home as impostors, we made our way through the entrance gates and onto the MGM lot. We walked down a street lined with clapboard buildings, but this was emphatically not Wall Lake; a neon sign overhead proclaimed METRO-GOLDWYN-MAYER STUDIOS and ahead of us were the huge hangar-like buildings housing the soundstages.

I was so busy staring up at their towering walls that I almost walked straight into Lana Turner, who had just come out of a door in one of them. I tried to apologize, but faced with the most beautiful and glamorous woman I had ever seen in my life, the words died on my lips. I dropped my gaze from that perfect face and, to my mixed horror and delight, found myself staring into her cleavage instead. I burbled some meaningless sounds and then, blushing crimson, stumbled past her and hurried on down the lot, pursued by the silvery sound of her laughter. For the next couple of years, even if I saw Lana Turner only on a movie screen, I'd find myself blushing in memory of that encounter. On that first morning alone we also passed Ava Gardner and Mickey Rooney going to or from the sets of their next movies, and once more I showed my true colors — a starstruck, tongue-tied Iowa farm boy trying and failing to show some sophistication — and blushed my way past them as well.

We had been granted an audience with Louis B. Mayer himself that morning, and after waiting outside his office for twenty minutes as a queue of supplicants came and went, we were shown into an office the size of a small aircraft carrier. Mr. Mayer was just visible at the far end, presiding over a vast semicircular white desk on which a series of 1940s executive toys — a white telephone, a marble penholder, a silver cigarette box, and some photographs and ornaments — were neatly arranged. The Venetian blind covering the window behind him was closed, but he was as brightly lit as if he were on a movie set, the lights shining on a forehead that looked as if it had been polished with Turtle Wax.

As he rose to shake hands with us, I noticed that his chair was set on a podium, raising him above us by a few extra inches, and that the chair was high-backed and leather-upholstered, while those for his visitors were tubular steel and canvas. No visitor to Mr. Mayer's office could be left in any doubt about his relative status. He greeted us with a smile that seemed friendly enough although his eyes, half hidden by the light reflecting from his glasses, had a calculating look. He rattled through what, from the speed with which he delivered it, must have been his standard speech of welcome to "the Metro-Goldwyn-Mayer family," told us that he was "expecting great things from us," pressed a button under his desk, and his secretary reappeared and showed us out. The whole interview had taken less than two minutes.

Although we were now contracted to MGM, they hired us out to Warner Brothers for our first movie, *Janie,* and a couple of weeks later we turned up to begin work at the Warner Brothers lot in a state of high excitement. We had very small parts: four soldiers singing around a piano during a party at Janie's house when her parents were away. It passed in a blur, and I can recall very little about the making of the movie, but I can still remember Mom's excitement a couple of months later when the whole family went to Grauman's Chinese Theatre on Hollywood Boulevard. Before we went inside to watch our movie, we looked at all the stars' handprints in the cement of the Walk of Fame, and Dad inevitably told us that if we practiced hard enough, our handprints might be there one day.

While working on the Warner Brothers lot, I also picked up my first solo singing role in the movies, although I didn't appear on-screen. I still hadn't finished high school then but was taking my lessons in the school on the studio lot. When I had done the work I'd been given one afternoon, I went to the office of the musical director, Dudley Chambers. He had his back to me, fumbling for something in a drawer. I waited a moment and then cleared my voice and said, "Excuse me, Mr. Chambers. I've finished my homework. I'd like to go outside and play a little baseball." He froze and then turned around, stared at me, and said, "That's the voice I've been looking for." Nineteen-year-old Lauren Bacall was making her first movie, *To Have and Have Not,* which featured the "You know how to whistle, don't you?" dialogue that was to make her famous, but her singing voice wasn't quite good enough for a number she had to do in the film. Mr. Chambers had been auditioning scores of women, including Bob Hope's wife, Dolores, to sing for Bacall, but because she had a low, husky voice, none of the singers he auditioned had the sound he was looking for. He had now decided that a sixteen-year-old boy whose voice had only recently changed was the perfect match for Bacall.

Mr. Chambers took me straight over to a soundstage, handed me some sheet music, and then stood me in front of a huge movie screen. The projectionist ran the footage of Bacall singing "How Little We Know," and Mr. Chambers told me to sing along with her. I ran through the number a couple of times, and although the lip sync was by no means perfect, the sound was good enough for him. "That's it," he said. "We've got it. Come back in tomorrow, and we'll make it." I left thinking that this was a very strange way to make movies. In her autobiography years later, Bacall admitted that I dubbed the song for her but said that they wanted to use her own voice saying part of the lyric — "You can tell" — and because my voice didn't match her speaking voice well enough, in the end they decided to use her recording, not mine, as originally planned. I'm not sure what the truth of it was, but I'm not going to argue about it with the formidable Ms. Bacall!

The Williams Brothers appeared in half a dozen movies, most of them instantly forgettable. The titles *Kansas City Kitty* and *Something in the Wind* give a fair idea of what they were like. All of them were filmed in a matter of a few weeks (the scripts read as if they'd been written in five minutes), and each of them featured us as a quartet, standing around a piano and singing at a party.

America had been at war since the horror of Pearl Harbor, and the navy yards and the docks were running twenty-four hours a day. There were more men in uniform on the streets and more war movies being made on the studio lots, but our day-to-day life had remained largely unaffected until the day Bob received an official-looking envelope in the mail: his draft notice. When he was drafted into the army, Don and Dick at once enlisted in the merchant marine, in line with another of Dad's schemes. He had sent all of us to evening classes at Santa Monica Technical School to learn how to be radio engineers because he thought that if we learned that trade, we could join the merchant marine for the duration of the war. When it was over, we'd be able to quit the service at once and get straight back to our singing career, whereas if we were in the U.S. Army or Navy, we might not be demobilized for a year or more.

He also thought that the merchant marine would be a nice safe place for his boys to serve out the war. He didn't make many mistakes, but that was certainly one of them. It was a matter of pure luck that he didn't lose two of his sons; in a convoy to Australia, the boats on either side of the one in which Dick and Don were both serving were sunk by Japanese torpedoes with the loss of all crewmen. Ironically, Bob was drafted before he could volunteer, and he finished up serving in the army where, contrary to Dad's theories, he saw far less action than his brothers in the merchant marine.

Although they were in the service, Dad continued to push them to keep up their singing and even bought Dick and Don a small organ that they could use to accompany themselves. When they were on shore leave in Australia for a few weeks — their ship's boilers blew up, and it took a long time for replacements to be shipped there — they even got a booking to sing in a couple of Sydney restaurants.

With my brothers unavailable for the foreseeable future, I sang with a few other close harmony groups instead, including the Starlighters. Through them I first got to know Bob Hope. We worked on Bob's radio show, sang the "Poor Miriam" commercial, and toured with him to Chicago, New York, and a few other cities. I also sang with a group called Four Hits and a Miss. They were originally called Six Hits and a Miss, but two of the guys were called up by the army. Pauline Byrnes was the Miss, and I was one of the Hits. There weren't many guys around who could sing the high parts of harmonies, and, anyway, I was one of the few male singers left who hadn't enlisted. I was still too young to serve in the armed forces at the time.

While under contract to MGM, I also met Kay Thompson, the studio's vocal and choral director and the vocal coach to such stars as Lena Horne, June Allyson, and Judy Garland. (Later, Kay was godmother to Judy's daughter, Liza Minnelli.) Kay didn't want to use traditional trained singers on the sound track in MGM musicals but preferred a more modern sound, with singers who could swing. She knew my voice from the Williams Brothers, and from then on, although I never appeared on-screen, I was used whenever Kay put out a chorus call at MGM, and my voice can be heard on the sound track of musicals like *The Harvey Girls, Good News,* and *Till the Clouds Roll By.* Even now I can still sing my part in *Harvey Girls;* I may not remember what I did yesterday, but I can remember what I did in the 1940s!

When I turned seventeen in December 1944, I also became eligible for the draft, but in line with Dad's master plan, I volunteered instead and, like Don and Dick, joined the merchant marine. On my first voyage I sailed on a ship with them. Because a merchant ship could carry only two merchant radio operators plus one navy operator, despite my qualifications, I had to sign on as a messman, the lowest of the low in the ship's hierarchy. I didn't mind; at least I was with my brothers. I was probably the worst messman in the history of the merchant marine. I was seasick all the time, and having to serve food to everyone didn't help. Many times I had to rush off to be ill yet again.

I had been in the merchant marine for only six months when, with the war winding down, the government stopped drafting anyone under twenty-one and released anyone of that age who was already serving. I got off the ship as soon as we made port in Los Angeles, and while waiting for my brothers to return home, I rejoined the Starlighters for a while and also sang with the Little Sisters on a show called *California Melodies* on the Mutual Network.

I was drafted again in 1948 when I turned twenty-one, but by then I was suffering from a stomach ulcer and, with no more fighting going on, the military wasn't interested in anybody who was less than a perfect physical specimen. I was accordingly rated 4-F, and my far from glorious military career was over.

4

By the end of 1946, Dick and Don had gotten out of the merchant marine, Bob had finished his time in the army, and the reunited Williams Brothers were ready to resume our singing career. But the entertainment landscape had changed, and in the postwar period the kind of lightweight musical pictures that we had been making earlier were few and far between. Then Kay Thompson, who had just left MGM, came up with an offer we couldn't refuse: "Let's get out of this movie business and get into the nightclub business instead." The reaction from Bob was instantaneous and completely predictable: "Are you crazy? That'll never work. We're not nightclub performers. We've never even been in a nightclub." Just as predictably, the rest of us shouted him down. We wanted to hear more.

Kay was a multitalented singer, dancer, pianist, and comedienne. She would later famously play a magazine editor in *Funny Face* opposite Audrey Hepburn and Fred Astaire, in which she had the big stand-out number "Think Pink." She was also the author of the hugely popular Eloise children's books. A striking-looking woman, very thin, almost gaunt, with angular features and a prominent nose, she wasn't conventionally beautiful but there was certainly something about her that set her apart from anyone else, and she had energy and enthusiasm to burn. She often wore tailored suits or trousers, and with her hair cut short, she could look almost androgynous. But she could also be very feminine and was always glamorous.

She had been married twice, first to a jazz trombonist, Jack Jenney, and then to William Spier, a highly successful producer of radio shows such as *Sam Spade* and *Suspense,* but when we began rehearsing with her, she was in the process of divorcing him. I had a huge crush on her, but I was just seventeen years old then, naive and painfully shy. She was almost twenty years older, a poised, sophisticated, and worldly woman. I never thought my feelings about her would ever come to anything, and I kept them secret, even from my brothers. I suppose I was afraid that they would either laugh at me or embarrass me by telling Kay.

At that time singing groups typically just stood around a microphone and sang, but Kay and her friend Bob Alton had come up with the idea that we should do a review, almost a small Broadway musical but in a nightclub setting. If it worked, it would be unique: a high-octane fusion of singing, acting, comedy, and dancing performed at breathtaking speed.

Bob was a great choreographer who had done a lot of Broadway shows and big musicals for MGM. He was flamboyantly gay — another revelation for these Iowa country boys — and also had a rather disconcerting habit of using his feet rather than his hands to gesture or point to something he wanted doing. But he was inspirational, brilliant at choreographing huge set pieces — almost a latter-day Busby Berkeley, and an absolute perfectionist. He could have been earning a lot more money working on a movie or on Broadway, but he was devoted to Kay. She had approached him and said, "I have an idea for a show with these four Williams brothers. They can really sing, but they can't act and can't dance. They're choirboys, Bob. Help me do something with them." Either the idea for the show or the chance to turn four ugly ducklings into swans captured his imagination, because he threw himself into it.

It was a grueling show to rehearse and perform. Kay was relentlessly professional; everything had to be perfect, practiced, and rehearsed until it gleamed. The dance moves Bob gave us were really punishing, tremendously hard, physical work for non-dancers like us, and he was as pitiless as Kay in pushing us to do them over and over until we got them right. I had to do some stage falls in the act, and Bob taught me how to land on my back by keeping my hands at my sides and then, to break my fall, pushing down hard a split second before my body hit the ground. Bob had me practice it many times on an exercise mat in his house where we were rehearsing. Then he led me down to the cellar and said, "Now do it here. And you'd better get it right. That floor is concrete." It was a swift but very steep learning curve; I got it right and never hurt myself, then or later.

We rehearsed day after day, week after week, and none of us has ever been fitter in our lives. It took us a long, long time before we were able to complete the act without collapsing like runners after a marathon. Of all of us Bob found it the toughest. Dick was always a natural performer, and Don and I weren't bad. But Bob never was a natural and had to work especially hard at it. Once he learned the steps — and it was a painstaking process — he could do them the same as the rest of us, but it was never less than laborious for him, and the effort really showed.

The act was so physically demanding that when we came offstage, Bob could literally wring the sweat out of his suit; it was completely saturated. He looked as if he had been wearing it in the shower — and it had to be cleaned after each show. He also spent a lot on ties because they were also so sweat-soaked that the knot was often rock-solid by the end of the show, and the only way to remove it was to cut it off.

After four grueling months of rehearsal, we were finally ready to unveil our act: Kay Thompson and the Williams Brothers. We showcased the act in the ballroom at Arnold Kirkeby's house in Bel Air, the house where *The Beverly Hillbillies* television series was later filmed. Arnold Kirkeby owned hotels all over the country, and we auditioned for him and a couple of dozen agents and bookers for clubs, hotels, and casinos. We were nervous before we started, but the nerves soon faded. I knew that we had taken care of every variable and had rehearsed the act literally to the point of exhaustion, and we knew our material inside out, upside down, and every way in between. There was nothing we could do to improve the act any further; we just had to perform it for an audience, and a very tough audience at that.

When we began, we were moving too fast and concentrating too hard to take in the reaction, but the applause at the end of our first number was loud and seemed genuine. I shot a swift, incredulous look at Don. These were agents and bookers; they didn't applaud, did they? We went into our second routine. Kay was a good dancer, but it hadn't come as easily to us and we had learned each routine by numbers. As a result we all danced in exactly the same way — we were the same height, were dressed alike, and looked alike. We moved in unison, so much so that when we did a high kick, our feet all finished at exactly the same height. The pace and precision of it, coupled with the hard-hitting, tight vocal sound, simply blew our jaded, world-weary audience away. After we finished, the agents clustered around Kay before we had even left the ballroom floor. We picked up our first bookings straightaway: two weeks at the El Rancho Vegas in Las Vegas, followed by two weeks at the Tahoe Village at Lake Tahoe, two weeks back in Vegas at the about-to-open

Flamingo Hotel and Casino, and then a ten-week residency at Hollywood's most glamorous nightclub, Ciro's.

For the first time ever we would be traveling without Dad. He had been the dominant force in our lives and careers until then, had shaped our original act, and used every wile and guile to find us work on radio and in Hollywood. He must have felt a little shut out, knowing that he would no longer be so closely involved in our careers, but even he had to concede that we were now working in areas about which he knew nothing and could offer no useful advice or guidance . . . not that it stopped him from trying. It was difficult because he had put his whole life on hold to make his vision for his sons come true, and the success we had enjoyed until this point was largely due to his efforts, but even he now reluctantly accepted that it was time to step aside. Kay Thompson had now become the mentor and guiding hand for all the Williams brothers, and for me in particular. She took me under her wing and taught me how to be a professional performer, and the professionalism and perfectionism that Kay instilled in me has stayed with me ever since.

Even someone as experienced as Kay had things to learn however, when transferring movie techniques to nightclubs. Sound, for example, was a problem. Microphone technology was quite primitive then; there were none of the headsets and lapel microphones that performers use today. Handheld microphones were out, because the act involved so much movement, and we needed both hands for the dance routines and to do all the things that were an integral part of the act. In the end we used a series of microphones suspended from the ceiling above the stage, hanging just over our heads. The sound wasn't perfect, but it worked better than anything else we could devise.

We also had to rein in some of Kay's wilder ideas. She was so eager for the show to be a success that she rented a pair of huge searchlights to light up the night sky wherever we were appearing. We had to point out that not only was it not our job to do so, but the cost and the logistical difficulties of moving these massive lights around would be enormous, and anyway, we weren't presenting the premiere of some new Hollywood blockbuster; we were doing a supper club show in rooms that held only four hundred people.

Our first booking was at the El Rancho Vegas. It was essential for the casino business to make it very easy for people to get there.

In 1947 there was a train running from Los Angeles to Las Vegas, but air flights were very inexpensive as well; you could get a round-trip ticket for just $29. Once you arrived, they wanted to keep you there as long as possible, so everything was dirt cheap; hotel accommodations and meals were often virtually given away. The casinos counted on your losing enough money at the tables to make their profit. When we went there, Kay took a plane while my brothers and I, along with our pianist, Joe Marino, piled in the car. Pulling a U-Haul trailer containing our luggage, we drove through Barstow and across the Mojave Desert to Las Vegas.

Las Vegas was then in its infancy as a tourist destination. Casino gambling in Nevada had been legalized in 1931, part of a package of measures, including instant weddings, quick divorces, and legalized prostitution, that was passed by the state legislature in an effort to boost tourism and protect Nevada from some of the worst effects of the Depression. Gambling halls soon opened in downtown Vegas, but resort casinos, offering a range of facilities and entertainment along with the chance to gamble, did not begin appearing until the 1940s.

The Old West–style El Rancho Vegas had opened on April 3, 1941, on an isolated sixty-acre site just south of the city limits. Running past it was a dirt road, Highway 91, later better known as the Strip. According to the legend fostered by El Rancho's builder, Thomas E. (Tommy) Hull, his car had broken down on a blazing hot day, and while waiting for help he decided to build a hotel with a swimming pool at that exact place — an oasis in a desert of sand and sagebrush, although cynics suggested that the endless procession of tourists in their automobiles passing this lonely spot was Hull's true inspiration. Already the owner of the San Francisco Bellevue, the Los Angeles Mayfair, the Hollywood Roosevelt, and several other hotels, Hull built the first of the themed resorts that would come to dominate the Vegas Strip.

Although it was a pretty basic "spit and sawdust" place by today's standards, for a handful of years El Rancho Vegas was the leader of the pack, the biggest and busiest of the three hotels then operating on the Strip and the first that visitors driving up from Los Angeles passed on their way into town. Its huge billboards towered above the highway, and its neon-lit windmill on top of a tall square tower was an unmistakable landmark, a beacon to guide the new breed of visitor: newly affluent workingmen and -women driving automobiles and with money in their pockets who came in ever-growing numbers from L.A. and all over the Southwest and Midwest.

El Rancho Vegas had covered wagons and other Old West mementos scattered around a site laid out as a rustic dude ranch, complete with riding stables. In keeping with the theme, the Show Room was decked out like the interior of a giant barn; it had cartwheels for chandeliers, tables laid with white linen cloths and red napkins, and lighting from hurricane lamps with stitched leather lamp shades. The guest rooms ($5 a night) were in low, tile-roofed, concrete, mock adobe wings in Spanish mission style that spread out from the main buildings or in separate chalets built around the edge of the complex, each with its own manicured lawn.

If gambling was the engine that drove El Rancho, the crowds were also drawn by the promise of top-class entertainment in the Opera House Showroom, drinks in the Nugget Nell Cocktail Lounge, good food in the Stage Door Steakhouse, or cheap eats in the ninety-nine-cent Chuck Wagon Buffet. There was also the chance to relax by the pool, clearly visible from the highway, and soak up the desert sun that shone 365 days a year, or to stroll or ride through the sprawling grounds where avenues of palm trees led to a man-made waterfall.

We made our public debut with our new act at the El Rancho Vegas in August 1947. Even though the agents and bookers had loved the act back in Los Angeles, there was no guarantee that an audience of vacationing couples and men with gambling on their minds would see it the same way, and we were riddled with nerves before opening night. Although the act was physically demanding, it had to look effortless and fun to do, and as we stood in the wings ready to go on, Kay tried to defuse the tension by reminding us of the old showbiz maxim: "Eyes and teeth, darlings!" I did my best to oblige, smiling like the Cheshire Cat as we went through our routines, and I had such a rictal grin on my face that by the end of the act I had practically given myself lockjaw. When I tried to stop smiling, I found I couldn't. It kept Kay and my brothers amused for the rest of the evening. They told me the saddest, most heartbreaking stories they could think of, and I'd grin like a maniac through each one. I was still smiling when I fell asleep, and although my face was back to normal in the morning, my jaw muscles ached all day.

I had my own problems on our opening

night. There was no raised stage; we worked on the polished dance floor in front of the band. To fit in as many paying customers as possible, the tables were arranged very close to us. In one number, "Pauvre Suzette," we took up positions at the four corners of the floor, and Kay moved between us, like a woman choosing a partner. Kay first danced over to Bob on the left front corner and said, "There was always the man she loved," and Bob pushed her away. Next she moved to Dick on the right corner and said, "There was always the man she didn't love." Dick fell to his knees and grabbed her around the legs, but she shook him off and moved on to Don on the back right-hand corner. "There was always the man she loved too often," she said. Don put on a dreamy expression and sank to his knees as if exhausted, which always got a big laugh. Then Kay moved on to me at the back left corner and said, "There was always the man she loved too much," which was my cue to spin around and fall flat on my back.

We then all held our positions, staying absolutely motionless until Kay gave the signal — a clap of her hands — which was our cue to jump up and go to our original positions at the four corners of the stage, ready for the next part of the routine. The whole sequence

97

was repeated three times.

When I spun around and fell flat, just as Bob Alton had taught me, I slapped my hands down and pushed hard to break my fall. The floor was so highly polished, however, that I went under the nearest tablecloth-draped table where a couple was watching the show. I came to rest between their legs under the table, among the bits of spilled peas and carrots from their dinner. As I lay still waiting for the clap of hands, I heard a woman's voice say, "Henry, he's looking up my dress."

"I promise you I'm not," I whispered. "I have to stay here until I get the signal. It's part of the act."

I heard the handclap, shot out from under the table, and took up my position as Kay started the sequence again. "There was always the man she loved. . . . There was always the man she didn't love. . . . There was always the man she loved too often. . . . There was always the man she loved too much." Once more I did my fall and slid under the table. "Henry," the woman said. "He's doing it again."

"Get out of there," a male voice said in a thick Brooklyn accent, "or I'll —"

The handclap again rescued me. I shot out from under the tablecloth and went back to my position as Kay started again. I was dreading this next fall because I knew I would be back under the table again, and, indeed, as I disappeared under the tablecloth, I heard the male voice say, "That does it!" and a pair of tasseled loafers started kicking out at me. I moved my head from side to side, trying to avoid the flying loafers, until Kay clapped her hands for the third and last time, and I was able to make my escape. We got a standing ovation at the end of the show. The only people who didn't join in were the two diners who were still glaring at me as we took our bows and left the stage.

Our two weeks at El Rancho Vegas were a big success with SOLD OUT signs outside the showroom every night. We were in great spirits as we moved on to our second booking at Tahoe Village on South Shore at Lake Tahoe. Kay had one of the few guest rooms at the casino. The rest of us stayed in a couple of log cabins a mile down the road, and when not rehearsing or performing, it was a real pleasure to sit on the porch, shaded from the fierce heat, or walk by the cool water of the lake. It was so cold, local legend had it, that it would never give up the dead said to have been dumped in it by the Mob.

Tahoe Village, reached by a dirt driveway, was a long, low building. Its whitewashed walls were blinding in the fierce sunlight. An awning over the entrance gave the only hint of shade, and after the glare outside, the foyer seemed as dark as the entrance to a cave. It took a moment for my eyes to adjust to the gloom. There was a cigarette stand on one side of the foyer and a souvenir stand facing it, manned by a bored-looking young man and woman who, after giving us a cursory once-over, went back to staring out the window at the blue waters of the lake. The coat-check booth was empty, but the casino, visible through a wide doorway on the far side of the foyer, was busy with people playing the banks of slots and the gaming tables. The casino was functional rather than decorative, with wood floors and walls bare but for signs reading CHANGE and NO LIMIT, and a sign showing the number of jackpots paid out by the slots that day. Throughout the two weeks we spent there, the tinny whir and clank of the slots, punctuated by the occasional rattle as a machine paid out, never stopped for a minute, night or day. The noise, the bare walls, and the constant movement of people reminded me more of a factory floor than a casino.

The billboard slogan that had greeted us as we pulled off the highway was TAHOE VIL-LAGE: SOMETHING DOING EVERY MIN-

UTE, and that proved to be true although most of what was doing was as crooked as a hairpin bend. Tahoe Village was run by two gangsters. "Russian" Louie Strauss was linked to the Chicago Mob and was said to be a member of Murder, Inc. He was tall and thin with a long face and eyes as cold and lifeless as a fish on a marble slab. His second-in-command was "Sir" Abe Chapman — the title was ironic, as I don't think the king of England had been consulted about it. He was also known as Abe the Trigger. Their front man, Harry Sherwood, was a WASP whose principal function, apart from acting as casino manager, was to keep the Nevada Gaming Board off the mobsters' backs. Sherwood himself was no stranger to organized crime, since he was formerly the partner of Tony Stralla, a notorious West Coast bootlegger.

Considering that he and his business associates were gangsters, Sherwood was a curiously refined character, well-read and well-mannered, and he even took afternoon tea every day like a regular English gentleman. He invited us to join him on the day we arrived, and we all sat there sipping tea from china cups and talking about the latest books and movies with him, while the desert sun blazed down outside and the mob-

101

sters' mood music of choice — the tinkle of slot machines and the clack of chips being played — could be heard from the casino downstairs. Even Sir Abe and Russian Louie seemed like the acceptable face of gangsterism, always immaculately turned out in suit and tie, and always polite and friendly to us whenever we passed one another in the casino. Sir Abe in particular took a real shine to us and would often invite us to join him for a drink or dinner, take a drive to another casino, or use his boat on the lake.

We all felt a curious ambivalence about the gangsters for whom we worked. Like a lot of people then and now, we perhaps found it too easy to be seduced by the spurious air of glamour and excitement — and the whiff of danger they projected — and to forget or downplay the lawlessness and brutality that was their stock in trade. The money they were paying us to perform in their casinos probably made it even easier for us to forget the darker side of these characters and dismiss them as no more than likable rogues, dangerous but somehow almost endearing.

There was certainly no possibility of avoiding the gangsters because even more than Vegas, the whole of Tahoe was crawling with them at the time. The Nevada police put up roadblocks every night trying to catch some of the more notorious characters from out of state, but very few ever seemed to be picked up; either the gangsters came cross-country, or some of the cops were pocketing bribes to look the other way. Bob came across some of that kind while coming back from a trip to another casino with Sir Abe and a couple of other characters one night. Sir Abe was drunk and driving very erratically when a flashing light appeared in the rearview mirror, and the cops pulled him over. "Wait here," Sir Abe said, peeling a couple of $50 bills from a fat roll. "I just have to have a word with these boys." Two minutes later he was back in the car and swerving his way down the highway while the cops turned off their flashing light and headed back in the opposite direction.

Apart from our act, the only other entertainment was a line of a half-dozen showgirls who danced while the orchestra played a few bump-and-grind tunes. The showgirls were housed in a Quonset hut behind the casino — a long, open room with a series of iron-frame beds and a small wardrobe and cupboard for each girl. Don had eyes for one of the dancers, and one night she took him back to the Quonset hut. They were making love in total darkness to the accompaniment of squeaks from the rusty iron bed frame, twangs from the bedsprings, and suppressed giggles from the other showgirls eavesdropping from their beds farther down the room when Don felt cold metal pressed against the back of his head and heard Sir Abe's guttural accent: "If I didn't like you kids so much, I'd blow your fucking head off. Now get out of here."

Don didn't need a second invitation. Not even stopping to pick up his clothes, he sprinted out of the hut and, stark naked, ran a mile down the highway to the log cabin where we were staying. Who knew that the dancer was Sir Abe's girlfriend? Don was understandably nervous when we went back to the casino the next day, and he kept well away from her, though her makeup did not entirely conceal a black eye. Sir Abe, though, seemed content that the lesson had been learned on both sides and had gone back to being charming and polite.

We didn't gamble in the casino because there wasn't a straight game in the place. Decks were stacked, dice were loaded, roulette wheels were tampered with. Everything was done to make sure the suckers never got anything approaching an even break. The season at Tahoe in those days was only eight weeks long; the casino had to make its money in that brief summer period, and the

Tahoe Village's owners made sure that the odds were always in their favor.

One night we were resting in our dressing room between shows when the pit boss of the casino, the son of the Mafia don of Philadelphia, a guy called Tony Bonano — no prizes for guessing his nickname — suddenly burst in. "Take those," he said, shoving a stack of playing cards at us and diving out again. Curiosity overcoming cowardice, we leafed through the cards; there were endless aces, kings, queens, and jacks, and a tiny handful of other cards. "Must be the dealer's," Bob said with a wink. A few minutes later the door burst open again. "Give me those," Tony said, snatching the cards and then disappearing again.

On the morning after our last show, Sir Abe and Russian Louie came to Kay's room to pay us. It was early September but still a broiling hot day, and even with the windows open, it was stifling inside Kay's small suite. The two mobsters entered, dressed as usual in dark suits. After a few minutes' small talk, Sir Abe, with sweat rolling down his brow, turned to Kay. "Miss Thompson, it's awfully hot today. Would you mind if we removed our jackets?"

"Of course not, boys. Go right ahead," she said, but her smile froze as they took off their jackets, revealing the pistols that both of them were packing in shoulder holsters. Throughout the rest of the conversation, try as she might, Kay could not drag her horrified gaze away from those guns.

Russian Louie took an envelope from his pocket and held it out to her. "That's your check, Miss Thompson," he said, "but I wonder if I could ask you one small favor. Would you mind very much not cashing it for five or six days?"

"I'll never cash it! I'll never cash it!" Kay said, her gaze still fixed on the guns and her voice rising an octave as she spoke.

"No, no," he said. "It's fine to cash it. We really want you to cash it. You've all been great. Just please don't cash it until next week."

Kay now seemed to have lost the power of speech altogether, and for understandable reasons, Don was keeping pretty quiet, too, so I broke the silence and said, "Don't worry, we won't."

"Now," Sir Abe said, business having been completed, "how are you good people getting out of here? Miss Thompson, you don't have a car, do you? There are no taxis up here, and if you're not driving, the only way to Reno is the milk wagon leaving at five in the morning." He paused and favored her with a smile. "So Louie and I would be honored to drive you down to Reno."

Kay looked as if she would rather have been skinned alive and fed to the coyotes, but she gave a weak smile and said, "That would be very nice. Thank you." So while the Williams Brothers and our pianist squeezed into our car and set off over the precipitous mountain road toward Las Vegas, pulling the trailer-load of luggage behind us, Kay got into Sir Abe's black Cadillac with white-wall tires and was driven down to the small airport in Reno. None of us thought to say good-bye to the tea-sipping casino manager, Harry Sherwood, and we didn't get a second chance to do so.

It turned out that Sherwood had a gambling problem. His main problem was that he had taken all the money in the casino safe, gone to Reno, and lost it all at a rival casino. That was the reason Sir Abe and Russian Louie had asked Kay not to cash our check immediately; there was no money left, and they needed a couple of days to cover the check with the bank. It was also the reason that, having dropped her at Reno, they then drove back to Tahoe, walked into the foyer of the casino, and shot Harry Sherwood in full view of his two children who operated the cigarette and souvenir stands on either side of the foyer. Sherwood survived long enough to undergo surgery to remove a bullet lodged near his spine but died of his wounds two weeks later.

Russian Louie was arrested in Carson City, and a .38 pistol was retrieved from the glove compartment of his car. Sir Abe and another associate, George "The Professor" Kosloff, were also arrested, but charges against them were dropped. When Russian Louie stood trial, no witnesses to the killing could be found — not even Sherwood's children — other than two casino employees who claimed the shooting was in self-defense. Russian Louie was duly acquitted, but justice of a sort was served when he in turn was murdered. Like many other victims of Vegas's lawless past, his body was said to have been buried in the desert and has never been found.

Las Vegas and Tahoe remained with wall-to-wall gangsters until Howard Hughes began to buy up Vegas piece by piece. Hughes brought in his own people and his own corporate methods, and the town's old freewheeling, high-rolling days were numbered. When the Mob ran Vegas, virtually everything — rooms, food, drinks, entertainment — was inexpensive or even free. When Hughes took over, every single part of the casino operation had to turn a profit. His investment brought increased respectability to Vegas as well as increased profitability to the Hughes Corporation, but if it rid the town of some of its Mafia taint, it also took away much of the character and flavor that made Vegas unique.

In the wake of the Hughes-inspired cleanup of the town, Vegas even tried to reinvent itself as a family-friendly destination for a while, but whether owned by the Mob or legitimate businessmen, Vegas has always revolved around drinking and gambling, with more than a little prostitution on the side. How casino owners ever thought they could combine those vices with a family resort is beyond me, yet for a decade the message was "Bring the family." Then there was a moment of clarity, and the slogan ever since has been more realistic: "What happens in Vegas stays in Vegas," a tacit invitation to indulge your fantasies without anyone back home ever finding out.

5

After three months honing our act in Vegas and Lake Tahoe, we were ready to perform for a tougher showbiz crowd at Hollywood's hippest supper club: Ciro's on Sunset Strip, "the hottest nightclub on the planet." It was a magnificent venue: Outside was a largely featureless concrete façade, broken only by Ciro's name, but the interior was a gloriously over-the-top collection of the most baroque fixtures and fittings money could buy. Even the dressing rooms would not have been out of place in the Taj Mahal.

The show went down even better at Ciro's than it had in Vegas and Tahoe. We did five encores on opening night, and our reviews were astonishing: "Lightning in a bottle." "The most inspired thing I have ever seen in my life." "Like the finest watch you can imagine, everything was precision, and it just blew everybody away." As word spread, we became the hottest ticket in town; everybody seemed to want to see us, and the place was packed with Hollywood stars every night. Walter Winchell saw the show, loved it, and wrote about us almost daily in his syndicated column. Lena Horne was appearing at the Clover Club at the same time, and Nat King Cole was at the Trocadero, both on the Sunset Strip, but the show that everyone was really talking about was Kay Thompson and the Williams Brothers.

It was a sign of how celebrated the act had become in such a short time that when Ciro's held a benefit night for charity, it was a group that included Danny Kaye, Van Johnson, Jack Benny, George Burns, and Jack Carson that appeared as Kay Thompson and the Williams Brothers. Danny Kaye took Kay's part and was hilarious. Van Johnson was me and had to do the stage falls that I did. He had never learned how to do a fall, so he just crumpled to the floor in a heap every time. It was still funny.

Sadly, no film of the real Kay Thompson and the Williams Brothers show survives. Film and TV companies routinely burned the film or tapes of shows in those days. Storage space was a problem, and, ironically, in view of the vast sums the companies make now from endlessly recycling old shows, they didn't think their back catalog would ever be worth anything. All the music and arrangements of the songs we did have been lost, but in 2008, Liza Minnelli revived three of our old songs in a show at the Palace Theatre in New York. (They had survived because we had recorded them on Columbia Records.) Liza took the Kay Thompson role and had four singer-dancers playing the Williams Brothers. It was very well done, and I couldn't think of a more appropriate person to have revived the show; after all, Kay had been Liza's godmother.

With the whole of Hollywood acclaiming our act, these were heady days for us, and it was hard not to be carried away by all the adulation. I can't ever recall asking the others or even myself if we were happy, if this was what we really wanted. There didn't seem to be time to do anything other than hang on to the career express train we were riding.

Everywhere we went flashbulbs were popping, people were asking for autographs or trying to buy us drinks, and good-looking women were letting us know in more or less subtle ways that they were interested. We had money in our pockets, and, with the exception of Bob who went home to Edna and the kids after the show every night, we were young, free, single, and ready to party. This was not the 1960s, but, among the young at least, the war years had changed attitudes about casual sex, and although I was only a country boy, I was growing up fast. I certainly didn't reject all the offers that came my way, but any relationships I had were very short term. My torch continued to burn for Kay Thompson, but still I told no one, least of all Kay herself.

We did spend a lot of time together offstage, and one night when we were appearing at Ciro's, Kay took me with her when she went to dinner at George Platt Lynes's house. He was a famous photographer for *Vogue,* and one of his favorite models, a very beautiful girl named Duggie, was there with her boyfriend, Bill Harbach. Bill was a television producer and son of the composer Otto Harbach, who had had a string of hit Broadway shows, including *No, No, Nanette,* and had written "Smoke Gets in Your Eyes," among many other songs. After we had been there a couple of hours, I asked George where the bathroom was. "I'll show you," he said and led me up the stairs and along the landing to the bathroom. When I turned to thank him, he suddenly grabbed me and kissed me full on the mouth. It was another new experience for a boy from Iowa, but not one I was eager to repeat. I was so shocked that all I could think of to say was, "Don't you ever do that to me again." Just to make sure of that not happening again, when I got back downstairs I told Kay what had transpired and that I didn't want to stay any longer, and we left straightaway. It was okay with me if you wanted to walk on that side of the street, but it wasn't for me.

After a ten-week residency at Ciro's we took the show on tour, playing the finest supper clubs in America. At each new club or theater we played, Bob always had a struggle to adapt; his having learned our routines parrot-fashion wasn't always helpful when we changed venues. The stage lights were so bright that you couldn't easily see the audience, and Bob had gotten so used to facing one way at Ciro's that on opening night at the next place we played, Don, Dick, and I found ourselves singing to the audience, while Bob, playing from memory as if we were still at Ciro's, wound up working to the wings.

We rarely appeared at venues bigger than supper clubs, but when we did, it gave us another headache — on one occasion quite literally. We were booked at the Roxy, a five thousand–seat movie theater in New York, and at the start of our act two of us would run onstage from one side and two from the other. We'd come together in the middle of the stage and go into our routine, building up to Kay's entry. However, the stage at the Roxy was much wider than the ones we were used to in supper clubs, and on the first day there the stage lights were so dazzling that the four of us sprinted on from opposite sides and, blinded by the lights, ran straight into one another. We all finished up flat on our backs, and although it wasn't part of the act, it got the biggest laugh of the night.

The booking was a strange one. The Roxy was a cinema, and just as Frank Sinatra used to do at the Paramount Theatre in New York when he was starting his career, we did a series of short sets in between showings of the movie. We were there from lunchtime until mid-evening, performing a total of five twenty-minute shows in between screenings of *Apartment for Peggy*. The Roxy was so huge that it was not really suited to so intimate a show, but we always got a good reception even though the audience at the back was so far from the stage that some of Kay's fan letters were addressed to "Mr. Thompson."

Wherever we went, we were appearing at the very best small clubs and earning incredible money, and we also fitted in an occasional lucrative private booking. While playing a ten-week residency at Le Directoire in New York, an exclusive, brand-new, and, as it turned out, very short-lived club in the old Café Society building on East 58th Street — a sort of East Coast equivalent of Ciro's in Los Angeles — we were offered $5,000 to perform for fifteen minutes at a party given by one of New York's grandest "grandes dames," Mrs. Cordelia Biddle. She divided her time between New York, Paris, and the Hamptons, and her famous friends and acquaintances included Cole Porter, Charlie Chaplin, and, curiously, the notorious bootlegger Legs Diamond, whom she visited in jail and described as "such a nice little fellow." She was now hosting a party in honor of the Duke and Duchess of Windsor, or Eddy England, as Ethel Merman (who was there with Randolph Hearst Jr.) called him to his face; he seemed to like it.

We arrived, as instructed, at the servants' entrance at the back of the building and were then kept waiting for fifteen minutes until Mrs. Biddle appeared to give us our orders. She looked Kay up and down, with the sort of expression of distaste that a preacher's wife might reserve for the madam of the local whorehouse, and then said, "How long are you intending to perform?"

"Fifteen minutes," Kay said. "That's what

you asked for, isn't it?"

Mrs. Biddle's lips pursed in disapproval. She was clearly used to being addressed with a lot more deference.

"Very well," she said. "You will begin at nine o'clock promptly, and you will wait out of sight here in the servants' quarters until it is time for you to perform." She turned on her heel and went back to her party.

Bill Harbach, the television producer, was at the party with us. He was a bit of a society figure and an invited guest of Mrs. Biddle, but our agency had asked him to act as our unofficial agent for the night. Kay stared after Mrs. Biddle for a moment and then said to Bill, "I'll need a check from her for five thousand dollars before we go on."

Bill was aghast. "You can't ask Mrs. Biddle for a check. She's a billionaire, for God's sake. Of course you'll get paid."

"I know," Kay said. "I just want to make that bitch go and get it for us now. No check, no performance." She was absolutely adamant, so with the look of a condemned man on his way to the electric chair, Bill went to find Mrs. Biddle, who was now busy fawning over her special guests and wasn't exactly pleased to have to break off, go upstairs to the library, and prepare our payment.

When she returned, stone-faced, she

handed it to Kay and said, "There's your check, Miss Thompson," with ice dripping from every word. She then issued some further precise instructions: "You will remain here until it is time for you to perform, and as soon as you have finished your act, you are to leave immediately by the servants' entrance at the rear of the building. Under no circumstances whatsoever are you to attempt to mingle or socialize with any of my guests. I hope I have made myself absolutely clear."

Kay pocketed the check, returned look for look, and said, "Honey, if we'd known we wouldn't have to mingle with your friends, we'd have done the show for twenty-five hundred."

A few months later we returned to New York for a six-week booking at the Persian Room in the Plaza Hotel, an eighteen-story building modeled on a French château and overlooking the southern end of Central Park. The Persian Room had just been redesigned by Henry Dreyfuss, an interior design consultant on luxury liners, and the room had something of that feel. The bell captains and waiters at the Plaza all seemed to have been there for years and looked and acted more like bank presidents.

While we were at the Plaza, Kay introduced

me to a more friendly and approachable society figure, Stanley Marcus of the Neiman Marcus department stores. He was a big collector of art, and I talked to him for hours about modern art and the paintings and sculptures he owned. He saw that he had caught my imagination and told me that if I really wanted to learn about modern art, I should go in every art gallery up and down 57th Street, day after day, and become familiar with the work of the different contemporary artists shown there. I did exactly that, and before long I was amazing myself by being able to spot the differences of a Picasso, a Braque, and a Juan Gris. It was the real beginning of an interest in art and antiques (my brothers have been known to call it an obsession) that has stayed with me throughout my life. Kay also encouraged us to broaden our interest in art and even taught us a song to help us remember the names of the Impressionists:

Toulouse-Lautrec, Renoir, Bonnard,
Manet, Monet, and Degas;
Van Gogh, Goya, Gauguin,
Sisley, Cézanne, Matisse;
Mary Cassatt, et aussi,
George Seurat, et aussi,
Toulouse-Lautrec, Renoir, Bonnard,
Manet, Monet, and Degas;

Van Gogh, Goya, Gauguin,
Sisley, Cézanne, Matisse.

She wrote another ditty using the names of literary greats:

Thackeray, William Makepeace, 1811, 63;
Stevenson, Robert Louis, 1850, 1894;
Walpole, Whitman, Whittier, Oscar Wilde,
 Voltaire,
Boswell, Browning, Emily Brontë, Balzac;
Cicero, Caesar, Euripedes, Aristotle,
 Aesop,
Dante, Darwin, Dickens, Dumas, Conrad;
Ernest Hemingway, Michelangelo.
We read them all in the Brooklyn branch of
 the New York Library.
We read them all in the Brooklyn branch of
 the New York Public Library.

While we were playing the Persian Room, we stayed at the Plaza Hotel, and it was there that Kay started writing the first of her Eloise books. Eloise was a six-year-old spoiled brat who lived at the Plaza with her parents, although they were very social and almost always away. Her main companions were her nanny and a pet turtle, Skipperdee, who lived in the bidet in Eloise's bathroom. My brothers and I would sit around Kay's hotel room after the show and act out the various characters' parts for her while she scribbled notes. The books' humorous, slightly surreal take on life proved an instant hit with children, and the Eloise series became very successful.

As well as touring we also made a couple of records for Decca with Kay, but because the special material that we did for our stage show relied as much on our dance moves and acting as on the songs, and because Kay's voice wasn't really that of a pop singer, they were never likely to be hits.

In the fall of 1950, after more than three years of being continuously on the road, Kay decided it was time to take a break, and we all went our separate ways for a while. Bob, who by now had three children, didn't want to spend all the money that he had been able to save and was eager to get a job of some kind to tide himself over until we got back together with Kay. "You know something?" he said. "I'd like to be a milkman. The deliveries are in the early morning, and then I'll have plenty of free time to spend with Edna and the kids." So he got a job delivering milk. Because he was the newcomer, the older milkmen made sure he got all the worst jobs, like the second-story deliveries. On his first day he delivered milk to Buddy

Lester, a comedian who had opened for us in one of the clubs. He had always said that Bob was "the funniest of all of you. He really cracks me up." So when Bob himself turned up on his doorstep in a milkman's uniform, he started laughing, convinced that this was some kind of zany routine that Bob was trying out. It took several visits and quite a few bottles of milk before Bob convinced him that he really was a milkman and not setting up a stunt.

While Bob was delivering milk, Dick decided to take it easy, play golf, and work on a musical he was writing with a friend of his, which he hoped would one day reach Broadway. Don was doing much the same thing — playing golf, relaxing, reading, and enjoying the time off before we were to resume our act with Kay.

I, however, soon tired of sitting around doing nothing much, and hearing about a television show that Martin Gotch was putting together for Chico Marx called *The College Bowl,* I auditioned and was hired as one of several high school kids. Joan Holloway played my girlfriend. *The College Bowl* was broadcast live from New York, and for the label it was probably the worst TV show ever made. Chico's character managed a soda fountain in a drugstore, and every episode would begin with us drifting into his establishment and sitting around drinking sodas. It was similar to the characters in *Friends* who used to sit around drinking coffee in Central Perk. The only difference was that *Friends* was pretty good.

Chico was fairly old by then, and it was quite a sight to see him getting ready for the show. He would give himself a face-lift by pulling the folds of loose skin upward and outward and then hold them in place with strips of tape at his temples that were hidden under his wig. He did the same thing with his neck, sticking the tape around the back where it wasn't seen because he spent most of the show standing behind the counter, facing the camera. It was unfortunate that he didn't put as much effort into learning his lines; he was constantly forgetting them, though that wasn't all bad, given how terrible the scripts were. When Joanie and I came in together, he would say, "Hiya, Andy. Hiya, Joanie," in his best fake Italian accent. Then he would forget his next line and wave his fingers around as if trying to pull it out of thin air. Joan would mouth "Football" at him, and he'd smile with relief and say, "So, Joanie, you still playing football?"

"Er, no, Chico. It's *Andy* who plays football."

"Oh, yeah, yeah, that'sa right." There would be more finger waving and then, "Andy, you stilla the besta-looking boy in school?" That line wasn't in the script and didn't have much relation to my next line: "So, Chico, what are you going to wear for Easter?"

He managed to remember that bit — "Anything that you getta for me" — and I then had to respond with the punch line: "Oh, you'd better wear more than that." Even the canned laughter machine had trouble working up much enthusiasm for jokes like that. I watched a tape of one of those old shows recently, and all I could think was: *My God, that's the worst thing I've ever seen.* It was beyond terrible, and after a start like that, it's a wonder I ever worked in television again.

When not working, Chico seemed to spend all his time either on the phone to his bookmaker or playing cards with the stagehands, and never — even in the rigged games at the Tahoe Village — had I seen anyone lose as consistently as Chico. Whatever salary he was paid for *The College Bowl* wasn't enough to keep pace with his losses; he was always broke, always borrowing money, and always telling people, "I'll pay you back Friday."

After the demise of *The College Bowl* in 1951 — it was more of a mercy killing than a cancellation — I went back on the road with my brothers and Kay Thompson, who was now rested, refreshed, and ready to give it another go. We even made our first visit to England to play at the Café de Paris. Now a disco, it was then the most sophisticated nightspot in London. Noel Coward had appeared there just before us, and Marlene Dietrich took over after we left.

We were very excited to be appearing in London for the first time, but before we could open, King George VI died suddenly on February 6, 1952. He was a much-loved figure, and because the papers had hidden the extent of his illness, people were thunderstruck at the news. The king's death cast a fresh pall over England, which was only just emerging from the years of wartime austerity. The country, or those parts of it that we saw, still seemed exhausted, physically, mentally, and financially. Everything appeared gray, drab, and dirty, from the smoke-blackened buildings to the dense fog swirling up from the Thames to engulf the city, sometimes for days on end. The people also often looked pinched and poor, and the displays of food in the shops can have done little to lift their mood; the greengrocers had endless rows of cabbages, turnips, and potatoes, and not much else. Reconstruction of the bombed sections of London had barely begun — or so it seemed to us — and whole areas, particularly in the East End, were rubble-strewn wastelands. There were, however, great sights to see, too — Buckingham Palace, the Houses of Parliament, and St. Paul's Cathedral — and on our trips out of London we loved everything from the great stately homes to the little thatched cottages and country inns. And there were other things — Big Ben, London buses and black taxis, red telephone boxes, Guardsmen with bearskin hats — that were at once so strange and yet so familiar from movies and newsreels that we'd seen. If there were still traces of the wartime resentment of Americans — "oversexed, overpaid, and over here," in the famous phrase — we never encountered any, and the years of austerity seemed to make the people even more determined to enjoy themselves when they had the opportunity.

After the king's funeral and the period of public mourning were over, we opened at the Café de Paris to a packed house of invited Londoners. It was a gloriously over-the-top place with velvet drapes, gilded ceilings, chandeliers, and ornate plasterwork. It had an atmosphere of opulence and decadence, as musicians and film stars rubbed shoulders with politicians, financiers, fortune hunters, aristocrats, and members of the royal family; Princess Margaret and the Duchess of Kent were both regular visitors. A secret stairway led from the balcony to the street, useful both for the discreet arrival and departure of royalty and for throwing out drunks, gate-crashers, and troublemakers. The show was a smash, and we wound up playing the Café de Paris for ten weeks. The audiences were as noisy and enthusiastic as any we ever played to. We all loved our time in London, apart from one thing: the food. It was still in very short supply, and what we could get was often a bit of an acquired taste. Meat was always very well done, for example, or, as we straight-talking Americans would say, "Burnt!" — but we managed to get used to the warm beer. We went to a lot of pubs and fell in love with the game of darts, so before we left, we bought a dartboard and a few sets of darts to take back home. When we returned to the States, we hung the dartboard on the back of our hotel door. After a few drinks we'd go back to the room and play darts, but we missed the board so often that when we left, we had to buy the hotel a new door and pay for repairs to the wall. I came to love England so much that, as well as darts, I even played a game of cricket on a subsequent visit there, although I must admit that I did use a baseball bat rather than a cricket bat.

Having played at the Café de Paris in London, we also paid a visit to Paris itself, but not to work, just to see the city. We had all made an effort to learn a little French before our trip there — all of us except Bob, that is, who steadfastly refused to learn even a word. "Why do I need to speak French?" he said. "They'll understand me in English."

On our first day there we went to a restaurant for lunch. Dick, Don, and I managed to order what we wanted in halting, heavily accented, but still comprehensible French. Bob, on the other hand, adopted the classic tactic of the ugly American abroad: If those damn foreigners refuse to understand you the first time, just keep repeating yourself, louder and louder.

"Two eggs over easy," Bob said the first time, using his hands to indicate "over easy."

There was a pregnant pause. *"Comment?"*

Bob tried again: "Two . . . eggs . . . over . . . easy."

"Je suis désolé, mais je ne comprends pas, monsieur."

"TWO EGGS OVER EASY!" Bob bellowed at maximum volume. That appeared to solve the problem, because the waiter disappeared in the direction of the kitchen, while Bob turned to us and gave us a satisfied look.

Ten minutes later the food arrived. Dick's, Don's, and mine were exactly what we had ordered. Now all eyes turned to the plate the waiter was placing in front of Bob. *"Voilà, monsieur."*

Looking up at Bob from his plate were not two eggs over easy but two scoops of ice cream. The rest of us burst out laughing.

When we returned to the States, we went back on the road, playing many of the same rooms we had played before, but this tour was like a lingering death. Television was taking over America and steadily killing nightclub attendance, as people chose to stay home and be entertained in their own living rooms. In the end we all felt the same: We had gone about as far as we could with the act, and there were no new venues to play. We were just treading water, and we realized that we all needed to go our own ways. So in the summer of 1953 we stopped performing and split up for good.

We had spent our entire lives as a group, and it sometimes felt as if we were glued together. We were still very close, but we were tired of living in one another's pockets, spending virtually every waking moment together. Even when we went to a party, the four of us would often wind up in the same corner, talking to one another. In our different ways, each of us also had ambitions to stretch his wings and try something on his own rather than forever being just one-quarter of the Williams Brothers. We were no longer boys: Bob was thirty-four, and even I, the baby, was twenty-four. To a greater or lesser extent, we all felt it was time to grow up and make our own ways in the world. There was no acrimony; we had just reached a parting of the ways.

Bob had never liked performing and was tired of touring and always being away from his family. Having had enough of being a milkman, he now decided to join my dad in the real estate business he was running in the San Fernando Valley of Los Angeles. Don told me that he wanted to be an agent, so I phoned my friend Jerry Perenchio, who had just formed a new agency with a variety wing of Music Corporation of America, called United Talent Management (UTM). Jerry instructed Don: "Just sit in my office a couple of weeks, and you'll see what an agent is supposed to do. You've been in show business all your life, so this shouldn't be difficult for you to learn." After a few weeks Jerry said to Don, "Do you think you're ready to join the agency?" and Don said yes. When General Artists Corporation bought UTM about a year later, Don became an agent at GAC, and eventually he opened his own management company, handling a string of top-line acts that included Ray Stevens, Roger Miller, and Jack Jones.

Meanwhile, Dick accepted an offer to join the Harry James orchestra as a vocalist, stayed with the band for two years, and then became a regular on the Tennessee Ernie Ford daytime television show. He went on to build a very good career, first as a session singer and composer and performer of advertising jingles, and then as a studio singer and arranger.

Janey had gotten married and had a couple of children, and she devoted herself to her family when her kids were young. Her husband, Bob, worked for a telephone company at the time, but later on she and Bob both got their real estate licenses and began selling real estate out in the Valley, where they lived. Bob also got his pilot's license and began working with the Coast Guard and the Drug Enforcement Administration, making spotter flights off the coast to look for potential drug smugglers and, over land,

131

searching for areas that were being used for marijuana cultivation.

So, with my brothers and my sister all pursuing their own careers, there I was, aged twenty-four, suddenly all on my own. Singing was all I knew, and having tasted success with my brothers and Kay, I was desperate to be successful again. Until then I had never even thought about going solo, and doing so at this point in time came as something of a shock. I was not prepared for it at all, but prompted by Kay, I moved to New York and set about developing a solo act under her guidance. She was now living at the Plaza Hotel, and I stayed in a small hotel nearby while I worked with her on an act. She did everything: She chose the songs, arranged the medleys, gave me some dance steps, and even wrote some lines of patter to link the songs.

Our relationship also now became more than strictly business. Despite the age difference — Kay was nineteen years older than me — I was still absolutely fascinated by her, and now, living and working in New York, and spending so much time alone with her, I couldn't help letting my feelings show. To my surprise and delight, she admitted that she felt the same. We made up for lost time over the next couple of years, but even though we were now lovers, it remained a completely private affair. Kay never mentioned it to anyone, and, taking my cue from her, I never said or did anything in public that would have revealed our relationship. Although I still never even told my brothers, I'm sure they guessed what was going on. Like the office romance where the two lovers think they're being carefully discreet but everyone else knows exactly what is happening, I'm sure Kay and I weren't as subtle as we thought. Looking back on our affair with the benefit of hindsight, I wonder whether it was not only Kay who attracted me but also the glamour and aura that surrounded her, the artistic and literary circles she moved in, and the famous people she knew. Whatever it was, I loved everything about her.

Our personal relationship didn't affect our working one. Kay remained a perfectionist in working hours, never letting anything pass until it was as good as we could possibly get it. As well as the new act I was working on with Kay, I was now also trying to strengthen the lower register of my voice. While singing with my brothers, I always had to sing the top parts in the four-part harmonies because I was the youngest, and as each of my older brothers' voices changed, they dropped lower. Mine had, too, of course, but someone had to sing the top line, and so I had developed an upper register in order to cover it. I was a tenor at a time when all the popular male singers — Bing Crosby, Frank Sinatra, Dick Haymes, and Vic Damone — were baritones. Since the Beatles came along, all the popular singers have tended to be tenors, and most of the voices now are higher than mine. Back then, though, all the successful singers were baritones, and I certainly wanted to be successful. I even went to a voice trainer, but it didn't really make a difference. I remained a natural tenor, and, as things turned out, not being a baritone did not prove too much of a handicap.

6

Although I was very focused and felt I knew where I wanted to go and what I wanted to do, I was still quite nervous about going solo. I really missed having my brothers with me, both offstage and on. I was usually petrified before I went onstage, and although I was able to control my nerves so that they didn't show in my voice, this was the period when I really grew to hate performing.

Many of my fellow artists are so in love with singing that they probably start when the refrigerator light goes on, but throughout my career I never truly enjoyed concerts and appearances. I suppose it was because I was too uncertain, too insecure. It was a strange paradox: Singing was what I wanted to do, and I desperately wanted to be a success, but I always heaved a sigh of relief when the show was over and I reached the sanctuary of my dressing room. As I always said to myself when the show was over,

"Fooled 'em again!"

Part of the reason was that I can relax only when the musicians, lighting, sound, and everything else are as good as I or someone I trust can possibly make them. If the musicians are not properly rehearsed or are just competent, or if the sound system is poor or the lighting amateurish, then it is torture for me.

My fears were often justified in those early days. My first engagement was at the Blue Angel, one of New York's more popular small clubs on the East Side. The guy who owned it, Herbert Jacoby, was a remarkable character. Born in Paris of a French-Swiss mother and an English father, he spoke English before he learned French but had a strong French accent all his life. Educated in Paris and London, he became a French diplomat and then a journalist and a press agent. One of his clients was a Parisian nightclub, which is where he began to develop the ideas that he later put into practice in his own club.

He was very tall, well over six feet, dark complexioned, and always wore a black slouch hat and a long black cape. He also walked with a strange flowing gait so that he seemed to slide rather than walk, and would slither into a room. We called Herbert the "Prince of Darkness," not because he was the epitome of evil but because of his dark outfits, his Bela Lugosi–type voice, and the fact that, since he was in his club until dawn and then would sleep all day, he was seen only at night.

His first club, Le Ruban Bleu in Paris, opened on the day that the French liner *Normandie* claimed the Blue Riband for the transatlantic speed record. George Gershwin, Cole Porter, and some of his other American friends and clients who loved the club persuaded him to come to New York, where in 1937 he opened a similar nightspot, also named Le Ruban Bleu. While performing there, one of his acts, a young unknown pianist called Walter Liberace, decided to shorten his name and began putting candelabra on his piano.

Six years later, Herbert opened The Blue Angel on East 55th Street. It was named after the 1930 film that introduced Marlene Dietrich in the role of a nightclub singer. Herbert also said that blue was his lucky color, though I never saw him wear anything but black. The club was an immediate success. Instead of a single continuous show, Herbert pioneered a more informal approach to club entertainment with short sets, often by new talent, punctuated by periods when his customers could just sit, talk, and relax while a pianist played. Herbert claimed to audition some five hundred acts a year and said he felt it was worth it if even two of them turned out to be good enough to play at the Blue Angel. Yul Brynner, Harry Belafonte, and Pearl Bailey were just three of the big names who got their break through appearing at the club.

The Blue Angel was a great venue. The Herman Chitterson Trio were the terrific backing musicians, and the audience was a sophisticated crowd, so everything went fine. I would happily have sung there every night for a year; but the Blue Angel changed acts every few weeks, and there were very few other clubs of that quality around.

I also made an appearance on *The Ed Sullivan Show,* entirely on the strength of having been part of Kay Thompson and the Williams Brothers. Ed Sullivan knew our act very well and loved it, so he booked me, introducing me as "one of the Williams Brothers, who's just starting a solo career." I sang "I've Got a Crush on You," but my performance didn't start any brushfires.

I began to realize that the success I had enjoyed with Kay and my brothers now meant virtually nothing; promoters weren't being offered Kay Thompson and the Williams Brothers. All they were getting was one-fifth of that act, and even at a lot less than one-fifth of the money, the name Andy Williams was not a draw, so there were very few offers. Kay had helped me immensely to develop my act, but I now had to take the show on the road, playing at any place where my new booking agent could get me a job, in the hope that I could build enough of a reputation and a following to start climbing the show business ladder again.

I left New York with very mixed feelings. I was now heading into unknown territory where clubs like the Blue Angel just didn't exist. Instead, I'd be playing small clubs in the East and Midwest: New Jersey, Pennsylvania, Maryland, West Virginia, Ohio, Michigan, Indiana, Illinois, Wisconsin, and Minnesota. Each time I arrived in a new town, I was at the mercy of the local promoters and their venues, and both were often inadequate. I was playing little 150- to 200-seat clubs, and sometimes when I went onstage, the lights wouldn't focus right; one time there were no lights at all — or at least none on me.

I didn't play an instrument, and I wasn't being paid enough money to carry a pianist, so I had to make do with whatever backing musicians were available in each place. Sometimes they were good, sometimes not so good. One of the first bands I encountered was a drum, violin, and accordion trio — a lineup that would have tested the skills of any arranger. Many of the backing musicians couldn't read music; they just played by ear. This could be a considerable problem, and I was too inexperienced to adapt my act to suit what they could actually play. An hour before showtime I'd still be trying to get the musicians to learn the arrangement of the Gershwin "S'Wonderful" medley that Kay had put together, instead of asking them, "Do you know 'Embraceable You'?" and just performing some standards that they could play.

After all the success and adulation I had enjoyed as part of Kay Thompson and the Williams Brothers, these early appearances as a solo singer were a brutal comedown. At some clubs people would carry on with their conversations or get up and dance while I was singing, leaving me standing there thinking, *I'm not a band singer. I'm doing my act. You're supposed to be listening.* At times I was in despair. This wasn't at all the way it was supposed to be. But I asked myself what else I was going to do and where else I was going to go, and then told myself that I had to stick it out even if it killed me. In the far recesses of my brain I could still hear my father's voice: "You're not as good as the others, so you have to work harder."

There was no question of giving up or refusing to go on even if the audiences were drunk and indifferent because I desperately needed the $300 that I would be paid. Yet sometimes I didn't get paid even after I had performed. At one club, after singing in front of a dismally small crowd of twenty or thirty people, I was told by the promoter, "I'm not paying you. You didn't draw at all."

"What do you mean?" I asked. "I did my job. Your job was to promote me. Did you do any advertising?"

He didn't answer but just kept repeating: "I'm not going to pay you."

My agency had sent a young agent along; he was about seventeen years old, and it was the first booking he'd ever handled. He was supposed to be there to get acquainted with the business, so I told him what the promoter had said to me. "We'll see about that," he said, storming off to the promoter's office. Five minutes later he was back, looking a lot less cocksure. "He doesn't want to pay you."

"I ALREADY KNOW THAT!" I screamed. "THAT'S WHAT I JUST TOLD YOU!" Somehow I don't think he had a long career as an agent.

I never did get paid for that show, but something did come out of it: I decided to get another agent. The new one wasn't much better, and there was still pitifully little work for me. Like my dad when he was waiting to see radio producers in Des Moines and Chicago, I used to sit for hours in the reception area of my new agency, just to be there if a job came in. Usually none did, and I'd leave empty-handed a few hours later. Every now and then, though, the agent would put his head out of the office and say, "If you want it, there's a booking Friday in Syracuse" — or Niagara Falls or Buffalo or Cleveland or wherever it was — and I'd get my bag and take the bus out of town.

Even at clubs where they liked me and my agent was able to rebook me, I found that the money being offered was decreasing every time. If I started at $400, the next time they booked me it had fallen to $350, and the time after that $300. I later discovered that the agency would sometimes get a booking for $600, tell me it was for $300, and pocket the rest, but even when they were straight with me, the money on offer was still going down. There was always an excuse: Business was bad; snow was forecast, and ticket sales would be off; the other acts had had to swallow a cut, and it wouldn't be fair to pay me more. But as I said to one club owner, "This isn't the way these things are supposed to work. If I appear here many more times, I'll wind up paying you." There was no question of turning any offer down, however. I was much too broke for that.

I was earning such little money that I couldn't even afford to have my tuxedo cleaned and pressed, so I made it a rule never, ever to sit down in it. I would change out of it as soon as the show finished, but sometimes there was no dressing room, so I had to change in the men's room or in a meat locker — a cold store. It was freezing, but there was one advantage to leaving my tuxedo hanging up in there: By the time of the next show, it was as if it had been cleaned and pressed. It was frozen stiff and absolute torture to put on, but once it had thawed a little, it looked really smart.

There were other problems, too. One night I was appearing at a tiny basement bar-restaurant in Pittsburgh with the plush name of The Monte Carlo. The name was pretty much the only thing that Pittsburgh and Monaco had in common. I was standing by the cash register at the end of the bar, waiting for my cue to go on and listening to the club owner — one of the Clark candy bar family — who was onstage wad-ing through an apparently endless series of announcements of coming attractions to an audience of about forty or fifty people. Suddenly, I felt a gun pressed into my back, and a voice growled, "Open the cash register."

I nearly wet my nicely pressed tuxedo right there. "I can't," I spluttered. "I don't know how."

"Whaddya mean you don't know how? You're the manager, aintcha? You're wearing a tux, aintcha? So open the fugging register, or I'll put a bullet in you."

"I'm not the manager," I said. "I'm just the singer. I'm waiting to go on."

I don't know what would have happened next if Mr. Clark hadn't finally reached the end of his preamble. "Now I saw this kid at the Blue Angel in New York," I heard him say. "I thought he was okay, so I'd just like to see what you think of him. So here he is, Andy Williams." As stage introductions go, it left a lot to be desired, but on this occasion I wasn't going to quibble; I had a gun pressed into my back. "That's me," I said. "I have to go onstage now." With the hairs on the back of my neck standing on end and fearing that every step might be my last, I bolted for the stage.

There was no gunshot and no searing impact throwing me to the ground. When I took the stage to a polite ripple of applause and raised my eyes to look at the bar, the man was still standing there with his gun in his hand. It didn't even occur to me to shout, "Call the cops!" or anything, and, besides, I needed the money, so I went straight into my act.

Surprisingly, there wasn't even a tremor in my voice as I sang the opening number, and by the time I finished it, I saw the robber heading out of the back door empty-handed. Perhaps he didn't like the act. I don't think the audience reaction was much better than Mr. Clark's introduction, but at least I got off the stage alive.

Whenever I was on the road, I took the cheapest hotel rooms I could find: $3 a night. The one in Pittsburgh was called The Pitt, though The Pits would have been more appropriate because it was the most godawful place I ever stayed in. It was damp and dirty, had cracked linoleum in the hallways, black mold in the bathroom, and bedding that had clearly been used at least once since it had last seen the inside of a washing machine. But it was cheap, and that was the number-one priority. Everywhere I went, I carried a little hot plate with me in my suitcase. I'd plug it in and heat up canned food, usually a can of ham and beans or a can of vegetable soup. I couldn't afford to eat out. I never had a date, or took anyone out for dinner or to a movie because I simply didn't have enough money.

While I was back in New York between road trips, I auditioned for a very popular television show, *Arthur Godfrey's Talent Scouts,* but I was turned down. I can see why I didn't make it now; I was doing the wrong kind of material. I should have been singing the *American Idol* kind of song, where you change key halfway through — the audience always goes wild when you change key and get louder — but I sang my supper club material, and it just didn't make it.

By now, whenever I was in New York I would actually cross the street to avoid show business people I had known when I was performing with Kay and my brothers. I couldn't face the "So what are you doing now?" questions and the looks — a mixture of pity, incredulity, and half-concealed amusement — when they discovered that I was doing two-bit shows in one-bit nightclubs.

For the next two years I kept crisscrossing the country, performing in small clubs in such places as Philadelphia, Pittsburgh, and Cleveland. One of my more bizarre bookings was at the Steel Pier in Atlantic City,

New Jersey. Atlantic City in the 1950s was a fading, sepia-tinted relic of the bustling resort it had once been. Its long boardwalk was so decrepit that it was rotting away in places, and you'd have to dodge the holes as you walked along. Louis Malle's film *Atlantic City* captures something of the melancholic flavor of the place. The Steel Pier was exactly that: a rusting pier jutting out into the sea, lined with popcorn and souvenir stands. I was booked to perform at the end of the pier and had to do seven shows a day, each only six or seven minutes long — just time for two or three songs. Even stranger than this, however, I was appearing with a flying horse.

At the end of my act, after a suitably dramatic buildup, the horse was led up a ramp onto a high platform like the top diving board at a swimming pool, and after a roll on the drums and another dramatic pause, it would canter along the platform and launch itself into thin air. It plummeted into the ocean with a huge splash, to the delight of the children and adults who lined the rails of the pier to watch, and then it swam to the beach and was toweled off by an attendant to be ready for its next appearance. Today animal welfare groups would have the show banned within five minutes. I never saw anyone use a whip or anything else to get the horse to dive, so it can't have minded doing it too much — and maybe even enjoyed it.

I tried very hard not to dwell on the humiliating thought that after topping the bill in the best venues in America with Kay and my brothers, I was now playing second bill to a flying horse. Yet at some other venues things could be even worse. At one club I performed with a ten-piece band — they all wore plaid jackets, black trousers, and white socks — for an audience of eight people. At least I had some musicians there; when I showed up at another club, the manager asked, "Where's your band?"

"What do you mean, where's my band? I don't have a band. There's just me. You're supposed to be providing the musicians."

After arguing for a few minutes, it was clear that not only didn't he have any musicians he could call, but he wouldn't have paid them even if he had. In desperation — I needed the money — I went across the street and borrowed a phonograph. I had never made a record of my own, so I bought a record of another singer (I forget which one) and then took it back across the street. When it was time for me to appear, I turned on the phonograph and did my best to lip-sync the songs, complete with the hiss of the needle on the record and the gaps between each track, which gave me enough time to say, "Thank you, and the next song is . . ." before the start of the next track. There was a longer pause when the record got to the end of side one, when I had to turn it over. The audience, such as it was, sat in silence. I don't think they could believe what they were hearing, but I did get paid at the end of the night.

By now it wasn't a matter of being ambitious for greater things; my only focus was where the next meal was going to come from. The bottom of the barrel came in Cleveland in early 1954 when I didn't have two cents in my pocket and was staying in one of the less savory hotel rooms I had found on the road. Its cracked window, framed by filthy curtains, looked out on a blank wall and a fire escape, behind which one of the local streetwalkers plied her trade. When I turned off the light at night, I could hear the scrape and scuttle of cockroaches on the linoleum. I had nothing to eat all day, and the only company I had was canine. A while before, Kay had given me a boxer dog, Barnaby, as a present. Barnaby normally stayed in Kay's apartment in New York when I was on the road, but on this particular date I had brought him with me for company. At least he was pleased to see me when I appeared.

That evening I was cooking up some Alpo dog food for Barnaby, big chunks of horse-meat and gravy. I was so hungry and it smelled so damn good that I tried some and then ate a whole plateful of it. I took Barnaby for a long walk just to get out of that place, but eventually I had to return to that bare, cold, filthy room and the remnants of my meal on the table. I was close to tears. How had I come to this? Only a couple of years before I was earning good money and playing to packed houses at some of the best and biggest clubs in the country. Now I was apparently such a has-been that I'd been reduced to eating dog food.

I was on the edge of the abyss. If I couldn't somehow reverse the process, I'd have to kiss good-bye any thoughts of a singing career and start stacking shelves in a supermarket for a living. I could imagine myself years from then, boring my workmates on our coffee breaks with tales of the days when I used to play Ciro's, while they rolled their eyes and laughed at me behind my back. "There goes Andy, babbling on again about his great showbiz career. If he was that good, how come he's working here?"

If I needed a wake-up call, a dose of dog food certainly supplied it. I was desperate. If I stayed on the road, touring ever-smaller clubs in ever-more obscure and out-of-the-way places, I was on a one-way ticket to oblivion. I decided I had nothing to lose by rolling the dice.

My destiny so far in my sorry solo career had been in the hands of Kay Thompson. She had been doing everything for me and was never interested in compromise. She loved witty, erudite, supper club material, and that was what I had been performing. She had put a lot of time and effort into helping me develop my solo act, but now it finally dawned on me that all her effort had been completely misdirected.

Everything she had written for Kay Thompson and the Williams Brothers was perfect for an act playing clubs with very sophisticated audiences in large cities such as Chicago, San Francisco, Boston, and New York. She had written exactly the same kind of material for me, but I wasn't working those kinds of rooms. I was working clubs that sold more beer than martinis. I didn't need Kay Thompson material for them; in fact, it was actually hurting me. I asked myself a question: *What the hell was I doing singing songs like "Mad Dogs and Englishmen" to an audience of steelworkers or meat packers who had never even heard of Noel Coward?* Those audiences didn't understand that kind of material; they probably hated it, and it wasn't right for me, either. I wasn't a supper club song-and-dance man. I should have been singing pop songs like Perry Como and Frank Sinatra, and spending my time trying to get a record contract or an appearance on television.

Until that moment I had always let others — first my dad and then Kay — call the shots, and I had followed where they led, pushed and pulled by events but with no real strategy of my own. Now, in that moment of realization, I found the direction I wanted and had to take. For the first time I would take a grip on my own career. I knew I could sing, but if I was ever going to make an impression on major promoters and TV and radio producers, it would not be by doing shows in dilapidated clubs a thousand miles from the heart of the action. Somehow I had to get back to appearing in New York City.

Yet even after I had made this momentous decision, I had to ask my brother Don if he would lend me $100 (I was so broke, I had to call collect) and wire it to Cleveland. When the money came in, I bought a one-way bus ticket to New York, and as soon as I got there, I quit my booking agency and put in a call to the Prince of Darkness, Herbert Jacoby, at the Blue Angel. He agreed to give me a booking there in a couple of weeks' time. Even over the telephone he could probably smell my desperation — but I needed him a lot more than he needed me.

I spent the next couple of weeks staying at Kay's apartment and rehearsing a new act over and over again. Although the new mix of pop songs and well-known standards wasn't her style, Kay helped me and worked with me. I told myself that I just had to try this new approach, and if it didn't work out, well, I'd deal with that when the time came. To this day I don't know what I would have done if it had failed.

I rehearsed with the backing trio at the club on the afternoon before my opening night, then went to get some air and something to eat. By the time I headed back, it was dark and bitterly cold, one of those freezing nights when even the sounds of the city — traffic and car horns, muffled noises from bar and restaurant doorways, high heels clicking on the sidewalk — seemed to take on a harder metallic edge. Snow flurries were blowing through, and I pulled my coat tight around me and sank my chin into my scarf as I walked on the East Side streets. I was broke again. I had spent my last few dollars having my tuxedo cleaned and pressed, and was saving the cab fare.

The doorman waved me through. "May be a slow night tonight, Mr. Williams. It's cold enough for Christmas. You wouldn't have gotten me out of doors tonight if I hadn't needed the money."

I nodded and gave a vague smile, but my mind was only half on what he was saying. I was thinking ahead to going onstage, visualizing how it would be, mentally rehearsing the songs I would sing and the links and gags I'd use between them. I walked through the lobby, past the entrance to the clubroom, and went down a flight of stairs to a cramped corridor with exposed ducting and pipework overhead. The dressing room was halfway along the corridor. Small and smelling slightly of dampness, it had a straight-backed chair in front of the dressing table, a theatrical mirror surrounded by a semicircle of lights bright enough to show up even the smallest skin blemish, and, across one corner, a sagging sofa where a couple of guests could take a precarious perch. At the far end of the room there was a bathroom with a tiny shower cubicle. It wasn't the Ritz, but compared to some of the places I had been playing, it was a palace, and my spirits were lifted by the sight of two bouquets of flowers that had been delivered while I was out. One was from Mom and Dad, wishing me luck.

The other was from Kay; the card with it read simply, "Knock 'em dead, And."

I sat down on the sofa, lay back, and closed my eyes for a few minutes. I was too wired to fall asleep, but it did me good just to shut out the world and retreat into my own thoughts. Once more, as I lay there, I went over and over my act in my mind, running through the lyrics of each song. I even visualized the close of the act: the bow, the walk to the wings, and — if I was lucky enough — the return to center stage for an encore.

Twenty minutes before showtime I started getting ready, applying a touch of stage makeup and putting on my shirt and tuxedo pants. I left the shoes, tie, and jacket until the very last minute. There was a knock on the door to give me a ten-minute warning. I finished getting dressed, adjusted my tie, combed my hair, and gave myself a final check in the mirror. Then I was out the door. As I climbed the steps, I could hear the applause as the Herman Chitterson Trio finished their warm-up set. I waited in the wings as Herbert Jacoby began his lugubrious introduction.

I snuck a look from behind the curtain to see what sort of crowd there was, but the stage lights were too bright to see more than the first few tables. I knew Kay was there with a party of friends and well-wishers, but she was somewhere in the darkness beyond the pool of light. I let the curtain fall back and turned my gaze to the stage where Herbert was still speaking. Strangely, despite everything I had at stake, I wasn't even particularly nervous as I stood there. I think by then I was all out of nerves, and even though I was psyched-up, a kind of numb fatalism also crept over me. I just had to sing as I knew I could, give the new material a shot, and then see what happened. I was pondering what that might be when I heard the deep bass voice of the Prince of Darkness say, "And now, ladies and gentlemen, for your pleasure tonight, the Blue Angel welcomes back Andy Williams." There was a burst of applause as I walked out on the stage. As it faded, the trio played the introduction to the first song, and I took a deep breath and began to sing "A Romantic Guy, I."

My half hour passed in a blur, but as I finished the final number, there was loud applause and shouts of "More! More!" — by no means all of them emanating from Kay and her guests. I did two encores before heading back to the dressing room. I had just washed off my makeup and was drying my face when there was a knock on the door.

It is well known in show business that, no

matter how much talent you have or how much work you put in, you also need a large stroke of luck somewhere along the way. As it turned out, on that cold winter night when I opened at the Blue Angel, my luck was in. My old acquaintance Bill Harbach happened to be in the audience. (I had first met him at George Platt Lynes's house in Los Angeles and then again when we were appearing at Mrs. Biddle's private party for the Duke and Duchess of Windsor.) He clearly liked what he saw and heard this time because he came backstage after the show and said, "Andy, you sounded great. I'm producing a new five-nights-a-week network television show for NBC, and we're auditioning for singers. We already have two, Steve Lawrence and Eydie Gormé, and we're looking for another boy and girl singer. I'd like you to come to the studio and sing for Steve Allen."

"Terrific," I said. "By the way, who is Steve Allen?"

It turned out that Steve Allen was a very funny comedian and a skilled writer and songwriter who had already built a successful career as a host on local television. A big, round-faced, always smiling guy with black hair combed into a pompadour who wore black-rimmed spectacles that seemed almost as big as the TV screens on which people watched him, Steve made his first national appearance as a last-minute guest host on *Arthur Godfrey's Talent Scouts*. When he improvised the live Lipton commercial that Arthur always did, Steve ended it by making tea and soup and then pouring both into Arthur's ukulele. He made a big impression on the head of NBC, Sylvester "Pat" Weaver, who now decided to launch three new network shows: *The Today Show,* going out in the early morning; *Home,* in midafternoon; and *The Tonight Show,* a ninety-minute program airing from 11:30 p.m. to 1:00 a.m.

Pat chose Dave Garroway as the host of *Today* and decided that Steve, who was already doing a very similar show for a local New York TV station, WNBC-TV, would be perfect for *Tonight*. Steve introduced the first show by telling the audience, "This is *Tonight,* and I can't think of too much to tell you about it except I want to give you the bad news first: This program is going to go on *forever.* Boy, you think you're tired now? Wait until you see one o'clock roll around!"

So I went down to the NBC Studios on Fifth Avenue and sang for Steve. I was nervous throughout the audition because I had so much riding on it. If I blew the chance, I might not get another one. A couple of times I could feel my vocal chords tightening, but

I managed to control my anxiety and kept singing. Steve clearly liked what he heard because when I had finished, he turned to Bill and said, "Great choice, Bill. Sign him up. I love his work."

It was the break I was hoping for. Hallelujah, I was going to be on TV. The job was for only a week, but nobody said, "Don't come back," at the end of the first week, so I went back the next week and the one after that, and kept doing it for two and a half years.

The fourth singer they auditioned was a girl named Micki Marlowe, who had the most sensuous voice I've ever heard — like that of a young Mae West — and a body that just wouldn't quit. She sang "Life Is Just a Bowl of Cherries" in a fashion that somehow contrived to be breathy, husky, and sultry all at the same time. Every man in the studio was absolutely riveted, including Steve Allen, who invited her to come back the following week. Then he asked, "What will you be singing next time?"

"Oh, I only do that one song," she said. She either couldn't or wouldn't contemplate doing a different song the following week, and this fabulous and sexy young woman's meteoric television career came to an abrupt end. What a shame; she was gorgeous. Next came a lovely girl called Pat Marshall. She was terrific, but after a couple of months, she moved on. Pat Kirby took her place.

Pat and I alternated with Steve and Eydie, doing two nights one week and three nights the next. We were paid a starting rate of $280 for the two-night weeks and $340 for the three nights. Flushed with my newfound wealth, I immediately rented a room at the Algonquin Hotel on West 44th Street, a famous writers' hangout. It was once the haunt of Dorothy Parker, Robert Benchley, George S. Kaufman, and the other members of the Vicious Circle who skewered people with their wit while occupying the overstuffed chairs at the round table in the bar, segregated from the more mundane regulars by a velvet rope.

The bar was always buzzing and extremely popular, but perhaps I spent too much time there because my stay at the Algonquin came to an abrupt end when I discovered that my bill for the first week was $600. After that I beat a hasty retreat and rented a tiny apartment at 5 East 63rd Street for $129 a month. It was a terrific address, right off Fifth Avenue and with Central Park across the street, but it was so small and narrow that it resembled a railroad car. Originally a single apartment, it had been split down the middle to make two smaller ones. The ceilings were higher than the apartment was wide. I could sit on the couch on one side of the living room and almost put my feet in the fireplace on the other side, but it was my very first real home, in a city that was then the music, entertainment, and television capital of America — and I loved it.

My interest in art was still growing, and I spent almost all my spare time hanging around the galleries in and around 57th Street. Their staffs soon realized that I didn't have enough money to buy anything, but they let me come in anyway. I learned a lot just by talking with them and looking at the art on the walls. Although I couldn't afford original works, I covered the walls of my tiny apartment with French Impressionist prints that I bought for $2 or $3 apiece. I then framed and hung them on the walls beneath picture lights, transforming my apartment from a railroad car into a long, thin art gallery.

Soon after I began appearing on *The Tonight Show,* I got a record contract. Once more I owed a huge debt of gratitude to Kay Thompson, who arranged an audition with Archie Bleyer, the head of Cadence Records — a very hot small label — and even played piano for me while I sang for him. Archie didn't look like a typical music producer to me. With his business suit, white shirt and tie, shiny shoes, glasses, and slicked-down receding hair, he seemed more like a bank manager or a real estate salesman, but his appearance was deceptive. He knew the music business about as well as anybody and had a track record that few could match of producing hit singles, often by little-known artists.

Kay knew Archie from his years as musical director on Arthur Godfrey's show, the most popular program on daytime television. Godfrey was very possessive of everything on his show, including the performers, but in 1953, without Godfrey's knowledge, Archie set up a record company and started choosing songs for the resident boy singer, Julius La Rosa, that he thought might be hits. One of the songs received a tremendous audience reaction and lots of mail, so Archie made a record of it with Julius. When Godfrey found out, he was so furious that he fired both of them right there, live on his show. It made headlines in all the papers the next day, with Godfrey fuming: "How dare they make a record without asking my permission, a song they tested on my show? How dare they?"

That was how Archie got into the record business. He went on to produce hits for

Julius La Rosa such as "Anywhere I Wander" and "Eh Cumpari." He also had big hits with "Mr. Sandman," "Lollipop, Lollipop," and "Never on Sunday" with the Chordettes, who also had been featured on Godfrey's show.

When I auditioned for him, Archie, a man of few words, listened intently and then just said, "Fine. Let's make a record." He told me that my voice didn't sound like anybody else's, which was good, and that I could possibly have a record career if he found the right song for me. That was the hardest part, finding the right song, but he had managed to do it for the Everly Brothers, who had a string of hits with him, and I certainly wanted a hit, too.

Some producers have a trademark sound — such as Phil Spector's "Wall of Sound," and if you were produced by any of them, that was pretty much what you were going to get. Archie was much more eclectic and wide-ranging; you really didn't know what was going to come next with him. The first record we made together was a Christmas ballad, "Wind, Sand and Star." Archie was crazy about that song. He had cut it once before with a choir singing it, but he didn't think it had really come off and never released it. Now he thought it might work with my voice. Unfortunately, he didn't get the record released until a few days before Christmas, and since holiday records sell about as well in January as refrigerators in Alaska, it sold only ten thousand copies.

Next we did one called "Dreamsville," written by Henry Mancini and Johnny Mercer, which was quite modern, almost a jazz piece and a beautiful song. That one did a little better, but Archie's ability to produce hits was definitively demonstrated in August 1956, when he gave me "Canadian Sunset." It went all the way to number seven in the Billboard Top Hundred. My brother Don, who was living in Los Angeles, was driving down Balboa Boulevard when my record came on the radio. He was so excited at hearing his kid brother had a Top 10 hit that he damned near ran off the road. He told me later that he had to hit the brakes and pull over to the side until the song finished.

On the strength of my hit record, my agent booked me into a venue in Hartford, Connecticut, for a one-night show. All I had to do was go onstage and sing my hit song — nothing else — but since all the other acts were black, as was most of the audience, it was exactly the wrong place for me to be appearing. If I went out there and sang "Canadian Sunset," I was sure they would boo me off the stage or worse.

I shared a dressing room with the other acts on the show, and as I was getting ready, a guy from a popular doo-wop group saw me pacing up and down. "You Andy Williams?" he asked. "You have that record 'Canadian Sunset'? That's a great record, man, and you're a good singer. Why are you nervous, man?"

"Well, this just isn't my audience," I said.

"Oh, you want them to dig you, man, to scream and yell at you, too?"

"Well, yeah."

"Okay. Here's what you gotta do. When you get to the end of the first line of 'Canadian Sunset,' stamp your foot real hard and shake your head very fast, like this." He stomped down hard on the floor and shook his head. "Then do the same thing at the end of the second line. Try it."

I tried it out a couple of times, then went onstage, still feeling a bit nervous, but what the hell did I have to lose? I sang the first line: "Once I was alone . . ." *STAMP!* and shook my head. There were a few screams as I moved to the second line: "So lonely and then . . ." *STAMP!* Head shake! By then the audience was yelling and screaming. I finished the song with more stamping and head shaking. I thanked the doo-wop guy for his advice on my way out the door.

I assumed that for my follow-up record to "Canadian Sunset" Archie would pick a similar type of song. Wrong. It was 1956, a seminal year in pop music, and with Elvis Presley charting with "Heartbreak Hotel," "Hound Dog," and "Don't Be Cruel," and a host of other rock and rollers following in his wake, Archie showed me a rock-and-roll song called "Butterfly." I thought he was joking at first, and when I realized he was serious, I said, "Archie, I really don't know whether I can do this."

Archie gave me a long look. "Well, Andy, do you want to have another hit or not?"

"Yeah, of course I do."

"Just trust me," he said. "I guarantee you'll have a hit with 'Butterfly.'" So I went back to my apartment with an Elvis Presley album under my arm and listened to it over and over, hoping that some of it would rub off on me. It certainly wasn't the way I had intended to sing, but I wanted a hit. So I went to the studio with Archie, curled my lip, and started singing in an Elvis style:

You tell me you love me,
You say you'll be true,
Then you fly around
With somebody new

166

But I'm crazy about you — STAMP! —
You Butterfly.

It didn't sound like Elvis, but I guess it had what the song needed. Archie turned out to be 100 percent right about it, because in 1957, "Butterfly" went to number one in the Billboard charts, both in the United States and in the United Kingdom. It was my first number-one hit single.

I had eleven more chart hits with Cadence over the next four years, including "Baby Doll," "Lips of Wine," and "I Like Your Kind of Love." Archie wasn't trying to turn me into a poor man's Elvis; he was just trying to find hit songs. If they were rock and roll, then he wanted them sung that way. If they were ballads, I could sing them in my natural style. So I also recorded "The Village of St. Bernadette," "Lonely Street," "Are You Sincere?" and another huge hit, "The Hawaiian Wedding Song." Years later I met Burt Bacharach, who had worked for a while as accompanist to Marlene Dietrich, and he told me that she loved my recording of "Hawaiian Wedding Song" so much that she had a special album made. On side one, tracks one to six were all "Hawaiian Wedding Song," and if you flipped it over, side two was exactly the same.

Although Archie Bleyer always chose the songs that I released as singles, when it came to recording an album, he was much happier for me to take the lead. I decided that my first album for Cadence would be titled *Andy Williams Sings Steve Allen*. Steve was a good songwriter with some fairly big hits, such as "This Could Be the Start of Something Big" and the theme from the movie *Picnic,* but I chose his songs largely because I thought that if I recorded an album of Steve's own compositions, he might let me sing one or two on the show. It worked out even better than I had hoped. Steve loved my versions of his songs so much that he got me to sing a different one every night on the show until I had sung all eleven on the album.

The album did well, and I released several more with Archie over the next couple of years. He didn't bat an eyelid at my choice of material even when I told him in 1959 that I wanted to record an album in France produced by Quincy Jones, whose work I had admired for a long time. Quincy Delight Jones, to give him his full title, was multi-talented: a trumpet player, conductor, composer, arranger, record producer, film producer, television producer, impresario, and all-around musical genius. Black, bearded, shades-wearing, and French-speaking, he was also the epitome of *cool.* I had met him when he was a guest on *The Tonight Show,* and we got to talking about music, as musicians do. When he said he would like to work with me on my next album, I didn't need to think about it for more than a second before saying yes. There was only one small problem; Quincy had moved to Paris in 1957, and if I wanted him to produce my album, I'd have to go there.

Archie knew Quincy well and had great respect and admiration for his work, but I explained to him that Quincy wasn't the sole reason for wanting to make the album in Paris. I also loved the sound of French strings; musicians there played in a much softer, more delicate, and almost gossamer way than American musicians — Debussy, not Stravinsky. When I had finished my pitch, I waited while Archie put his fingertips together and thought about it for a few minutes. Then, a man of few words as ever, he just said, "Okay," and sent me off to Paris with a few thousand dollars to make the album.

My pianist, Dave Grusin, flew to Paris with me. I had originally met Dave after a friend suggested that I hear him play. "Dave's just graduated from the University of Colorado," he said, "and he really is great." I was doubtful if someone fresh out of college would have what I needed, and my doubts only grew when he turned up for the audition in an ill-fitting, shiny-seated blue suit. He later told me he had worn it to give himself an air of experience. Dark-haired, bespectacled, and quite intense, especially when talking about music, Dave also appeared very businesslike and took his job very seriously. I asked him to accompany me on "Danny Boy" in D-flat, and I knew in the first few bars that not only was he the right pianist for me, but he was also a very special talent, a beautiful piano player with a lovely jazzy feel. He could play any style of music, and he was the perfect accompanist. He was intelligent enough to know where to fill and what to play, and he had exquisite musical taste. He was also a very talented composer and arranger; in later years several of his compositions were nominated for Academy Awards, and he won an Oscar for the score of *The Milagro Beanfield War*.

At first I just asked him if he would like to go on the road with me for a couple of weeks while I was playing a room in the Roosevelt Hotel in New Orleans, but we worked so well together that the two weeks ultimately turned into seven years. We played a lot of medium-sized clubs, and in some cases the backing musicians might not have been the best, but it didn't really matter too much because I had Dave. We could easily have done the show with just the two of us plus a very good drummer I picked up along the way named Larry Rosen. Dave and Larry became pals and eventually formed a record company called GRP Records, specializing in jazz.

Before we went to Paris, Dave and I worked on the vocal arrangements for several days, mapping out the French songs we would do. When we got there, we met up with Quincy and showed him the songs. He began planning the arrangements with Billy Byers, who wrote a lot for Count Basie. Meanwhile, Dave and I had to find somewhere to rehearse. We were staying at a little place called the Queen Elizabeth Hotel, right next door to the George V, and Quincy suggested a jazz club he knew nearby that would be deserted during the day. He had played there in the past, so they knew him, and it wouldn't be a problem, he assured me — all we needed was the key.

"The manager lives in an apartment in a basement just around the corner," Quincy said. "Just knock on the door and ask him for the key to the Mars Club."

"And how do I do that?" I asked, a typical American in Paris. My French lessons with Kay and my brothers had long since been forgotten, and, like my brother Bob, my language skills now mainly consisted of repeating myself louder and louder — in English — in the hope that someone would eventually understand.

Quincy gave a world-weary sigh. "Just say, *'Avez-vous le clef pour le Mars Club?'*"

I repeated it a couple of times just to be sure I'd gotten the hang of it, then set off for the manager's apartment.

Two minutes later I was knocking on the door of a seedy-looking basement. No reply. I knocked louder, waited, and then knocked again, very loud. At last I heard the sound of movement from within, accompanied by a few French curses. The door opened a few inches, and a baleful and slightly bloodshot French eye contemplated me.

"Avez-vous le clef pour le Mars Club?" I asked.

He scowled, said, *"Allez-vous-en!"* and slammed the door.

I waited a few minutes and then knocked again. There was more cursing, and eventually the door opened again.

"Avez-vous le clef pour le Mars Club?"

He gave me a tirade of French abuse and then slammed the door again.

I waited a few more minutes, took a deep breath, and knocked again.

This time he threw the door wide open. *"Avez-vous le clef pour le Mars Club?"* He gave no response but just kicked me in the shins and then slammed and locked the door. I decided that, on balance, he probably didn't have *"le clef,"* and even if he did, he could keep it. I hobbled up the steps and back to the hotel. It turned out that I had been knocking on the door of the wrong apartment. For years afterward Quincy and I could always reduce each other to tears of helpless laughter by rapping with our knuckles on the table and saying, *"Avez-vous le clef pour le Mars Club?"*

We eventually found somewhere else to rehearse and went to the studio to record the album. I didn't know how much French musicians normally got paid, but I assumed they all worked on the same kind of scale as American ones. They looked like a fairly honest bunch, so at the end of each session — just as my dad did with the money under the carpet back in Cincinnati — I let them help themselves to what they needed. With the exchange rate then, you got an awful lot of francs to the dollar. I opened up a suitcase of French francs and told them to take as much as they were entitled to for a three-hour session. It wasn't quite as quixotic as it might have appeared since musicians have a definite pecking order in terms of pay. The scale for a guy who plays oboe, flute, and clarinet in a session, for example, is different from one who just plays the violin or trumpet. I was counting on the musicians to keep tabs on one another and make sure that no one got more than he was entitled to take.

The album we made together was called *Under Paris Skies*. I loved that album, but I must have been in a minority because it didn't exactly set the charts alight. It has stood the test of time, though, because it still sounds fresh and is one of my favorites even today. After experimenting with different types of material and ways of singing, as Archie and I searched for hit records, that French album also showed that I had now defined my own vocal style.

I owed Archie and Kay Thompson a lot for their help in setting me on the road to success. In addition to a debt of gratitude, I also incurred another sort of debt to Kay. Before I ever met Archie, I had said to her, "I'd give half my royalties for a deal with Cadence."

"Okay," she said, "you have a deal." It was then that she spoke to Archie, persuaded him to give me an audition, played piano for me while I sang, and then advised me on the deal. My first Cadence payment was small, and I hadn't minded giving her half of it, but before long I was writing her checks for hundreds of thousands of dollars and wishing I had said I'd give twenty percent of my royalties!

Kay's compositions also featured as the B-sides on a number of my records and although B-sides were virtually never played on the radio or even by the people buying the record, the composer got the same royalties as the composer of the A-side. Nonetheless, I never regretted the money I paid Kay; I owed her at least that for everything she had done to help my career, first with my brothers and then on my own. I did resent it, however, when she refused me permission to record a song, a setting of the Twenty-third Psalm, that I wanted to use on an album of songs of faith. When I asked her, Kay just said, "I don't think so. I want to save that for Leonard Bernstein and a full orchestra." I couldn't believe that she wouldn't allow me to perform the song. I had been with her when she wrote it, and I had sung it for her many times in her apartment.

I guess that was just Kay; she was very possessive about everything she worked on. A woman once wrote to the composer Johnny Mercer, saying, "I have an idea for a song:

'I want to be around to pick up the pieces when somebody breaks your heart.' Can you do anything with it?" Johnny wrote a song around that title and paid the woman half the royalties on it, because once you had a title like that, the song practically wrote itself. Kay would never have done that. She was very reluctant to give credit to anyone for things they worked on together. The illustrations drawn by Hilary Knight, for example, were a big part of the success of the Eloise books that Kay wrote, but she was so possessive about Eloise that she insisted on having complete control over every aspect of the character and would not allow anything done that wasn't exactly as she wanted it.

Her publisher, Simon & Schuster, was desperate to launch a range of Eloise merchandise but could not get Kay to agree to anything. They produced an Eloise doll to retail for $25 in the children's departments of stores all over the country, but Kay wanted only the best for Eloise. If there was to be an Eloise doll, Kay insisted that it be absolutely top of the range, with hand-sewn clothes and a $100 price tag. That would have priced it out of everywhere except stores like Neiman Marcus and Saks Fifth Avenue, but Kay refused to budge. When Kraft offered her $250,000 for the right to use the

Eloise name on a candy bar, she turned that down as well. In the end Simon & Schuster just gave up and washed their hands of her. Looking back now, I can see that in some ways she was overly possessive of me as well and to some extent took advantage of me, but I can't be too critical of her. Aside from the personal relationship we shared, she helped shape my career and my life. She put me on the road to success more than anyone other than my father.

7

After my years on the show business equivalent of Skid Row, I had at least learned something from my previous meteoric rise and fall. Although all the money I had earned with Kay and my brothers was long gone, this time when I started to earn some money again, I always made sure to put a little away.

Like me, *The Tonight Show* with Steve Allen didn't have much of a budget, and many of the things they did reflected that. They couldn't afford lavish sets and often just opened the studio doors and filmed the street outside and the reactions of people passing by. From that arose "The Man in the Street" segment with a guest comic posing as a passerby and answering Steve's dumb questions. It helped make stars of Jonathan Winters, Tom Poston, Don Adams, and Bill Dana, who did a character called José Jimenez. Steve might also have a guy in a gorilla suit in the background on the other side of the street; that was about as sophisticated and expensive as it got, but it worked.

Once in a while the show would go on the road to a different city to bolster the ratings, and Steve and Bill Harbach were always coming up with crazy things to do. When we went to Miami Beach, they even persuaded the Coast Guard to stage a mock invasion with several landing craft roaring toward the beach while people fired blank ammunition; several Miami matrons nearly went into heart failure. One of the other stunts they rigged up was to get me in a deep-sea diving suit and then, with a little baby shark and an eel and a few other big fish for company, send me down to the bottom of a pool, from where I had to sing a song. During rehearsal they called a break for the crew, and everyone left to have coffee or a cigarette, including the guy who was pumping oxygen down to me. He had forgotten that I was on the other end of the air hose.

The first I knew about it was when I started to get short of breath. I began to panic and was jerking frantically on the air hose, trying to get someone's attention. By the time anyone up above noticed the hose flopping around and remembered I was still submerged, I was close to unconscious.

They hauled me up, got me out of the suit, and resuscitated me. Then they had to cover me with blankets because I couldn't stop shivering. I was not much good for the next three days.

We also went to Niagara Falls for one show, but luckily it didn't occur to anyone to get me to sing while going over the falls in a barrel, because I was still young enough and dumb enough to have done it.

With the exception of my near drowning in Miami Beach, I loved every minute of my two and a half years on *The Tonight Show*. I was always a little restless, never wanting to stand still and constantly looking for ways to improve, and I learned a lot from just being around the show and working with pros like Steve, Bill Harbach, Dwight Hemion, and all the crew. Dwight directed the very first *Tonight Show* and stayed as director for three or four years, during which time we became great friends. After leaving the show, he became the most successful director in television and received eighteen Emmys in the course of his career, directing all the Barbra Streisand specials as well as those of Sinatra, Pavarotti, Elvis, Baryshnikov, Bette Midler, and many others.

Performing for television is very different from performing onstage. You're working to the camera, and it's important to be aware of which camera is on. If you're in a long shot, you might move a little bit more, but you don't want to move much if the camera is in a close-up. You don't want your hands suddenly appearing on the edge of the screen. It was a lot more disciplined than a live show, which is more freewheeling. My time on *The Tonight Show* made me a lot more aware of what worked and what didn't work on television. Although I didn't know it at the time, it was very good training for the years to come.

Steve Allen was hugely popular on *The Tonight Show*, but after a couple of years NBC offered him a one-hour slot on Sunday night, opposite Ed Sullivan on CBS. *The Ed Sullivan Show* had been the most-watched Sunday night program for years, and Steve absolutely died opposite him. Although the media concentrated on the "battle" between Sullivan and Steve for the right to call themselves king of the Sunday night ratings, it was actually *Maverick,* starring James Garner and airing on ABC at the same time, that finished as the highest-rated program. Faced with this formidable competition, Steve's ratings were so poor that the show was axed after one season, and his television career was never the same. It was a lesson for me in how transitory a TV career could be and how important it was to think very hard before agreeing to do a show that might make you but could also break you just as quickly. Although Steve didn't return to the show he had pioneered, *The Tonight Show* has remained a fixture of NBC's schedules to this day, under a series of hosts, including Jack Parr who did it for several years, Johnny Carson, who hosted it for thirty years, Jay Leno, and now Conan O'Brien.

Helped by my nightly appearances on *Tonight,* my singing career was taking off, but even though I had had some success on records and had been on some other variety shows on television, I was still being paid a lot less than comparable entertainers, and my agents, GAC, just couldn't seem to get an increase for me. Alan Bernard, a young agent at the company, was trying to book me on Dinah Shore's show. It turned out that Dinah was crazy about my hit record "Hawaiian Wedding Song" and wanted me on her show, so Alan managed to persuade her to pay me twice as much as anybody else at the agency had ever gotten me before. I was immediately impressed and asked, "Did you do that?" When he answered yes, I said, "Do you want to be my manager?" That was two yeses, and I had my first manager.

I made a few guest appearances on *The Dinah Shore Show* and then in 1958 I was given the chance to host my own television show, albeit only for the summer. All the big weekly series took thirteen weeks off in the summer and were replaced by programs that showcased up-and-coming talent. I was offered a stint as the replacement for Pat Boone on what was to be called *The Pat Boone Chevy Showroom with Andy Williams*. I already knew Pat, having first met him when I was on *The Steve Allen Show*, and helped by the fact that we were both country boys in the big city — Pat was from Nashville, Tennessee — we became friends. The friendship even survived Pat's discovery that years before, when I was twelve years old and appearing on the *National Barn Dance* on WLS in Chicago, I'd had a crush on Shirley Foley, the girl who eventually became his wife and the mother of their five daughters.

I had a real crisis of confidence before the first of those shows aired. Since childhood I had never been able to get out of my head the words my father had spoken to me: "You're not as good as them, so you have to work harder." If I wasn't good enough — and I was still convinced that I wasn't — what on earth was I doing hosting a television series? I still had the drive to succeed, but there were times when I wanted to bolt out of the studio, run down the street, and hide. I felt physically sick at the thought of going on, but I knew that if I didn't, I might never get another chance at a national TV show. So I talked myself around, battled my self-doubt, and forced myself to get through the first taping. Once I got out there, I was okay. The doubts I felt didn't show, and the producers and the audience seemed to like it. It got a little easier after that, but only a little.

The Chevy Showroom was a half-hour program, but it was very well produced by Bill Hobin, and there was a real feeling of class about it. Although it was still Pat's show, I presented it in my own way, with my own musical arrangements. Dick Van Dyke was a regular guest on the show but never spoke; he did only very funny mime sketches. The first week his sketch was based on my being interviewed by the legendary radio and news reporter Edward R. Murrow for *Person to Person*. Playing the role of my butler, Dick's character was so desperate to get in the shot during the interview that he first brought in a tray of tea, grinning at the camera all the time; next he popped up from behind the sofa to give a little wave; then he swung across the room on a chandelier; and finally he climbed out of the kitchen window of my apartment (supposedly on the twentieth floor), worked his way along the ledge, and appeared outside the living room window facing the camera. He was smiling and waving his arms frantically when he toppled over backward and disappeared from sight. A few seconds later he crawled back onto the ledge with his shirt half torn off, his arm in a sling, and his head wrapped in bandages. He was still grinning and waving as the sketch ended. That was one of his classic pieces, but he was so good at mime that his spots each week were always hilarious. He is a genius at physical comedy.

We also had three great dancers, the Bob Hamilton Trio, which featured Bob and two girls. One of them, Neile Adams, was dating a struggling young actor named Steve McQueen, who usually brought her to rehearsals. He was virtually unknown then, and none of us imagined that he would become an enormous star, but — and it's not just the wisdom of hindsight — there was an aura about him even then. He had great looks, of course, with those clear, almost translucent blue eyes, and was a guy that men liked and women adored, but it was more than just his looks; he had a magnetism that stopped you in your tracks.

We struck up a friendship that continued

after we both moved to Los Angeles a few years later, by which time he had married Neile. I liked and admired Steve a lot, and if I had ever wanted to model myself on someone, I think it would have been Steve. He loved motorcycles and dirt racing with his buddies, and even when he dressed up at night it was always jeans and a sports jacket. He got the material for the jeans in Mexico, and it was unusually thin. His housekeeper would iron them with a little starch to give them a slight crease, and they were the best-looking jeans I ever saw. If he had marketed them, he would have made a fortune.

It is the strangest feeling to see him now in those television ads where they "captured" him electronically and put him in a different context to sell cars. We have all moved on and grown old, and yet there's Steve, eternally young, still with those rugged good looks, clear blue eyes, and faint smile playing around the corners of his mouth that I remember so well.

The Chevy Showroom was a big success; even Kay Thompson, who was my harshest critic and seldom complimented me on my television work, conceded that it was good. It gave me some confidence that I might have a future on television, and I was given another opportunity the following summer, hosting a one-hour variety program on CBS, replacing *The Garry Moore Show.* Kay hated that one. It was too mainstream for her taste, very much in the model of programs like *The Perry Como Show,* which I loved, but the reviews were unbelievably good, and the show was a great success, leading to an offer to host a show of my own on NBC. It was hugely tempting, but the slot that was being prepared was opposite *Gunsmoke* on CBS, which had been on for years and was one of the most popular programs on television. Remembering what had happened to Steve Allen when he went up against Ed Sullivan, I turned it down.

The head of my agency, Tom Rockwell, whom I'd never even met, was livid and called me. "Are you out of your mind?" he screamed. "They offer you a prime-time show and you say no?"

"That's right."

"But it's a national prime-time show —"

Despite all his pleas and threats, I was immovable. I might not have known much about television, but I did know enough to realize that going up against *Gunsmoke* was a guaranteed recipe for disaster. No matter how good my show might be, it wasn't going to beat *Gunsmoke* in the ratings. I'd have had more chance of survival walking into a

Dodge City saloon with a placard around my neck that read I'M UNARMED, AND I CHEAT AT CARDS. The show would be cancelled, and I'd be lucky ever to be offered another one.

I also turned down a show called *Your Hit Parade,* which would have featured me singing versions of that week's hit songs in some kind of corny setting. If it was "How Much Is That Doggy in the Window," I'd be performing it outside a pet shop, and if it was "24 Hours from Tulsa," I'd better start packing a suitcase. Once more I didn't have to think long before declining, nor did I have to wait long before I got another call from Tom Rockwell, who couldn't believe that I had turned down *Your Hit Parade* as well, but I was convinced I was right, and I wouldn't give in. Although I had rejected those series, NBC did commission me to make a number of one-hour television specials, beginning with *Music from Shubert Alley,* which aired on November 13, 1959.

I also appeared on the Johnny Carson *Tonight Show* several times. Before one of those appearances he said to me, "Andy, I thought maybe you and I would sit on two stools, and we'd read cards with questions from the audience. You read one and answer it, and then I'll read one and answer it."

One of his writers, Herb Sargent, was a good friend of mine, and before the skit he took me aside. "It's really unfair of Johnny to do this bit with you," Herb said. "You'll see your question for the first time, but Johnny already knows what his questions are going to be and has a joke for each of them already written on the card. It's just unfair. He'll come off much better than you will because he has answers all prepared and they're very funny. So . . ." He looked around to make sure Johnny was nowhere in sight. "If you promise not to tell him, I'll give you jokes to tell when you get your cards, but for God's sake, don't ever mention this to anybody, or I'll get fired!"

When I got my card with the first question on it, my answer, supplied by Herb, got quite a laugh. Johnny looked a little surprised that I had an answer so quickly. Then he read his question and his funny answer. On my second question I had an even funnier answer, and when Johnny did his second one, it didn't get as big a laugh as mine. We had a few more prepared, but straightaway he said, "I think we've done enough of this, Andy. Why don't you sing a song?"

I was never invited back on his show.

Johnny Carson aside, my television career was beginning to develop, and my career as a live performer was also on the rise. In the early 1960s live entertainment in Las Vegas was really booming, and I was booked to headline at the Flamingo with Joe E. Lewis, a huge name at the time and a show business icon. Because I had had a couple of hit records, I was given top billing, which did not please Mr. Lewis at all. He was the star, he always got top billing, and he always closed the show. He wasn't at all happy to be playing second fiddle to some punk kid.

The golden rule in Vegas is "Keep it short." The owners book entertainers to draw people to the casinos, but once there, they don't want them wasting any more time in the showroom than is absolutely necessary when they could be losing money in the casino. Shows were not to be longer than ninety minutes. On our opening night Joe E. Lewis, intent on making his point, went on first and stayed onstage for two hours. By the time I began my set, the audience was worn out and the casino owners furious.

I kept my act very short indeed, and when I came offstage, I went straight to my co-star's dressing room. "Mr. Lewis," I said, "I was wondering if I could go on first tomorrow night and let you close the show."

"I thought you might come to that conclusion, kid" was all he said.

From then on I opened the show and did forty minutes, and he closed with an hour. The audience, the casino owners, and Joe E. Lewis were all happy again.

Over the next few decades I appeared regularly in Vegas with some really big names in comedy opening for me, such as Bill Cosby, Jerry Seinfeld, and Jim Carrey. The money they paid headliners in Vegas was huge for that time, and although all the casinos tended to offer similar rates, the way the owners treated their artists varied considerably. One of the best was Bill Harrah, who had casinos in Lake Tahoe and Reno. He went out of his way to woo star names, offering a beautiful house on the lake with servants, a boat to go cruising, and anything the star wanted — such as vintage champagne and Beluga caviar — would be flown in free of charge. As a result, he never had any trouble attracting the top names to perform at his casinos.

Jerry Seinfeld opened for me at Harrah's in Reno. I had never seen his act before, and I went straight to his dressing room after the show and said, "You're great, Jerry. You should be on television."

He shook his head. "I never want to do anything but stand-up."

"Yeah, but if people got to know your work through television —"

He cut me off. "I don't want any of that. I just want to do stand-up."

A couple of years later he had his own half-hour show on television, but the opening few minutes was always Jerry doing stand-up. I guess he got the best of both worlds. The show went on to become one of the biggest and best-loved situation comedies on television. He became a very big star and still does stand-up whenever he wants, wherever he wants.

While I was appearing at the Flamingo in Vegas in 1960, I met a beautiful girl named Claudine Longet. She had been driving her very first car, an old Chevy, along the Strip when it broke down. She and a girlfriend were pushing the vehicle along the street when my manager, Alan Bernard, and I stopped to help. It was partly because we wanted to be good Samaritans, but it was also because she was stunning-looking. She had straight dark hair, huge dark eyes, and full lips, and moved with a dancer's sensuous grace. All that and a French accent, too. I was smitten.

She had been living in Paris with her family when one day she ran into a girlfriend who told her she was going to Las Vegas as a can-can dancer in the new Folies Bergere show, which had been booked for the new Tropicana Hotel. Claudine was a trained dancer — she had studied ballet for ten years — so she auditioned for a part and was accepted. (It could have been a job for decades; the show opened in 1959 and ran for fifty years.)

Claudine didn't speak any English, and my little bit of French was useless. Somehow we were able to communicate enough to have dinner that night, and we dated for the entire time I was working at the Flamingo. After our shows we went to see Harry James and his band playing in the lounge at the Flamingo or Louis Prima and Keely Smith in the lounge at the Sands.

When I left to go on tour, I phoned Claudine every day. Her friend, who spoke reasonable English, took the calls and acted as interpreter. It felt more than a little strange to be carrying out a love affair via a third party. I flew back to Vegas whenever I could; my phone and airline bills were horrendous. I moved from New York to California later that year, which made the travel bills a little less expensive, and rented an apartment on Doheny Drive, just off Sunset Boulevard. One evening Claudine was flying in from Vegas, and since I couldn't get to the airport to pick her up, I gave her the address and told her to take a cab to the apartment.

When she arrived, she was looking very flustered and had an irate cabdriver in tow. She had never been to the United States before she went to Las Vegas and had flown there directly from Paris. She therefore thought that everywhere in America was just like Vegas. Casino gambling chips were as good as cash there — bars, cabs, and shops all honored them — and not having much cash on her and not realizing that what happened in Vegas didn't happen anywhere else, Claudine tried to pay for her Los Angeles cab ride with a chip from the Tropicana.

"What the hell is this, lady?" the driver asked with all the charm for which cabdrivers are famous the world over.

"It's a chip," Claudine said, pronouncing it *cheep*.

"You're goddam right you're cheap, lady," he said, "and I ain't taking it."

She still spoke virtually no English, so the standoff continued until she came running to the apartment, pursued by the cabdriver, and I paid him with some rather more widely accepted U.S. currency.

As well as a dancer, Claudine was already an experienced actress. She had appeared in *The Turn of the Screw* at the Edward VII Theatre in Paris when she was only ten, had done three years in repertory in French television, and had appeared in plays in Milan and Venice. However, her parents back in Paris, already concerned that their nineteen-year-old daughter was working so far from home in a place renowned for excess of all kinds, were further alarmed when she told them that she was dating an older man. That was the final straw for them, and they insisted that she give up her job with the Folies Bergère and fly home at once. I begged her to stay, but she didn't want to cause a breach with her parents. Not without a few tears on both sides, I saw her off at the airport.

By now I was head over heels in love with her and was terrified that she'd stay in Paris and forget me — it was that old lack of self-confidence once more. I thought, *If I don't marry her, I'll regret it for the rest of my life.* So, having finished my stay in Las Vegas, I flew to Paris. I introduced myself to her parents and eased some of their fears about the older man who was dating their daughter. Then I took Claudine out to lunch, poured us both a glass of champagne, and proposed to her. Her English must have been improving because it took her only a fraction of a second to say yes. One of the other diners overheard my proposal and spoke enough English to understand what was happening and explain it to the other French diners in the restaurant. The word spread rapidly, and the next thing we knew we were getting a standing ovation. Everyone in Paris loves lovers.

We flew back to Los Angeles together a couple of days later. My favorite record at the time was *My Fair Lady,* recorded by André Previn and the Shelly Manne Trio. I was playing it in my apartment later that day when the strangest thing happened. As the record came to the end, the music kept on playing. I thought I was losing my mind. I took the record off the turntable, stared at it suspiciously, and put it back in its sleeve. All the time the music kept going. I stared around me, trying to pinpoint the source, and when I glanced out the window, I saw, framed in the open window of the apartment in the neighboring building, André Previn himself playing the piano. He smiled and waved and asked us over for a drink.

It turned out that his house in Bel Air had burned down recently, and he took the apartment across the way until his house could be rebuilt. He had heard his record and just kept playing after it stopped. We had a glass of wine with him and his wife, Dory, and they were the first people in America we told that we were getting married.

We began looking for a house and found a really lovely little place just above Sunset Boulevard off Doheny, on a street named after a songbird, Bobolink; all the streets in the area had bird names: Blue Jay, Wren, Robin, and so on. On December 15, 1961, we were married at the Presbyterian church in Bel Air. The media treated it as a fairy-tale wedding, and I must say it seemed like that to me, too. I was happier than I'd ever been in my life. We spent our wedding night at the El Dorado Country Club in Palm Springs, honeymooned in Jamaica, and then set up home together in our little birdhouse on Bobolink.

8

When I left New York to move to Los Angeles, I also had to leave Cadence Records. I had had tremendous success with Archie Bleyer, and he was a man of great integrity in everything he did. When I told him I was relocating to California, he said, "Well, we really can't work that way, can we? If you're going to be out there and I'm going to be here in New York, it just won't work." He released me from my contract with Cadence there and then and didn't ask for anything in return.

Soon afterward I joined Columbia Records, and early in 1962 I was asked by the Motion Picture Academy in Hollywood if I would like to sing one of the five nominees for best song from a movie at the Academy Awards show. It was sheer chance — and my great good luck — that I was asked to sing one of the most beautiful songs I'd ever heard, "Moon River" by Henry Mancini and Johnny Mercer. I had first come across it a year earlier when I went to a Los Angeles restaurant called La Scala for dinner one evening. Johnny and Henry were sitting at a nearby table, and I went over to say hello. They had just finished recording Audrey Hepburn in a movie called *Breakfast at Tiffany's* and were full of the song they had written for her to sing in the movie, "Moon River." Henry said, "Andy, this would be a great song for you."

They even had the music with them because they had come straight from the studio to the restaurant. I took it back to New York with me and showed it to Archie Bleyer. Archie didn't think the kids would understand the lyric "my huckleberry friend." He thought it was too abstract and didn't think it would be a hit single, so he turned it down. Even Archie got one wrong occasionally. It became a big hit single as an instrumental by Henry Mancini and then as a vocal by Jerry Butler.

Now it was nominated for an Oscar, and everybody seemed to think it was a shoo-in. So I said to my new producer at Columbia, Bob Mercey, "Why don't I make a record of this? We could do ten or eleven other movie songs with it and call the album *Moon River and Other Great Movie Themes*." He and Columbia thought that was a great idea.

We recorded the album in three days, one session a day. We were pressed for time and ended up having to get the last four tracks down in just three hours because the studio had been booked by someone else after that. "Moon River" was the last of the four, and by the time we got to it, we had only ten minutes left; it was pretty much one take and that was it. "Moon River" duly won the Oscar for Best Song, was a smash with the audience on Oscar night, and, as it turned out, with the television audience at home. Columbia had backed their judgment by shipping huge quantities of my album to stores all across the country. They sold over four hundred thousand albums on the following day alone, a tribute both to a great song and to the hold that the Oscars exercise on the American imagination. *Moon River* has been selling ever since. I've never released it as a single, but it has become my signature tune, the song with which I'm always identified. When I hear anybody else sing it, it's all I can do to stop myself from shouting at the television screen, "No! That's my song!"

The night after the Oscars I received a phone call from my mom, congratulating me on winning my first Academy Award. "But, Mama," I said, "this wasn't an award for me. It was for the songwriters." Like proud mothers everywhere she wasn't having any of that. "I don't know what you're talking about," she said. "All I know is that four other people got up and sang songs, and you were the best one." That was my mom.

The following year I was asked by the Academy if I'd like to sing another Henry Mancini song at the Oscars: "The Days of Wine and Roses" from the movie of the same name. I loved that song as well. It was easy to sing and very nostalgic and evocative, an "our town" kind of song that anyone could relate to. Once more we released an album with the song as the title track; once more it won the Oscar; and once more the sales of the album went wild. It shot straight to the top of the album charts and remained there for sixteen weeks.

Once more, too, I received a call from my mom the following night, congratulating me on winning my second Academy Award in a row. "I don't believe anyone has done that before," she said. "Not even Walter Brennan has won two in a row."

"But Mama . . ." I said, but again she just didn't want to hear it.

The next year I went one better and ended up singing two songs on Oscar night. Yet again I'd been invited to sing another beautiful Henry Mancini and Johnny Mercer song, "Charade." Debbie Reynolds was due to sing one of the other songs, "Call Me Irresponsible," written by James Van Heusen with lyrics by Sammy Cahn, but on the day of the awards, Debbie called in sick with the flu and wasn't able to appear. The Academy immediately asked me if I could sing that song as well. How could I refuse? Perhaps feeling that three Mancini-Mercer songs in a row might be too much, the Academy this time awarded the Oscar to "Call Me Irresponsible," although I also recorded "Charade," which became a huge hit for me.

The following night my mom rang me again. "You got the hat trick," she said as soon as I picked up the phone. "Three in a row." By then I had given up trying to argue with her. Mom and Dad used to come to my house for dinner every Sunday night, and Mom would often ask to see my three Oscars. I always told her they were at my office and never felt guilty about lying to my mother about that.

On the strength of those Oscar-linked successes, Columbia signed me to a new contract — at that time the biggest recording contract in history. I would have hits with a number of other Henry Mancini songs over the years, such as "Dear Heart" and "In the

Arms of Love"; his songs were great for me, and I felt there was a special bond between us. We were near contemporaries — he was only three years older than I was — and I loved working with him. He had a very quick, dry sense of humor and made me laugh a lot. We became good friends, often went skiing together in Sun Valley, and did a lot of tours together.

In November 1963 we flew to Chicago for an engagement at McCormick Place. When we got to the arrivals area at Midway Airport, it was full of people but had none of the usual hustle and bustle of a busy airport. It was deathly quiet: no flight announcements, no lines of people shuffling toward the departure gates, nobody talking, and nobody moving around. All the thousands of passengers were clustered in groups around every available flickering television screen. We were too far away to see what they were watching, and Henry whispered, "What the hell's going on?"

"I don't know, but something bad has happened," I said. "Listen."

The only sound to be heard was that of people crying. We moved toward the nearest television, surrounded by another knot of silent people, and saw the images on the screen — so potent and soon to become so familiar that even now I can conjure them up at once by closing my eyes and casting my mind back to that afternoon: the black convertible limousine, the smiling figures of a man and woman, and then the impact, the mist of blood, and that same figure but slumped like a crumpled doll. President Kennedy had been shot in Dallas.

We eventually tore ourselves away from the telecast and took a cab into Chicago. It was a long somber journey. The show was postponed because of the assassination, and like many Americans, Henry and I spent most of the next couple of days in front of a television set, watching endless replays of the assassination; the almost immediate arrest of a suspect, Lee Harvey Oswald; the swearing-in of Lyndon B. Johnson as president; and then, after two days the assassination in turn of Oswald by Jack Ruby.

None of it made any sense to us. We just stared blankly at the screen, hour after hour, as if somehow an explanation for all these bizarre and horrific events would eventually appear. Finally, three days after the killing, we watched the last chapter on that same hotel television as the body of President John Fitzgerald Kennedy was buried at Arlington National Cemetery.

Henry was a friend of Robert and Ethel

Kennedy, and he talked often during those bleak days about what might now happen to them, and how Jack's death would change Bobby's life forever. All Americans remember where they were the day that JFK was killed, and I'll never forget how I learned about his death in that silent Chicago airport. I think our witnessing together the terrible events of those November days made my bond with Henry even closer. We continued to tour together, including one tour to the United Kingdom and another to Japan and other countries in the Far East, and I recorded several other songs of his.

If I was a good judge of Henry Mancini's compositions, I didn't always show the same sure eye for other people's songs. Although I did record "Can't Get Used to Losing You" in 1963, it was against my better judgment. I didn't think it was a great song at all and was sure it wasn't going to be a hit — which shows what I know because after "Butterfly" it was the biggest hit single I ever had. What made it a hit above all else was the arrangement, with its staccato plucked strings, and in retrospect, I have to admit that it was a damn good record.

The Bee Gees' Barry and Robin Gibb apparently also offered me their song "How Can You Mend a Broken Heart" before ultimately recording it themselves, and scoring their first U.S. number-one hit. If so, it was a shame, because I love the song, but have no recollection of having considered it. Either it never got further than my agents, or my memory isn't what it once was.

I also missed a chance to sing the Burt Bacharach and Hal David song "Raindrops Keep Falling on My Head" from the movie *Butch Cassidy and the Sundance Kid*. The producer of the film, John Foreman, lived down the beach from me in Malibu, and he told me later that he had wanted me to sing "Raindrops" in the movie. He tried to get hold of me to do it, but I was away on tour. It had to be recorded then and there, so he got B. J. Thomas to perform it instead. I eventually recorded the song on an album, but by then it had already been a huge hit and won an Oscar.

The year 1962 became even more spectacular for me when the huge sales of the *Moon River* album helped persuade NBC to offer me an opportunity to do a pilot for a potential television series. There were a lot of musical shows on television back then: Although he was off the air at the time, Milton Berle had a Tuesday night show that ran for years, and it was so popular at one time that it was watched by 75 percent of the available audience; *Ted Mack's Amateur Hour* talent show ran for twenty-two years; Perry Como's show was on the air from 1948 to 1963; and Ed Sullivan was a national institution from the 1940s right through to the early 1970s. Dinah Shore, Tennessee Ernie Ford, and Lawrence Welk also had long-running shows, but NBC felt there was room for another and I thought we could do something that was distinctly different from the shows that were already on the air.

Bud Yorkin and Norman Lear, who would go on to produce situation comedies such as *All in the Family, Maude,* and *Chico and the Man,* were chosen as executive producers for my pilot, and Dick Van Dyke, Andy Griffith, Henry Mancini and his orchestra, and a then unknown called Ann-Margret were the guest stars. The pilot aired on May 4, 1962, and was a big enough success for NBC to give me my own television series.

It was the chance of a lifetime, and I was both excited and very nervous about it. I had no perspective about my work at the time; I didn't think I was a great singer or comedian, and I didn't see myself as a natural television host, either. I couldn't even enjoy watching the broadcasts. I don't think I'm unique in that; many performers carry insecurities, worrying obsessively that one day they'll be "found out." Some film stars can't watch their own movies; some can't even watch the rushes.

The first show of my series aired in September 1962, with guests Peggy Lee and George Gobel. The critics loved the program from the start, but they were members of a small minority because practically no one else was watching. The ratings were so low that the show was cancelled after a twenty-six-week run, and it looked as if my career as host of my own series was over. However, although it had been dropped, *The Andy Williams Show* still won the award for outstanding variety series at that year's Emmys. Coupled with the support of one sponsor whose directors really believed in me, it was enough to earn us a last-minute reprieve. S&H Green Stamps offered to sponsor twelve specials of *The Andy Williams Show*. These aired between September 1963 and May 1964, and this time the ratings were so good that NBC reversed its earlier decision and gave the show another chance.

The new series began in October 1964, this time with Bob Finkel as producer. Our intention was to produce a musical variety show, the kind of program people could watch with their kids. It was an old-fashioned concept in some ways, harking back even past my early years in Iowa, to the days of the old music hall variety bills, but we aimed to present it in a fresh and modern way, and we were able to draw on some of the best available talent in front of and behind the camera: musicians and dancers, producers, directors, cameramen, and soundmen. That gave us production values that few others could match, and it showed on the screen.

Bob Finkel and I set out to give the show an intimate and informal atmosphere. It was still a musical variety series, but when we were first planning it, I told Bob that I'd really like to have a spot where I could just sit down among the studio audience, talk to them, and sing a few songs that they wanted to hear. Merely being out there, chatting with people, gave the show the warm and relaxed feeling I wanted. My wardrobe also strengthened that feeling of informality. Instead of jacket and tie, I wore a series of brightly colored sweaters that became the butt of a few gags from my guest comedians.

The orchestra was large — thirty-two pieces — and an eight-voice choir. Dave Grusin, who had moved out to Hollywood, was on piano, and I also took on a new conductor, Colin Romoff. A New Yorker, he had conducted Broadway shows and had a terrific feeling for show tunes. I had first heard his work in Eddie Fisher's show at the Desert Inn in Las Vegas, right after Eddie's breakup with Elizabeth Taylor. I loved the arrangements that Colin had done for him so much that I hired him for my television show.

For all his Broadway experience, however, Colin found live television to be too much. Sometimes if we were running a little long on the show, the director would yell, "Cut out the next verse!" right in the middle of the song. Also, the constant stream of instructions coming over his earphones from the director's booth was so distracting that he found it difficult to conduct at all. Just a few weeks into that first season he told me that he wanted to leave the show. When I asked Dave if he could take on the job of conductor, he just said, "Of course." Jimmy Rowles then became my pianist. Dave had very little experience conducting a big orchestra, but because of his innate musical skills and his ability to adapt to live television, he proved to be terrific. After he conducted the first show, the entire orchestra and technical crew stood up and applauded him.

Dave oversaw all the music. He arranged many of the musical numbers himself, and it was a relentless job: eight to ten songs on every show, week after week after week. We also gave him the freedom to bring in the best musical arrangers available to share the load a little, and we used many of the top arrangers in Hollywood, such as Billy May, Jack Elliot, Allen Ferguson, Dick Hazard, Johnny Mandel, and Bob Florence.

Dave had to talk to the arrangers about the style and reason for each musical number for me or Peggy Lee or Ella Fitzgerald or any of the guest stars, and he had to work with George Wyle, who did all the vocal arranging for the choir and the layouts for all the musical numbers with the guests. Dave also had to work with the accompanists of the guest artists who appeared on the program and collaborate with the choreographer and his musical requirements. Of course, on a weekly series the clock was always ticking down to the next program. The production schedule for a complex, fast-moving show, broadcast every seven days for thirty-nine consecutive weeks, was very demanding, but whatever we asked of Dave, he always delivered in style. He was with me for a few more years, but then one day announced, "Andy, I'm going to leave the show. I want to write for movies."

"Are you crazy?" I said. "You came with

me to Hollywood to be my pianist, and now you're the musical director of my show. You're making good money, you're settled here, and you want to leave all of this?"

He shrugged and said, "I know, but I want to write for movies."

Dave was a real musician's musician, and I was genuinely sorry to see him go. But I felt very fortunate to have had several years with him and couldn't stand in his way. He went on to write the scores for some of the best movies in Hollywood, using his piano playing and his orchestrations in such films as *On Golden Pond* and *Tootsie,* which was with the director Sydney Pollack. He is now one of the most sought-after movie composers in Hollywood.

Mom and Dad came to the studio every week to support me and sat among the audience while we were recording the television show. I was glad they were there even though Dad did try to teach the producer his job at one point by telling Bob, "You know, if you included a hymn in the show, you'd make a lot of friends." That might or might not have been true, but it wasn't the way we wanted the show to go. Bob showed remarkable restraint when he merely thanked Dad for his suggestion and then ignored it. However, Mom and Dad did make one unwitting contribution to the future shape of the show. I sometimes got them to stand up, and I introduced them to the audience. From that came the idea of involving my whole family in the Christmas program.

The audience grew so fast that by the end of that second season, *The Andy Williams Show* had become one of the network's top-ranked features. My parents' pride at that was probably exceeded only when I performed for five nights running at the state fair in our home state of Iowa and was presented with a symbolic key to the city of Des Moines.

During the state fair I was invited to play golf at the Waverly Country Club. When we got to the club, they were having some sort of tournament, and no golf carts were available. I had decided to play only nine holes anyway, but I really wasn't looking forward to carrying my bag for even that long because, being on the road, I had loaded it up with other things such as shoes and golf balls — and it was heavy. A little kid there, about twelve years old, said, "I'll take your bag for you, Mr. Williams."

I said, "Are you sure? It's pretty heavy."

He said, "I'm strong. I can do it."

For nine holes he carried my bag, and he stared at me all the way around. I would ask him for a nine iron, and he'd give me a six iron. It didn't matter. I'd say, "Oh, this is the wrong one," and he'd get me the right one. But he kept looking at me so intently that he wasn't paying attention to what he was doing.

When we finished the nine holes, I gave him $50.

"Wow!" he said. "Fifty dollars! Thanks." He hesitated, clearly with something else on his mind, and then said, "Mr. Williams, my mom and I came to see you last night at the fair. We couldn't get really close up to see you. We were sitting way in the back." He paused again. "Can I tell you something, Mr. Williams?"

I thought he was going to say, "This is the best day of my life" or "My mother has all your records" or something like that, but instead he said, "You know what, Mr. Williams? You don't look so good up close."

Despite that, I didn't hit the kid with the six iron he always gave me when I asked for a nine iron, and I even let him keep the fifty bucks.

9

The Andy Williams Show was a one-hour show, which meant forty-eight minutes of actual airtime, not counting the commercials, but a huge amount of work went into those forty-eight minutes. We rehearsed five days a week, and many of those days lasted well into the evening. I had the same attitude toward every aspect of my show. I would rehearse everything over and over so that when we went on the air, I really knew what I was doing. Only then could I relax and be the "natural" TV performer that the public believed me to be. The "spontaneous" part of the show, where I'd go out to sit among the audience, talk for a few minutes, and then sing a song or two, was unscripted, but it was blueprinted. I had an idea of the topics I wanted to cover and my own choice of songs, and I knew pretty much what I was going to say when I went out there; being spontaneous takes an awful lot of rehearsal!

Dustin Hoffman once told me — he was talking about acting, but it applies just as much to any performance — that you should be able to give exactly the same performance on camera as you did in rehearsal, but when the cameras start to roll or the curtain goes up in the theater, it's hard to do that because you think, *This is it!* and try to make more of it. I found that only if I had prepared every aspect of the show until it was bombproof could I give that "natural" performance.

That said, by now I was much more comfortable on television, and in large part that was because every aspect of the show — production, lighting, sound, musicians, dancers, etc. — was perfect. As a result I loved doing it. Although it was taped, we did the show as if it were live, straight through with no retakes. Even in its last two years, when some of the short novelty segments with Cookie Bear and the other zany characters had to be taped, we still did the rest of each episode as if it were live and we then edited those taped pieces into the mix. We never reshot anything afterward. If there was a fluffed line, we just left it in. Perhaps that added to the feeling of spontaneity. We also taped the dress rehearsal so that if something had gone really wrong, we could have used that, but we never needed to do so in all the years the show was running.

The shows were taped in the NBC studios in the Los Angeles suburb often lampooned as "beautiful downtown Burbank" in *Rowan & Martin's Laugh-In*. Fronted by a row of trademark L.A. palm trees, the studio was a boxy structure of concrete and tinted glass. Five days a week I would drive past the security guard on the gate, park my car, go through the artists' entrance into the long, low, rambling building, and walk down the labyrinth of corridors, a block long in some cases. There were vast warehouses where props were stored, construction areas where carpenters built the sets, the NBC commissary — the butt of a thousand Johnny Carson gags over the years — the makeup department, and the Aladdin's cave of the wardrobe department where they could fit you out as a pirate, a seventeenth-century French nobleman, a hobo, a talking bear, or almost anything else you could think of. After passing the production office and a series of rehearsal rooms of various sizes, right at the end I reached the studios where the NBC shows were recorded. There were two smaller studios and two larger ones, the latter designated as A and B, where the big variety programs were shot. We were usually in Studio A, and Dean Martin was right next door in Studio B.

Television studios always look a lot bigger on-screen than they are in reality. The huge audience you see on-screen is only two hundred or three hundred people. When we taped our show, the orchestra was in one corner of the studio with the choir nearby, while the set stood in the center, facing the audience. The control room was at the back, above and behind the audience, and in front of the audience were the six huge color television cameras, four feet long and two feet wide, boom microphones, and studio lights. All this equipment meant the audience could see only parts of the set and watched most of the show on big monitor screens at either side of the studio and overhead. In any case, you didn't play to the audience, you played to the cameras.

In addition to the production team in the control room, there were also a couple of dozen people on the studio floor: sound- and cameramen, makeup girls poised to dash in and touch up their handiwork, wardrobe girls ready with a change of costume, grips, gofers, runners, best boys, and other production members, and some people who stood around with clipboards while we were recording. In ten years I never discovered what they did. In the middle of all this, I'd be sitting on a stool, trying to look natural and relaxed as if it were just another day at the office.

Most shows then tended to use a laugh track — taped laughter added to the sound track to encourage the television audience at home to join in. It was often unsubtle, unlike the technique used by the comedian Milton Berle, who was an artist in the use of fake laughter. He used to record his television appearances standing in front of a curtain, with no audience present, but he had a little red lightbulb out of camera shot that the sound engineer would use to signal him. Milton would crack a gag, and the sound engineer would play what he thought was the right amount of canned laughter for the joke. As he began to fade the track down, he would make the bulb flicker so that Milton would be able to launch his next gag: "And not only that . . ." When it was all put together, the effect was so convincing that you'd have struggled to realize there wasn't a real audience there. However, we chose not to use "canned laughter." We had a warm-up man to get the audience relaxed, but we relied on their natural response to the show. Although the sound engineer might turn up the volume of their actual laughter, what you saw and heard was pretty much the way it was.

Somehow the television show struck a chord with audiences not just in the United States but all over the world. British audiences in particular really took to the program, and I've had a very loyal following there ever since. I didn't really understand why the British public loved the program so much until an English friend told me, "You have to understand what British television was like then, Andy. The home-produced entertainment programs we had then were things like *The Billy Cotton Band Show*. There was a band, one or two singers, a comedian, and that was it. There was one or at most two cameras filming from static positions, the costumes looked as if they had been run up by somebody's mother, the sets were made of cardboard and wobbled if anyone breathed on them, and it was in black and white — well, gray mostly, just like British life at the time. Then along you came with a show that embodied everything we found glamorous and exciting about America. It had high production values. It was entertaining, full of life, color, and movement, and packed with stars that everyone had actually heard of. It was like a window on another, almost impossibly glamorous world, and we couldn't get enough of it."

We wanted the show to be a first-class experience for the performers as well as for the audience, so we tried to make all the guests feel especially comfortable; that way we brought out the best in them. I loved having comedians on the show, and I think my favorite was Jonathan Winters, a big bear of a guy who appeared more often than anyone else, about twenty times altogether. Like me, he had gotten his big break in show business while appearing at the Blue Angel. He was spotted by Garry Moore, who was then filling in for Arthur Godfrey on his *Talent Scouts* show. At breaks in rehearsals or whenever we were sitting around shooting the breeze, Jonathan would keep us entertained by challenging us to name any character we wanted him to assume, no matter how wildly improbable. We could tell him to be anyone from Shirley Temple to Benedict Arnold, and Jonathan would drop straight into that persona and be blindingly funny as well.

He was also one of the bravest performers, forever taking chances and going out on a limb. When most comedians find something that gets a laugh, they'll work it to death, but Jonathan wanted his routines to be fresh. Even when he had done something really, really funny in rehearsal, he wouldn't want to do it again the same way; he would always try to find something new.

Although it wasn't my normal way of working, there was no point in trying to rehearse with Jonathan because he'd never do the same thing twice, and usually what he did the first time was the best. So we would talk in general about what we were going to perform, but we didn't have a script and we didn't rehearse. We would just go on the air and wing it. He used to say that we were like two little guys in the playground of life, and he was always hysterically funny.

Bill Cosby had a bit of the same quality. Part of his concert or nightclub show was preplanned, but he would also go out there for half an hour and not have any idea what he was going to talk about. He had a safety net: tried and trusted routines he could revert to if he had to. But most of the time he was just riffing about new material, and it was very funny. Mel Brooks, too, was just plain off-the-wall funny. You could toss him any subject, and he'd be brilliant about it right off the bat. One day when he was guesting on the show, we went to lunch, and he had our table dying with laughter. Soon the tables around us were laughing, too, and then everyone in the whole place was cracking up. He took over the entire restaurant! I remember his wife, Anne Bancroft, being asked what it was like being married to him, and she said, "Every day would just be a regular day, but every night when Mel got home, I'd think, 'And now the party begins.'"

When another very funny man, Phil Harris, guested on the show, we paired him with Pat Boone even though it was hard to imagine a less likely partnership. Pat had the most squeaky clean wholesome image in show business, whereas Phil was more of a Dean Martin–style performer — at least as far as the drinking went.

When we took a break from rehearsal, Phil immediately said, "Come on, Andy, let's go across the street and have a drink. You coming too, Pat?"

"I don't think so," Pat replied. "I don't drink."

"You don't drink?" Phil said. "Never?" Then he turned to me and delivered a line that was to become world famous: "Andy, can you imagine getting up in the morning knowing that's the best you're gonna feel all day?" I've seen that line attributed to scores of people over the years, including Dean Martin, but Phil Harris was definitely its originator.

"Anyway, Phil," I said, "I kind of like waking up every morning feeling great. I think nothing of walking five miles every morning."

Phil gave me a pitying look. "I don't think much of that, either, Andy."

The son of two circus performers, he was originally christened Wonga Philip Harris, and I could see why he decided to drop his first name. Phil was a big, cuddly guy, who was a close friend of Bing Crosby. After Bing died on the eve of his annual pro-am golf tournament, Phil substituted for him on the telecast of the tournament and began by saying of Bing's death, "I have grown up to learn that God doesn't make mistakes. Today I'm beginning to doubt that."

Originally a bandleader, Phil became a big radio star, appearing with Jack Benny for a long time before launching his own show with his wife, Alice Faye. He once said to me, "If it hadn't been for radio, I'd still be traveling with an orchestra. I played one-night stands for seventeen years, sleeping on buses. I didn't have a home, and I never even voted in elections; I couldn't register because I didn't have a permanent residence."

Phil then went on to reinvent himself again for the television age. He was a fine singer, a very funny man, and a brilliant voice-over artist, creating three memorable characters for Disney: Thomas O'Malley in *The*

Aristocats, Little John in *Robin Hood,* and most famously, Baloo the Bear in *The Jungle Book,* singing "The Bare Necessities" and scat singing with Louis Prima on "I Want to Be Like You."

The bandleader Lawrence Welk was another regular guest on the show and almost as squeaky clean as Pat Boone. Born on a farm in North Dakota, Lawrence was the son of German-speaking immigrants. He dropped out of school in the fourth grade and was twenty-one years old before he spoke any English at all, and he never really mastered the language.

He had his own very popular television show, based on a simple format: easy-listening music, which he used to call "champagne music," performed by his orchestra and his "family" of wholesome musicians, singers, and dancers. Lawrence himself played the accordion — one of many examples of his total lack of "cool" — and wasn't a TV natural at all, always looking stiff and slightly embarrassed to be in front of a camera. Coupled with his thick accent, it left him open to ridicule, but whatever the sophisticates might say about him, millions of people watched him every week and bought his albums. His show was on the ABC network for sixteen years, and even when network executives pulled the plug on it, claiming it was too old-fashioned to appeal to advertisers, Lawrence promptly set up his own TV network of two hundred independent stations and carried on broadcasting his show for another eleven years.

Lawrence had no sense of humor whatsoever, so whenever we booked him as a guest on the show, we always made sure we had someone who was off-the-wall, such as Buddy Hackett or Jonathan Winters or Phil Harris, to do sketches with him. His attempts to read the cue cards were a source of much unintentional humor. I remember him introducing "a medley of songs from Vorld Var *i*" — rhyming with eye — and at one rehearsal he told us that since the sponsor was going to be in the audience, we should be sure to "pee on our toes." He was also quite absentminded, as he demonstrated on one memorable occasion during his own show. "I vant to introduce you viewers to my grandchildren," he said. "Dis is my grandson Lawrence Welk III" — except that he called him Lawrence Welk duh Turd. He then turned to his other grandchild, who was gazing up at him expectantly. "And dis . . ." Lawrence said but then floundered to a halt. "Dis . . . dis is. . . . Vell, dis is duh udder one," he finally said, hastily signaling his orchestra to strike up the next number.

Not only was his English bad, but he was also something of a puritan and a complete innocent abroad. He fired Alice Lon, one of his Champagne Ladies (the singers on his show), for "showing too much knee." After being deluged with thousands of protest letters, Lawrence relented and asked her to return, but she was so furious with him that she refused and never performed with him again.

Another time, while we were rehearsing, I was chatting with Lawrence — which, given the language barrier, was not always the easiest thing to do — and I mentioned that I was about to play a couple of weeks for Bill Harrah at his casino at Lake Tahoe.

"I've been taking my band up zer for years," Lawrence said, "and ve always drive up from Los Angeles to Lake Tahoe on my buz. Vell, I have a sleeping compartment on my buz, and one time ven ve got up to Lake Tahoe, ve had a rehearsal in duh showroom viz my band. But ze trumpet player didn't show up. I had an idea vair he might be, so I vent down to my buz and peeked into my sleeping compartment. Do you know vot I saw?"

"No, Lawrence," I said, "I don't."

"I saw him in zer viz a lady." He paused dramatically. "And do you know vot zey vere doing?"

"I can only imagine," I said.

"He vas kissing her on duh titty."

"Goodness, Lawrence," I said, trying to keep a straight face, "what did you do?"

"Vell, I had to fire him, of course. Ve can't have a kveer in our band."

Sammy Davis Jr. was also on the show several times. Both of his parents had been vaudeville performers, and he certainly inherited their talents. He was a singer, a dancer, an impressionist, a comedian, a multi-instrumentalist, and a photographer; all that and he could do quick-draw tricks with six-shooters as well. In fact, there seemed to be nothing that Sammy couldn't do. He was also the hardest-working man in show business, even at the cost of his family life — and that was something I knew all about, too.

He overcame the loss of an eye in a car accident in 1954 and the racial prejudice that was never far from the surface in large parts of 1950s America. Mixed-race marriages were still illegal in around thirty states of the union at the time, and when Sammy married the Swedish actress May Britt, he was deluged with hate mail.

He told me that when he was dating May, if they wanted to go out for dinner or to a club — assuming they could find one that would admit black people at all — his white friend Buddy Bregman would come with them and bring a black woman. The black woman pretended to be with Sammy, while May was supposed to be with Buddy, which was the way they had to carry on their relationship. It was a horrible position to be in, and it made Sammy both angry and sad that almost a century after the Civil War, they still had to resort to such subterfuge just because of the color of his skin.

Astonishingly, when we were chatting before the show one time, he told me that he had never been aware of racism when he was growing up because his father and his adopted uncle, Will — his parents had split up when he was small, and he grew up with his dad — shielded him so successfully that he never realized it existed. "If people yelled insults at me in the street, my dad would tell me it was because they were jealous of my talent, and I believed him. It was only when I joined the army that I came face-to-face with prejudice because of the color of my skin, and overnight the world looked very different. It just wasn't one color anymore. Then I realized the protection I'd gotten all my life from my father and Will. I was grateful for that and their hope that I'd never need to know about prejudice and hate, but, boy, were they ever wrong."

A lot of southern theaters and clubs not only refused to allow Sammy to perform but would not even admit him or any other black person. Las Vegas casinos were also segregated, and even when Sammy's talent opened doors for him, they would often be slammed in his face as soon as he came off-stage. He headlined at the Frontier Casino in Las Vegas for several years, yet, like Nat King Cole, Count Basie, and other black performers, he wasn't even given a dressing room and had to wait outside between shows. Nor could he gamble in the casino, eat in the restaurant, or stay at the hotel. He had to live in a rooming house on the west side of Vegas; black performers weren't allowed as guests in any of the city's hotels at the time.

After he became a major star, Sammy, supported by friends like Frank Sinatra, broke through the race barrier by refusing to play any venue that practiced segregation, and he once told me that the thing he was most proud of achieving in his life was that he had forced nightclubs and casinos from Las Vegas to Miami Beach to integrate. I thought of Sammy when I was watching the coverage of the 2008 presidential election; how thrilled and proud he would have been had he lived to witness an African American become president of the United States.

Another time when Sammy was going to be a guest on my show, I arranged to meet him for lunch at the Brown Derby in Hollywood to talk about what songs and routines we'd be doing. Sammy had to do some wardrobe fittings, so he warned me that he might be running late and also told me that he might bring a guest. When I walked into the Brown Derby — the entrance was through a brown-painted concrete dome in the shape of a derby hat — there were very few people there and no sign of Sammy at all. As I looked around the room, however, I saw one guy sitting alone at a table beneath the rows of caricatures of movie and television stars that lined the walls. I went over, introduced myself, and sat down. We chatted until Sammy turned up fifteen minutes later and then ordered lunch. We began tossing around ideas on songs and the sketch we were going to do. Sammy's friend was very helpful, coming up with a couple of great ideas. We had been chatting for quite a while when Sammy said, "You know, Andy, you still haven't introduced me to your friend."

"My friend?" I said. "I thought he was *your* friend." It turned out that the guy was just about to have lunch by himself when I came in and introduced myself. He was a fan of mine and couldn't believe his luck when I sat down and started talking to him. Then when Sammy came in and we ordered lunch, he just went along for the ride. We finished lunch, and I happily picked up his tab. We actually used some of the ideas he came up with in our sketch.

Sammy was on the road all the time, so whenever he checked into a hotel, he brought with him absolutely everything that was important to him. His valet, George, would even take down the hotel pictures and hang Sammy's photographs of his kids. Sammy would always have all his cameras with him as well — he seemed to have hundreds of them — and all the guns that he used to do the incredible fancy-draw and fast-draw tricks as part of his act.

He even had a portable bar that George would set up in his hotel suite or in the studio when he was doing my show. Sammy would sip his preferred drink all day long — Jack Daniels and Coke. I don't know how much bourbon George put in there every time because he'd keep filling Sammy's glass all day and all night long, but I never saw

Sammy get even slightly tipsy.

Unfortunately, the same could not be said about Judy Garland. No one who grew up in America before the war would ever forget the impact of *The Wizard of Oz* when it was first released. Judy Garland went on to become a global superstar, a legend, and one of the greatest and most beloved stars of the twentieth century. The insecurities and the problems with prescription drugs that she had from a very early age were well known, and she was not in a good state when she arrived to rehearse for a guest appearance on my show.

We chatted for a few minutes before she started rehearsals. Judy had just appeared at the Greek Theatre and was still shuddering over the state of the dressing room when she arrived there. I knew what she meant because I had played the theater a couple of times myself and still had bad dreams about it. The star's dressing room was a dim, dank, cement cell directly beneath the stage. It smelled of mildew, and springs protruded from the stained seat cushions of the ugliest, most beaten-up couch in the world. There was no telling what had transpired on it, and I didn't really like to think about it. The dressing table was drab green, like steel office furniture, and although the mirror was rimmed with the usual bare lightbulbs, the electrical wires were sticking out.

"Well, when the stage manager showed me the dressing room," Judy said, "I told him 'Even Cheetah wouldn't dress in here!' If Cheetah wouldn't, neither would I, so I made them redecorate it for me."

We chatted a while longer, and then the choreographer, Nick Castle, took her off to rehearse a song-and-dance number she was going to do on the show. She worked on the number all day with Nick and eight dancers, but when she came in the next morning, she had no recollection whatsoever of the previous day and no idea how to even begin performing the routine they had so laboriously rehearsed. We were left with a four-minute spot to fill. After an uncomfortable silence Judy said, "Well, what if we do a skit where I show Andy how to put on makeup?"

It would have been a tough sell in a twenty-five-words-or-less pitch to a Hollywood producer, but at that moment we had a guest-star-shaped hole in the middle of the show that we had to fill with something. My producer and I both felt the same way about it: What do we have to lose? I said, "Sure, let's try it and see if it works."

Judy and I sat down at a makeup table with only a piano tinkling in the background, like an old silent movie. She began by carefully drawing a greasepaint mustache on my face and then drew one on herself as well. Then she drew eyebrows on both of us. "And this is how you put on powder, Andy," she said, dabbing a small pad of it on my nose, hard enough to raise a small cloud.

"Well, I guess you could use some, too," I said, dabbing her nose and producing another cloud of powder. Things steadily escalated from there, with ever larger pads being used until we were both covered in powder and the whole makeup table was almost buried under drifts of it.

"I think you need just a little bit more, Andy," she said, reaching under the makeup table and pulling out a great big pillow. She smothered it in powder and then whacked me in the face with it, producing a pall of powder that hung in the studio like fog and obliterated the pair of us completely. It was simple slapstick stuff, but she performed it with such brilliance that she turned what could have been a ho-hum moment into one of the funniest skits we ever had on the show. Even today I get buttonholed by people who remember it and want to talk about it. Kay Thompson saw the show, called me up the next morning and said "Well, And," — she always called me that — "you finally made it." It was one of the only unqualified compliments — if it was a compliment — that she ever paid me about my television work.

Judy was also supposed to sing her signature song, "Over the Rainbow," on the show. We were seated on stools side by side, but when she began to sing, I grew increasingly alarmed. Her voice was cracking a bit, and at one point she hesitated as she groped for the next words in a lyric that she must have sung a thousand times or more. She kept going, but when she got to a line near the end of the song — "If happy little bluebirds fly beyond the rainbow" — I could tell she was struggling to get air into her lungs for the final notes. I slipped my arm around her waist to support her and joined her in singing, "Why . . . oh why . . . can't I?"

I had only wanted to help her through it. We made it to the end of the song together and she shot me a grateful look while, still with my arm around her waist, we acknowledged the applause of the studio audience. The following week my mail was full of letters complaining: "Why did you butt in when Judy Garland was singing? We don't want to hear Andy Williams sing 'Over the Rainbow,' we want to hear Judy Garland sing it."

As soon as Judy got off the set, her entourage surrounded her and got her back to her dressing room, and then out to her waiting limo. It was the last time I shared a stage with Judy and also the last time I ever saw her. Judy's health and her drug problems continued to deteriorate, and in June 1969 she was found dead in the bathroom of a house she was renting in London, after what the coroner later described as "an incautious self-overdosage" of barbiturates.

Whatever drug problems Judy Garland might have had, they were nothing compared with those of Tallulah "Turps" Bankhead, who took substance abuse to levels that others could not even conceive. Her nickname was an acknowledgment of her willingness to drink even that if nothing else was available, and when she guested on the show, her first question to my assistant, Keats Tyler, was "Where's the medicine box, Keats honey?" She wasn't ill; she just wanted to see whether it contained any drugs she could take.

Despite the foibles of some of my guest stars, over the next few years, my television show went from strength to strength. The ratings were consistently good, and if in some ways the format of singers, dancers, and comedians was as old as variety and vaudeville itself, we somehow made it new-looking every time. We freshened up the sets and tinkered with the format and running order a little between seasons, but it remained basically the same show throughout the 1960s.

I always enjoyed dueting with other singers. The media might sometimes try to play us up as rivals, but I never felt that way. I wasn't out there trying to put one over on Tony Bennett or Bobby Darin or whomever; we all had our own style and our own following, and the shows I most enjoyed were those where we had two or three other singers as guests and we'd do harmonies together.

I particularly loved singing with vocal groups. After harmonizing with my brothers for years, it seemed very natural to sing "Scarborough Fair" with Simon and Garfunkel or "Kisses Sweeter Than Wine" with Peter, Paul and Mary. One day Mary brought her little daughter to the set, and I was standing next to her while they were singing "Puff, the Magic Dragon." "Aren't they wonderful?" I said. "Do you know who that is?"

"Oh, yes," she said. "That's Peter, Paul and Mommy."

Although I had some of the biggest stars in show business as guests over the years, one of the greatest thrills was when my childhood hero, Bing Crosby, agreed to be on the show. I hadn't seen Bing in almost twenty years, not since my brothers and I had made "Swinging on a Star" with him, but he had sent me a gracious letter when I recorded "Hawaiian Wedding Song," telling me how much he liked it. He loved Hawaiian music and had recorded many songs, including *"Ke Kali Nei Au,"* the original lyrics for "Hawaiian Wedding Song." Of course, I was thrilled to get that acknowledgment.

He was a guest on the show two or three times, including an appearance during my first season. When he stopped by my dressing room to say hello, he was wearing his trademark hat, smoking his pipe, and wearing an old cardigan. At one time I'm sure it had been a very lovely cashmere sweater — it was obviously one of his favorites — but now it had a hole in the sleeve at the elbow and looked a little weary all over.

Bing reminded me of my dad, who got so attached to his favorite jackets or sweaters that he would wear them forever. I can remember my mom despairing of ever smartening him up and once going as far as throwing his current holed and threadbare favorite sweater away. Five minutes later, as my mom settled down in an armchair with a magazine, my dad tiptoed out the back door, retrieved the sweater from the trash can, and was wearing it when we all sat down to supper that night. Mom looked up, gave an exasperated sigh, and said, "All right, Jay, you win, but at least let me darn the holes." He kept wearing it for a few more years until finally it was so shabby that even Dad had to concede its days were over.

Bing's cardigan wasn't quite in that state, but it had certainly seen better days. I don't know whether wearing his favorite old clothes relaxed him, but he was certainly in a mellow mood that day. Friends had warned me that Bing was quite a "buttoned-up" sort of person, but to my surprise he really seemed to relax and open up while we were sitting around chatting in my dressing room. He started telling me about his early days as one of seven kids growing up in Spokane, Washington. He had been christened Harry but was renamed after *The Bingville Bugle,* a parody of a hillbilly newspaper that started appearing in his local paper. According to Bing it was a very funny spoof, and he and his friends were forever quoting it to one another. As a result, his friends began calling him Bing from Bingville, and the name eventually stuck.

When he grew up, he went to college, intending to be a lawyer, but two things changed his life. The first was when he went to see Al Jolson perform at a local theater and was so blown away by the experience that he never forgot it. Forty years later, as we chatted in that Burbank studio, he was still in awe of that performance by Jolson, calling him "the greatest entertainer I ever saw." The other key event was when he sent away for a set of drums on mail order, taught himself to play, and then began playing and singing with a local band. "I made so much money doing that," Bing told me, "that I thought, *Why would I want to be a lawyer when I can make more money and have a lot more fun doing this?*"

I really felt I'd seen at least a glimpse of the real Bing Crosby that day, even if only for those few minutes, before a couple of network executives arrived, and Bing slipped back into his normal role; like so many big stars he had developed an affable but rather distant public manner, one that kept all but the most persistent Bing worshipers at arm's length.

When we recorded the show, I was as excited as a kid in a candy store to be sitting on a stool alongside Bing and singing a medley of duets with him. We even sang "Swinging on a Star," just like the Williams Brothers had done with him all those years before. I was a reasonably well-known performer by then, but Bing was in an entirely different league — the first and greatest singing star of the modern era and the man who paved the way for all the singers, like me, who followed him. I found it both humbling and hugely exciting to be sharing a stage with him, listening to that wonderful relaxed delivery and that still silky smooth and beautiful voice.

After guesting on my show, Bing called me one afternoon and said, "Andy, I've been asked by Princess Grace to sing at the annual Red Cross Charity Ball in Monaco, and I just can't do it. I'm making a movie, and I can't get away. Would you fill in for me?"

The next day I had a call from Monaco confirming all the details, and a few weeks later I flew to Monte Carlo and went directly to the Hotel de Paris. The following evening, beneath a gilt-encrusted ceiling with crystal chandeliers I found myself standing in front of the toughest audience I'd ever seen — even in the dark early days in Pittsburgh and Cleveland. I was introduced by Charles Aznavour, and when even he was having difficulty getting the audience's attention, I knew I was in for a tough night. The people in the audience were the crowned heads of Europe: People listened to them; they didn't listen to anyone, least of all a mere entertainer. Half of them had their backs to me when I started singing, and they stayed that way, continuing their conversations with one another all the way through my performance. Every time I reached the end of a song there was a glacial silence, broken only by a faint ripple of applause, most of it coming from Prince Rainier, Princess Grace, and David Niven, who was sitting at their table.

As I looked at the impassive, indifferent faces of the audience, I began to wonder whether Bing really was making a movie or had worked this crowd before and wasn't eager for a repeat. I died a thousand deaths before I got to the end of my last song and slunk back to the royal table in a deafening silence. "I'm sorry I went down so badly," I said to Prince Rainier. "On the contrary, my dear boy," he said, "that was the best reaction we've had since Nat King Cole played here." If so, I'd have hated to be there on a bad night.

The following year my agent rang me to say that he had received an invitation for me to sing at the ball again. "You're joking," I said. "I never want to perform for an audience like that again."

"But they're desperate for you to do it," he said. "You're hugely popular there. 'Love Story' and the theme from *The Godfather* have been massive hits, and they're insisting that it be you. No one else will do."

Eventually I allowed myself to be persuaded, but I was determined not to have the kind of reception I had had the previous time. I thought long and hard about how to do it, and finally I came up with an idea. If they liked "Love Story" so much, I'd give them a "Love Story" they couldn't ignore.

On the night of the ball, as I took the microphone, the crowned heads and distinguished guests were, as usual, ignoring me and talking among themselves. I signaled for a drum roll. "Ladies and gentlemen," I said. "Tonight I'd like to pay tribute to the greatest love story of them all." The lights went down, and a single spotlight swept across the room, settled on Prince Rainier and Princess Grace, and stayed on them. Then a second spotlight hit me, and I began singing the theme from *Love Story*: "Where do I begin, to tell the story of how great a love can be . . ."

The crowned heads and VIPs could scarcely ignore their hosts and fellow royals, so they fell silent and turned to face them. I had the audience's attention for the moment, but I was determined not to give them the chance to applaud at the end of the first number. I knew that if they did, they'd consider their duty to their hosts done and go back to their private conversations. I segued straight from *"Love Story"* into "Dear Heart" and then "Moon River," and so on, until I completed a twenty-minute uninterrupted medley by segueing back into *"Love Story"* for the climax. All that time the spotlight stayed on Princess Grace and Prince Rainier.

When I finished, there was a moment's silence and then the place erupted. People were applauding, shouting "Bravo!" and "Encore!" and were even throwing flowers onto the stage. I didn't care if they were applauding me or Prince Rainier and Princess Grace. Either way, I had finally beaten those rude bastards.

10

As well as having Bing Crosby and many other great entertainers of his and my eras as guests on my television show, we also uncovered some of the biggest stars of the next generation. My dad called me one day and told me that he had seen four boys on a television talent show. "They were wonderful," he said. "You've got to put them on your show, Andy. They're the same age that you and your brothers were when you got started. You boys had a helping hand along the way, and now you've got to help these kids."

There was nothing I could say other than "Okay, Dad, we'll give them an audition." A couple of days later my dad brought them to the studio, and they sang for us. They were all nice-looking kids in matching red jackets, white shirts, black trousers, and bowler hats, and they sang excellent barbershop harmonies, so it was no problem to put them on the show. I introduced them by saying, "Here's a quartet of brothers who sing together just like my brothers and I used to do when we were little. I thought you'd like to see them, so ladies and gentlemen, here they are: the Osmond Brothers." They launched right into one of their barbershop songs.

The youngest one in the group was Jay, a cute-looking kid with a gap in his front teeth where his baby teeth had fallen out and his adult ones had not yet grown in. When they started singing, his three brothers looked straight ahead, but for some reason Jay started searching for the little red light to see which camera was on. His eyes were darting from side to side until he spotted the light, and then gave a gap-toothed smile and kept looking at that camera until the director switched the shot. At that point Jay started swiveling his gaze from side to side again until he found the camera that was now being used. This gap-toothed kid grinning from ear to ear, with his eyes twitching from one side to the other, was getting plenty of laughs from the audience, so the director started changing cameras faster and faster, just to keep Jay rolling his eyeballs around. By the end of the song, everyone in the studio was cracking up.

I had originally thought that having the

Osmonds on the show would be a one-shot event to please my father, but the NBC switchboard lit up after their appearance. People were calling to say how much they had enjoyed those cute little boys, and our mail indicated the same, so we asked them if they'd like to come back the following week. They kept coming back week after week for about six years. We never had a contract with them; as I had done on *The Steve Allen Show* all those years before, they just kept turning up, and we kept using them.

They were talented, hardworking kids, and they were like sponges, absorbing everything they were told — and they were learning from some of the best people in the business. Our choreographer, Nick Castle, taught them to dance and worked out routines for them. Our musical director, George Wyle, started writing for them, wonderful harmonic arrangements like the Four Freshmen used. Then one day I said to them, "Have you ever thought of playing instruments like the Beatles do?" They went straight out and bought instruments for themselves, and within six months they were playing like professionals.

They used to come in the day before the show: George Wyle would give them their vocal arrangements, Nick Castle would give them their dance steps, and then they'd go home. They rehearsed in their garage and must have rehearsed all night long, because they would come in the next day having memorized their song and the dance routine so that they were absolutely word- and move-perfect. They knew everything upside down and inside out; we called them "The One-Take Osmonds."

The following season Donny made his debut on the show when he was just five. He told me later that unknowingly I had been his vocal teacher when he was a little boy because his mom used to play my records all the time, and Donny would spend hours singing along. His favorite song of mine was "You Are My Sunshine," and the arrangement I used was a complicated jazzy one written for me by Dave Grusin. Donny sang it perfectly on the show, and another Osmond star was born. His kid sister, Marie, also made her debut during that same 1963 season when she was just three years old. She looked like a little princess, wearing a dark green dress with a diamanté necklace and silver high-heeled shoes. Her dad carried her over to the stage and said, "Honey, walk over to that man over there, and then he's going to dance with you." She wobbled over to me, and I introduced her as "the youngest Osmond brother, their little sister, Marie." We then waltzed our way across the stage while the audience went wild.

I would sometimes see my dad and the Osmonds' father, George, off in a corner together, talking animatedly. I'd smile wryly to myself at the sight of these two driven Svengalis comparing notes on how to turn their kids into superstars. However they had done it — and I suspect the Osmond technique wasn't much different from my dad's — it had certainly worked. The Osmond Brothers stayed with my show into the early 1970s; they also did Caesars Palace and toured with me several times.

The year Donny joined the group we played a few state fairs. Alan Bernard, my manager, was also along for the ride. The Osmonds always had two hotel rooms for the six of them, including their father. I went to their rooms early one morning to tell them of a change in the schedule for an interview. There was no answer at the first door, so I moved down the corridor to the second door and knocked. Donny answered the door in his pajamas. Across his shoulder I could see the other five Osmonds in the bed. They all greeted me cheerfully.

"Why are you all crowded into one bed? You always have two rooms," I said.

George spoke up: "The boys all like to be together. We always end up in one room and one bed at night."

Donny looked up at me. "Don't you sleep with Mr. Bernard?"

I checked his expression, but there was only childish innocence in that five-year-old face. "No, I don't," I said. "He's my manager, not my roommate. He has his own room. Don't worry, Donny. He doesn't mind sleeping alone."

Our first booking was at the Washington State Fair, and in addition to Alan Bernard and the Osmonds I had a sizable entourage with me: Keats Tyler, my assistant; Norman Morrell, the assistant producer of my television shows who came along as stage manager; the Goodtime Singers, a group who appeared for a year or so on my television series; Dave Grusin; two female backup singers; my rhythm section — drums, bass, guitar — plus eight strings and an electric keyboard player who were provided by the promoter. The promoter had also added a comedian, Candy Candido, who was about four and a half feet tall.

When we arrived at the motel the night before the show, Norman went straight to the fairgrounds to check the outdoor stage where I was to perform. He always sent a stage plan to the local promoter, showing the space required to accommodate the orchestra and conductor, and an "apron" on which the performers could dance and sing.

It was a stormy night, and Norman returned to the motel with bad news: "There is no stage, just a forklift pallet about four feet square standing in the middle of a very muddy racetrack. We can't do anything about the weather, but I think I can resolve the lack of a proper stage. But first of all I'm going to go and shoot the illiterate promoter!"

Norman called a local trucking company and ordered the largest flatbed truck they had, attached to a six-wheeler rig. It had arrived by the time we all went to rehearsal the following day, but the showground was a pitiful sight — a sea of mud — and the makeshift stage was ugly and also covered in mud. Norman had rented a trailer for my dressing room, and it was parked a number of feet behind the flatbed. A plank walkway had been set down in the mud to make a dry path between the two. There was so much mud that the planks were practically floating. The Goodtime Singers and the Osmonds had to dress for the show at the motel and were driven up behind the flatbed for their entrances. Candy Candido had a tiny trailer just big enough for him to sleep in; it was parked behind the flatbed, and hitched up to his old Pontiac sedan.

Candy opened the show with a ten-minute set and was followed by the Goodtime Singers, who performed for about fifteen minutes and then introduced me. I made my entrance by emerging grandly from the house trailer onto the planks and running to the flatbed, splattering mud all over my white outfit in the process. I sang a few hit songs, which were very well received by the grandstand audience seated on the other side of the muddy field.

Then I started singing the "Hawaiian Wedding Song." The local strings, which were prominent in the introduction, were very out of tune, and the sound was excruciating — like fingernails on a blackboard. I stopped the music and asked Dave to mute the strings and let the electric keyboard player play the string parts instead. We restarted the song, but the keyboard player sounded even worse than the strings had, so in the middle of the song I walked over to Keats and yelled at him loudly and firmly: "Pull the plug!"

We finally got through the "Hawaiian Wedding Song," without either strings or electric keyboards, and I then introduced the Osmond Brothers: Alan, Wayne, Merrill, and Jay. They did a couple of songs alone and then I joined them for "Aquarius/Let the Sunshine In," after which I introduced Donny, still only five years old, for his first state fair appearance. He did "Red Roses for a Blue Lady" and a rendition of Ray Charles's "I Got a Woman." The audience really went wild! All five Osmonds exited to thunderous applause, and for the finale I went into "Moon River."

Meanwhile, some distance up the racetrack and unseen in the darkness by me or the audience, the Royal Canadian Mounties had assembled, ready to make their entrance for the grand finale of the show. Their cue was supposed to be when I finished "Moon River" with a big flashy ending and took my bows, but for whatever reason someone signaled their entrance when I was halfway through the song. The cavalry bugler sounded the charge, and horses and riders thundered down the track and onto the showground. The impact of their entrance was overwhelming, as it was intended to be, and the audience roared in excitement, leaving me with the words of "Moon River" dying on my lips, my big finish in ruins, and egg on my face!

I hurriedly made my exit and crawled into

Candy Candido's tiny trailer: Candy was already behind the wheel of the Pontiac sedan. He drove me across the muddy track, swerving to miss being trampled by the mounties' horses, and got me to the other side. It was just another glamorous day on the fair tours circuit.

As well as the Osmonds, I also worked with Michael Jackson when he was with his brothers in the Jackson Five. Michael's father was another show business parent like my dad and George Osmond, but I never warmed to him the way I had to George. There was a harsher, ruthless edge to him that I didn't like. Michael, however, was a lovely little boy then, and a few years later when he was on his own, I admired his ability as a singer and dancer when he was making his big splash with records like "Thriller" — produced by my old friend Quincy Jones. I was always a supporter of Michael because he was such a talented guy. He was also very shrewd. He knew the value of creating a mystique about himself and never contradicted the rumors about him, no matter how weird they might be, because they only increased the mystery and strengthened his hold on his fans' imaginations. For example, Michael had a viral disease, vitiligo, that causes the skin to lose pigmentation. It is nonfatal, noninfectious, and noncontagious, but it is unsightly, and for obvious reasons it is particularly visible on black skin.

Anyone who suffers from it has to avoid exposure to the sun because the lack of pigmentation means that the affected skin turns white and is particularly vulnerable to sunburn. Michael's left hand was affected much worse than his right, so to hide it, he took to wearing a glove. Despite waves of speculation about the glove, he never tried to explain it, preferring to allow ever wilder explanations to circulate that only increased the Jackson mystique. When his face lost its pigmentation, he started using a parasol to shield his face from the sun, but again he made no attempt to stifle all the claims that he was bleaching his skin. When he had plastic surgery on his nose, the rumor circulated that he wanted to look like Diana Ross. This, too, was untrue. He had been told his nose was too large and his lips were too thick, and he wanted to improve them. He may have gone to extreme with his nose reconstruction, but he made no excuses. It certainly wasn't because he wanted to look like Diana Ross. His musical genius will live on long after he fades away.

One other superstar also made his TV debut on *The Andy Williams Show*. My friend and agent Jerry Perenchio called me one day and asked me to feature an unknown singer as a guest. "He's great, Andy," Jerry said. "He's made a great record. It's going to be a smash hit, and he's going to be a big star."

"Jerry," I said, "we're in competition with the other networks for ratings. We need people who are big stars *now*. We need Bob Hope and Bing Crosby and Judy Garland and Herb Alpert and the Tijuana Brass. We don't need this guy. Nobody even knows who he is. I've never heard of him."

"Andy," he said, "you're going to have to trust me on this. The guy is dynamite, and you've got to do this for me."

I thought about it and then grudgingly agreed. "Okay, Jerry, you win. Ask him to come by the office tomorrow, and he can meet with me and the producers and the writers. We'll listen to this new record of his that you think will be such a smash." The small two-story office building that I owned then was at 916 La Cienega Boulevard. Upstairs there had been an art gallery with big windows and high ceilings, and on the bottom floor was a beauty parlor. After I bought it, I used the second floor as my office and divided up the ground floor into several offices for the staff. When I arrived the next day, the unknown singer was already there.

He had on big horn-rimmed glasses encrusted with rhinestones and was wearing a black cape. I thought, *What a strange-looking guy. He is really different.*

I had already pretty much promised Jerry that I would book the guy for my show, so now it was just a matter of getting to know him and hearing the record. It was called "Your Song," and I immediately loved it, so much so that I later recorded it myself. After talking to him and having him sing for us, there was no doubt in anyone's mind that Jerry was absolutely right. We had just met a very special artist with a unique talent: Elton John. We recorded the show with Elton as guest star. It sat in the can for a couple of weeks, and by the time it went on the air, "Your Song" was already a hit. It broke very quickly, and as it turned out, it was a coup for us to be the first to showcase this new singer. After that his career really took off — not because he had been on my show but because he was so talented and continued to make such terrific records. I wonder what ever happened to him?

By now I had sold millions of records for Cadence and Columbia Records, and when I heard a rumor that Archie Bleyer was selling Cadence, I called him to ask if the rumors were true and whether he would be willing to sell me the masters of my old Cadence recordings. The Cadence catalog included not only my own early work but that of such artists as the Everly Brothers, Lenny Welch, the Chordettes, Johnny Tillotson, and a then unknown singer-songwriter named Jimmy Buffett. Archie was thinking of selling Cadence to Pickwick Records, a cut-rate company that sold to drugstores and supermarkets, and didn't want to start splitting off parts of it. I'd have to take all of the Cadence catalog or none of it. When he told me the price he was asking, I said I would buy it.

Being a man of few words, Archie just said, "Okay, Andy, you've got it."

A jazz label named Candide also came as part of the deal. It had some great jazz and blues artists, such as Charles Mingus, Lightnin' Hopkins, Phil Woods, Coleman Hawkins, and Memphis Slim, but it wasn't really my field, so I sold it to an English company, Phonoco, that specialized in jazz. However, I added another artist to my new stable by purchasing Ray Stevens's master records from Monument. Ray had appeared on my television show several times; we became good friends, and I loved his work. He was a genius at making his particular style of records — musical, very funny, and completely different from anything else that was being put out at the time. Ray also happened to be managed by my brother Don, and when Don mentioned that Ray was ready to make a move from Monument and that it might be possible to buy the catalog, I didn't hesitate.

At first I began reissuing some of my old Cadence material, such as the "Hawaiian Wedding Song" and "Canadian Sunset," at Columbia, but then I set up Barnaby Records, named after my dog, and put out future releases on that label. The early Barnaby releases included a double album of the Everly Brothers and all the old Ray Stevens records, including "Guitarzan," "Ahab the Arab," "Mr. Businessman," and "Along Came James." I then signed Ray to the Barnaby label, and we recorded new songs with him, including "The Streak" and "Everything Is Beautiful," which became big hits. We also released the first album by Jimmy Buffett, *Down to Earth*.

I also felt the Osmond Brothers were ready to record by now, and we released two singles with them, neither of which did much. Then they were approached by Mike Curb, who had his own record company, Curb Records. He recorded "One Bad Apple" with them, which became an instantaneous hit. They then left me and my record label so fast that all I saw was a dust cloud, but I don't blame them for that; I was glad for their success. They were more than ready to take the world by storm, and as Archie Bleyer told me years before when I first signed with him, the hardest part was finding the right song. Mike Curb found it, and the Osmonds then had many other big hits with him and became worldwide stars.

Some artists like to produce their own records, but I never saw myself as a producer or a record industry mogul, and Barnaby Records was never more than a sideline for me. My real interest was in performing and television. The show I always enjoyed doing above all others was the Christmas show, and it was the one that the audiences loved the most, too; it always had the highest ratings of the entire season. To this day people stop me on the street and tell me how much they cherished the Christmas shows and how much it meant to their whole family. I've always loved Christmas, and for me it really is "the most wonderful time of the year," as the song says. Because Christmas is above all a time for families, I took to inviting my own family — Mom, Dad, my sister and brothers, and Claudine — to join me on the show. I loved our all singing together as a group; it always sent shivers up my spine.

Dad and Mom both looked forward to doing those shows. Dad finally realized his dream of being a performer — he was a little bit of a ham, but it was great — and Mom was a real trouper. We had a running gag where we'd be in the kitchen, and my brothers and I would take turns trying to open a jar, but nobody could turn the top. Mom would then wander in, absentmindedly pick up the jar, and open it without even breaking a sweat. It always got a big laugh.

The number of family members that I could include in the Christmas show was steadily increasing. In 1963, Claudine and I celebrated the birth of our first child, whom we named Noelle, and we went on to have two more children, Christian, who was born in 1964, and Bobby, born in 1969.

My parents' show business careers never went further than the Christmas show, but after her guest appearances, Claudine began to get offers for acting parts. Her beauty and French accent won her a number of television roles as a femme fatale on such TV programs as *Hogan's Heroes, Dr. Kildare, and Alias Smith and Jones*. As part of her role on the show *Run for Your Life,* she had to play guitar and sing a bossa nova song, "Meditation." She learned enough fingering to look as if she was actually playing, and she did the song. When the program aired, the network switchboard lit up with people calling to ask about the French singer.

Herb Alpert and the Tijuana Brass were extremely popular then, and Herb had just started a record label with Jerry Moss — A&M Records. I called him and told him what had happened after the show aired. "I'd like to hear that song," Herb said, so I sent him a tape of the show. He loved Claudine's sound and immediately signed her to his label. He then put her in the very capable hands of producer Tommy LiPuma, who recorded an album with her called *Claudine* that went on to sell over a million copies.

Not long afterward we were on holiday in Hong Kong when a call came through from Blake Edwards offering Claudine a starring role in the film *The Party,* playing a Hollywood starlet who becomes involved with Peter Sellers's character. He said he would need her right away. I didn't want to cut short our holiday, but I also didn't want to stand in the way of what might be a big break for her in films. We packed our bags and were on our way back to Los Angeles within hours.

Claudine never thought of herself as a singer, and although she enjoyed recording, it wasn't her passion. People loved her voice and her sexy singing style, however, and A&M released another four albums of her performing easy-listening songs in that distinctive breathy and very sexy accent. I then asked her if she would like to come over to my record label, Barnaby, and we issued two further Claudine Longet albums: *We've Only Just Begun* and *Let's Spend the Night Together*. She also had four Top 100 hits, including "Love Is Blue." When I asked her what she wanted to do with the money she had made from her records, she said, "I want to buy some property on the beach." Very excited, Claudine asked my dad, who by then had been working in real estate for almost twenty years, to help her look for a lot, and they soon found one in Malibu that had a forty-foot frontage on the ocean. Dad helped her get the permits and do all the things necessary when you're planning a home, and eventually we built a wonderful two-story house on that site. It was a perfect place for us, with the beach on our doorstep, floor-to-ceiling windows from the first floor to the second, and a magnificent ocean view from the top floor.

When we started building the beach house at Malibu, we moved into the Four Seasons Hotel until it was completed, but we didn't want to lose our maid, Lula, who was a treasure. She had worked for us for several years and become a real part of the family; she was not only a maid but also the children's nanny from time to time. We were deeply fond of her, and even though there was no work for her to do, we kept paying her throughout the fourteen months it took to complete the house. Finally it was ready, and I called Lula and said, "Great news. We're moving into the house on Friday."

"I can't come Friday," she said. "You should know by now, Mr. Williams. Friday is my day off."

There were several things I could have said at that point, but I settled for "Of course it is, Lula. How about Saturday?"

It became a great home for us, and some of the happiest days of my life were spent there, just playing with my children, watching them grow and develop as the years passed, helping to shape their characters, and teaching them to enjoy the music and art that have played such a huge part in enhancing my own life.

It was fascinating to see the way their characters developed as each became an individual, distinct from one another and from their parents. Noelle, the oldest, was always quite serious and the most bookish of the three, but she had a lovely, warm personality and her mother's beautiful looks. She would help anyone, anytime, and was so gentle and caring that she was always bringing home baby frogs or birds that had fallen out of their nests, or crabs or starfish that she found on the beach. Christian, a tousle-haired "surfer dude," was a real laid-back character — smiling, relaxed, and a charmer; nothing worried him, and nothing fazed him. That mellowness had its downside because sometimes it could be hard to get him to concentrate on his schoolwork, but he was a lovely guy. Bobby had a little bit of me as a child about him, cheeky and fun-loving. Though he was quite shy behind that façade, he was also a very good athlete — a gift he certainly didn't get from me — and a real worker and a perfectionist who was never willing to let anything go until it was as good as he could make it.

Much as I loved them, Claudine inevitably played the major role in bringing them up because I was so often away on tour or working on the television show. In danger of becoming a workaholic, I was so obsessed with building my career that everything, including my family, suffered as a result.

The old cliché says that if you can remember the 1960s, you weren't there. Well, I was there all right, but my memory of them is blurred — not by any drugs I took but by the relentless pace of the schedule I set myself throughout that decade as I struggled first to make it in recording, concerts, and television, and then to consolidate my success. Sometimes on the road I would wake in the middle of the night in yet another anonymous hotel suite and, groping for the light switch, be unable to remember what town or city I was in. I would even open the draperies and look out on the neon-lit panorama of the city streets below me and still struggle to decide: Was this Chicago? Boston? Dallas? Denver? The outline of a familiar building might give me a clue, but more than once I had to find the hotel brochure to tell me where I was. And by the next night — another flight, another limousine, and another show later — I'd be in yet another hotel in yet another anonymous city.

My workload was self-imposed, but perhaps feeling that if I turned work down, I might never be offered any more, I took everything that was put in front of me. I was working so hard and was so self-absorbed that many of the great events of that seminal decade seemed to pass me by like the ghostly shapes of cars on a fogbound street. The release of the Beatles' *Sgt. Pepper's Lonely Hearts Club Band* album, the Paris riots of 1968, and Altamont — where Hell's Angels stabbed a man to death during the Rolling Stones' free concert — barely registered on my consciousness at the time, and even the Vietnam War, a constant presence on TV and in the news, seemed remote from me, almost a background noise.

While my television show was on the air, from September to March of every year, I spent five days a week at the studios, often not finishing until well into the evening. In the breaks from taping the television show I would either be in the recording studio working on my next album or on tour in America or Europe or Australia or the Far East, and every summer I was still playing an eight-week season, two shows a night, in Las Vegas. In between all that there were personal appearances, charity events, guest spots on other television shows, and all the planning, preparation, and rehearsals needed before going into the recording studio or on the road.

My first priority should have been Claudine and the children, but they often had to make do with the scraps of time I had left when all my other commitments had been fulfilled. It was crazy, but I was on a merry-go-round of fame and fortune and didn't know how to get off, or perhaps — and I'm ashamed as I admit it now — I didn't even want to get off.

In between all these commitments, I also found time for my one and only straight acting role in a Hollywood movie, although I did sing one song in the film: "Almost There." I co-starred with Sandra Dee, Robert Goulet, Maurice Chevalier, and Hermione Gingold in what one critic called a "comedy soufflé": *I'd Rather Be Rich,* released in 1964. Bob Goulet was a classically trained singer whose style was a world away from my more relaxed, pop-oriented delivery, so I never saw us as rivals except in that we were both singers. I don't think Bob saw it that way, either, despite what happened while we were filming. As competing suitors for Sandra Dee's character, we had to stage a fight, a rolling brawl that went on for some time, starting inside her house and finishing on the lawn outside. We rehearsed the fight sequence with the director a couple of times and then went for a take.

Since Bob had no more experience with fight scenes than I had, nobody had told him that you don't wear a chunky ring with spikes in it if you're doing a stage brawl. As a result, when he caught me accidentally — at least I *think* it was accidentally — with a punch, his ring split my left eyebrow wide open. It must have looked good on-screen — there was blood everywhere — but filming had to stop while I went off to get it stitched. I finished the movie with a thick layer of makeup over the stitches, which is why almost every shot after that one shows my right profile rather than my left. When Bob told his manager what had happened, he just said, "In the throat, schmuck. Next time hit him in the throat!"

Although the reviews were lukewarm, the movie did well at the box office. I had a few offers of other film roles, but the sheer boredom of waiting around for the next scene drove me mad. I was used to completing the filming of a forty-eight-minute television program in one week. In movies, 95 percent of the time was spent just hanging around waiting on lighting or technical matters. An entire day's work produced no more than a minute or two of actual screen time, so it took months to shoot a ninety-minute picture. The thought of doing that again was more than I could stomach, and I went back to my day jobs: television, concerts, and recording.

My television show and my recordings had by now made me an international name, and I was appearing in some big auditoriums as well as the one-thousand-seat Latin Casino in Cherry Hill, New Jersey. There was no negotiation about fees with the owner, Dave Duchoff. I had first met him a few years before when I was much less well known. "You're a good singer, kid," he said to me then, "but I'll tell you what I tell everyone. I got an A-list and a B-list. The A-list has stars who I know will bring me a lot of people; they get five times as much as B-list people, who are good entertainers but won't draw an audience." He looked at me appraisingly. "You're on the B-list."

"Okay," I said. "I'll pass this time and come back when I'm on the A-list." After I had the hit television series, he called me up and said, "Okay, kid, now you're on the A-list," and I played the Latin Casino several times after that. Dave had a bit of Vegas flair about him, and although his pay rates were inflexible, he never had trouble attracting top acts because, like Bill Harrah at Lake Tahoe, he would do anything to please them — other than increase their fees. If you wanted fresh strawberries in the middle of winter, Dave would have them flown in just to keep you happy.

The 1960s were probably my peak years in terms of fame and fortune. My television show was a hit, and I was releasing three albums a year. (If you get one out a year now you're very lucky.) Everything then was recorded live — singers, session musicians, orchestras, choirs were all in the studio with you at the same time. Editing wasn't digital; it was all done with razor blades and splicing tape, and about the most you could do was splice, say, sixteen bars of one take of the song into another take. So we would rehearse and then do the song. If it wasn't the way we wanted it, we'd do the whole song again until we got it right.

The process might have been crude compared to today's electronic wizardry, but there's a lot to be said for making live records, and whatever we were doing, it seemed to be working. I was selling millions of records and touring throughout the United States and Europe, Australia, and the Far East. I also hosted the first nationally televised Golden Globe Awards ceremony, which went out as a special segment of *The Andy Williams Show* in 1964 and 1965.

The Golden Globes were awarded by the Hollywood Foreign Press Association. When it was set up in the 1940s, the HFPA was so short of members that it didn't take much to be recognized as a foreign press correspondent. If you were a headwaiter in a popular restaurant, there was every chance the HFPA would welcome you as a member with open arms. As a result, it had no credibility whatsoever in the Hollywood community; in fact, it was thought of as a hoot. The movie stars who went to the awards dinner every year did so as much to have fun and get drunk as to pick up an award.

My press agent, Jim Mahoney, who also represented Johnny Carson, Lee Marvin, Frank Sinatra, and George C. Scott, among many others, went to his first Hollywood Foreign Press Association annual dinner in 1949, held in some hokey hotel on the beach. He attended the event to take a few photographs of his clients; it was such a low-key, low-rent event then that the Los Angeles press barely bothered to cover it.

Among the HFPA members were the Unger twins, Gustaf and Bertil, who were Swedish tap dancers and occasional correspondents for a couple of Scandinavian newspapers. They both wore monocles, and the only reliable way to tell them apart was that Gustaf wore his monocle in his right eye, and Bertil in his left. That first dinner turned into a barroom brawl when the Unger brothers found another pair of twins occupying their seats and started a fistfight. When Jim Mahoney took photos of his clients to the *Los Angeles Mirror,* the editor said, "We don't want pictures of the stars; we want pictures of the two sets of twins fighting!"

I was always hearing stories that the HFPA chose its Golden Globe winners at that time on the basis of who they could get to show up to accept them. That seemed to be confirmed by a phone call that Bertil Unger — by then running the HFPA with his brother — made to Jim Mahoney one year. "We want to give the major award this year to Frank Sinatra," Unger said. "He has contributed so much to the industry over the years and made so many fine pictures, he truly is the world's film favorite."

"Well," Jim said, "that's very nice, but Mr. Sinatra is going to be in Australia on tour during the time of the show, so he won't be able to accept the award in person, but I'm certain we can get one of his daughters to accept it for him."

"We don't want one of his daughters to accept the award," Unger said. "We want Frank Sinatra."

Jim thought for a moment. "Well, I'm afraid Mr. Sinatra's definitely not available. What about Steve McQueen instead?"

"You can get Steve McQueen?"

"Of course we can get Steve McQueen," Jim said. "He's a client."

"Okay," Unger said, "Steve McQueen is now the world's film favorite." And they duly gave him the award. That shows the credibility of the HFPA back then. Even by the 1960s it still represented a relatively small group of often part-time journalists working for organizations based outside the United States. As a result, the awards were not taken too seriously by the movie industry, and attempts were made to give them more legitimacy by including more bona fide writers and critics in the association. Some in Hollywood still see the Golden Globes as a joke, but because of the television exposure — among award shows, only the Oscars and the Grammys draw larger audiences — it has become an important barometer for actors, films, and television shows.

I also did a Christmas tour with Bob Hope to entertain American servicemen and -women at bases overseas; one stop was the now infamous Guantánamo camp, the Manhattan-size piece of Cuba that has been a U.S. military base for over a century. Zsa Zsa Gabor was also part of the group, and when we flew in at two o'clock in the morning, Zsa Zsa's only comment as she was being greeted by the sleep-deprived general commanding the base was "I vant a down pillow."

We all said, "Oh, come on, Zsa Zsa. It's two o'clock in the morning." But she was adamant, and in the end they found a down pillow for her. Perhaps she was right to be so picky, I soon discovered when I used the latrine — an eight-holer. I hadn't seen anything like it since the three-holer we had down the field in Wall Lake. I thought it would be fun to use one again, but before long I started itching in an embarrassing place. When I went to the camp doctor, I discovered that I had picked up crabs. I know it's the classic excuse of every man who gets crabs: "Honest, honey, I must have gotten 'em from a toilet seat," but in this case it was true. When I went back to take another look at the eight-holer, I could actually see the little critters crawling around in there. To my great embarrassment, news of my affliction soon leaked out, leading to endless variations on "Are there crabs on the menu tonight?" jokes.

Meanwhile, Zsa Zsa continued making incessant demands — for changes to her hair, makeup, costume, food, accommodation, etc. — alienating everyone in the place. The entire staff of the tour absolutely hated her, and I have to admit that she could be a major pain in the ass at times, but she used to make me laugh a lot, and I spent quite a lot of time with her. That may explain why I was taken aside by one of the other cast members, a woman, who pressed a large rolled-up paper into my hand. "Andy, I have a petition here," she said. "It's been signed by everybody: cast, production crew, and absolutely everyone in the costume, hair and makeup departments. We're all sick to death of Zsa Zsa, and we want payback, so we all want you to sleep with her and give her the crabs." I didn't feel I could oblige them; apart from anything else, it wasn't in my contract.

By now I was earning a lot of money and trying to invest it wisely, helped by my dad. He got a lot of books, talked to a lot of people, and taught himself enough about tax and business to advise me on some investments. Some of the things he suggested were pretty shrewd, such as always buying corner lots of property because they would eventually be the most popular and valuable, but if we had thought on a more ambitious scale, instead of chicken farms on agricultural land fifty miles out of town, we could have been buying corner lots on Wilshire Boulevard and making some very serious money.

On Dad's advice I also invested in some citrus groves in California, and my brother Bob took over managing them. He always had an interest in horses, so I also bought some purebred Arabians. He began breeding them and ended up with forty or so. One

Christmas I gave them to him as a gift. He phoned me at the end of the first year and said, "I've just been doing my accounts. My God, do you know how much it costs to feed these horses?"

"Why do you think I gave them to you!" I said.

I also became a part-owner of the NBA Phoenix Suns. I wasn't a follower of the team and didn't even watch basketball at the time, but the franchise was up for sale and my lawyer, Larry Kartiganer, who was representing three businessmen in the negotiations, asked me if I'd like to join them as a limited partner. If I was going to put money into the venture, however, I wanted a voice in how it was spent, so I held out for a general partnership — a full share in the business. After days of discussion they agreed I could have one-fourth ownership, and we bought the franchise.

I started the team's first game in Phoenix by throwing the ball up between the two centers. A chair was brought for me to stand on so I could reach high enough. After the game I went into the locker room. It was a fairly disconcerting experience: I found myself in a room full of giants standing around stark naked, and my eyeline was on a level with their groins. I didn't stay long. We ran the Suns for three years, but my three partners then all wanted to take their profit and move on. I didn't want to sell at all but found myself outvoted. It was a good investment but not nearly as good as it would have been if we had held on to it. Major-league sports franchises now change hands for hundreds of millions of dollars.

I was also buying a lot of paintings and sculptures at that time. I still had no formal training, but I had remained fascinated with art since those early days in New York, when I was buying cheap reproductions and hanging around the galleries on 57th Street. I think I had a good eye for art from the start, and the amount of time I spent in galleries and museums all over the world enabled me to absorb a bit of knowledge along the way, if only by osmosis. No two individuals experience abstract paintings in exactly the same way, but standing in front of them and letting them speak to me — Mark Rothko's paintings are a notable example — can give me a spiritual, almost mystical feeling. It is different and remote from everything else in my life, and it gives me a sense of peace and fulfillment that has greatly enriched me.

Next door to my office building in Los Angeles was a gallery owned by Nick Wilder. I went in there regularly and became acquainted with him, and he got me interested in the American color-field painters of the 1960s. We made a trip to New York together, where I bought some beautiful paintings by Morris Louis, Helen Frankenthaler, and Kenneth Noland from the Andre Emmerich Gallery. My neighbor across the street from my little birdhouse in the hills on Bobolink, Terry DeLapp, was also a dealer, working out of his home. He and his wife, Gus, became good friends of ours, and I bought a couple of paintings from him, including a small Picasso oil. He later became close to Steve Martin, too. Steve had been collecting the Hudson River School for years, but after seeing some of the paintings at my house, especially the 1960s color-field painters, he also became interested in modern art and now has a remarkable collection.

Steve knows about art in an intellectual way. I don't. I buy by the seat of my pants, using my own judgment and my own eye, which has improved tremendously over the years, though I still relied for advice on dealers I knew who were knowledgeable and honest, such as Terry, Richard Gray, Jimmy Goodman, and Nick Wilder. I never lost money on anything that they sold me or recommended that I buy — not that making money was the motivation. I just had the collecting bug. I look at every one of the paintings on my walls every morning and every night when I come home, and I continue to take enormous pleasure in them.

I have pretty much stopped buying now, but only because I have run out of wall space. If I saw something I really wanted, I would have to sell something to make room for it because I don't believe in putting art in storage; I want to enjoy it. Some people want to get rid of their possessions as they get older and simplify their lives, but I love my art too much to do that. It'll be around my house as long as I am, and what happens to it after that is up to my children.

I also learned an awful lot about art and life from a man who was one of the great characters in the world and one of the three or four greatest friends of my life. I first met Billy Pearson at Sun Valley in Idaho when Claudine and I took the kids skiing there. Billy certainly caught my attention because he was quite an arresting sight. A former jockey, he was only five feet two inches tall and wore immaculate tweed plus fours and a deerstalker hat at a jaunty angle, and he carried a swagger stick — a short cane with a silver knob. He also had a very striking-looking woman with him, a model, and he seemed quite undeterred by the fact that she was a foot taller than he was. Billy and I got talking and became fast friends, and I used to stay with him from time to time in San Francisco, where he had an antiques gallery.

Billy had been brought up in Chicago. He never knew his father, and his mother was an army nurse. By the time Billy was nine he had a corner in Chicago where he sold papers, and he had to fight for that corner with other boys who wanted it. So he had grown up struggling for his existence and was street smart. He did not graduate from high school but read voraciously — anything and everything interested him. Small but strong, he went on to become a very successful jockey. He rode with all the greats, such as Willy Shoemaker and Eddie Arcaro, and had two thousand winners in his career. Billy would say with a trademark wink, "I made a lot more money riding the ones that lost than I ever made on the ones that won." According to Billy, he and the other jockeys would sometimes agree among themselves which horse was going to win a particular race. All of them would then put a bet down on it and make sure it won by holding their own horses back while the jockey of the chosen horse would be whipping it on to the winning post. It was unsporting, unfair to gamblers who were trying to back a winner, immoral, and highly illegal, but it was also very lucrative when they got away with it — and according to Billy, they got away with it often.

He had started dealing in art and antiques when he was still a jockey, and he was a shrewd negotiator. Once when riding in the Far East, he took his fee in fine silks and artifacts instead of cash and then sold them at a substantial profit back in the States. After retiring from horse racing, he set himself up as an art dealer, and although the racehorse and art businesses might seem worlds apart, they both attracted characters looking to cut a few corners and make a quick buck. That description would certainly have fitted Billy, but he was far from a shyster. For a man with no formal training in the arts, he had a bewildering and eclectic range of interests. As Billy said, "I collect everything, mostly wives" — he was on his third by then — and his interests included folk painting, Oceanic, African, and pre-Columbian artifacts, Native American blankets, Americana, antique Japanese wedding kimonos, netsukes, and scrimshaws. He had a remarkably keen and sure eye for quality work and also had a photographic memory. He loved primitive art because, he said, it was pure truth; the artists were all anonymous, and you had to judge the work on its own merits, not be swayed by who had made it.

Billy had also appeared as a contestant on the TV show *The $64,000 Question,* answering questions on art. The first ever big-money quiz show, it was so popular that it was said you could shoot a cannon down any American street while *The $64,000 Question* was on and not hit anyone because they would all be indoors watching it. The three most popular contestants they ever had on the show were the psychologist Dr. Joyce Brothers, who was an expert on boxing; a shoemaker, Gino Prato, who was an expert on opera; and Billy, who was an expert on art.

Like many quiz shows of that era, what you saw on-screen was rather less spontaneous than it appeared, but while another show, *21* — on which the movie *Quiz Show* was based — was completely fake, with contestants coached not only in the answers to give but even in when to pause, mop their brows, hesitate or stumble over a question, the results on *The $64,000 Question* were tailored in a rather more subtle way. When I asked Billy if there had been any cheating or help given to the contestants, he said, "No, they didn't have to resort to that. Each of us had to take a very extensive examination to prove we really were experts in our field, and from that examination they knew what you knew and what you didn't know." If a contestant was popular with the viewing audience and they wanted to keep him on, they would ask a question in his particular area of expertise. If they wanted to drop a contestant, they knew his weaknesses and would ask him a question in one of the areas where he was least knowledgeable. The producers could therefore pretty well control who would stay or who would go. Since Billy was very popular with the audience, he went on to win the contest and $64,000. He and his good friend, movie director John Huston, immediately flew to Vegas and blew it all in a couple of days.

Billy and John both lived life to the absolute maximum. John was also a big collector; he bought tons of objects and artifacts from Billy, and, just like Billy, he wasn't averse to cutting a few corners. When he was directing *The Red Badge of Courage* on location in Texas, the star, Audie Murphy, had his own small airplane, and every night John and Billy would take the plane (without permission) and fly across the border into Mexico. There they would rendezvous with some tomb robbers that Billy had somehow gotten to know, buy pre-Columbian artifacts that they had stolen, load up the plane, and fly back across the border into Texas. Some years later I asked Billy if he wanted to go to Cabo San Lucas with me, but he told me that he couldn't go to Mexico at all because a Wanted poster with his picture on it was in all the post offices down there. Once again, just like fixing horse races, tomb robbing was immoral and highly illegal, but I think it was the adrenaline rush as much as anything that kept them doing it. They just loved the artwork, and virtually all of it ended up in their private collections.

When they did have money, Billy and John could go through it faster than a dog can eat steak, and they were invariably broke again within a few days. One time when John was making a movie in France, they were both broke when a residual check — quite a healthy one — from one of John's movies arrived by post. John cashed it immediately, and they then headed for a casino to celebrate. On the way there they passed an art gallery where they saw a Monet painting of water lilies, priced at the equivalent of $10,000.

When they got to the casino, they went to the baccarat table, where John hit such a hot streak that at one point he had $100,000 in front of him. He then decided to stake the whole $100,000 on a single hand. It was such a large bet that the bank couldn't take it all but could only cover $90,000 of it, so the croupier pushed the other $10,000 worth of chips back to John.

He promptly went ahead and bet the $90,000 and just as promptly lost it. That left him with $10,000, and without batting an eye, John turned to Billy and said, "Well, kid, it looks as if we just bought the water lilies." The next morning, as soon as the gallery opened, John did precisely that. He was now broke again but the proud possessor of a beautiful Monet. It hung for years in his Georgian house in Galway, Ireland, and was eventually sold for millions of dollars; some you lose and some you win.

John also gave Billy a brief acting career when he cast him as the stationmaster in his film *The Life and Times of Judge Roy Bean*. Starring Paul Newman, it was a heavily fictionalized account of the already extraordinary life of an eccentric saloonkeeper and "hanging judge" in a small town in Texas.

Judge Bean also wrote long impassioned letters to Lily Langtry, the British music hall star and mistress of many leading figures in British society, including, so it was rumored, King Edward VII. Judge Bean begged her to come and live with him, promising to lay down his life at her feet if that was what she wanted. In return, all he would ever receive were formal acknowledgments from a secretary: "Miss Langtry thanks you for your letter." The judge was eventually killed and his town was burned to the ground, but in the final scene of the movie a train pulls up at the station with Lily Langtry, played by Ava Gardner, aboard. She had not been seen at all throughout the rest of the movie except in the judge's collection of pictures of her. Intrigued by those impassioned letters, she had traveled to Texas to see Judge Roy Bean and his town for herself, but the town was now a smoldering wreck, and the only man who remained there was the old stationmaster, played by Billy. He was seen in various other scenes throughout the movie, helping people on and off the train, but this was to be his finest moment and his only line.

"Now, Billy," Huston said to him as they set up the shot. "The train is going to come into town, and you're the only one who is still here. The train is going to stop on that mark, and then you're going to walk up to Miss Gardner as she stands on the caboose of the train and say your line. The sound doesn't matter, though. We'll loop in the dialogue later, but the scene has got to look just right. She is costing me $50,000, and I only got her for this one day. The sun is going down, and we're losing the light, so we have only one good shot at this. Make it count."

Billy listened to all this with a suitably serious expression and then went to his mark. The train rolled in and stopped in a cloud of steam. Ava Gardner stepped out onto the caboose and took in the smoking ruins of the town. Then Billy got his cue and walked forward. "Why, Miss Langtry," he said, "welcome to our town. Have you ever had your pussy eaten by an old man, Miss Langtry?"

Ava burst out laughing, and after he had called "Cut!" John chased Billy all over the lot, screaming, "I'll kill you, you little bastard! I'll kill you!" But when he went to look at the rushes, he saw that Ava Gardner was enough of a seasoned professional to have put her hand up to her mouth and turn her head to hide her laughter. They managed to use the shot and loop in the dialogue. John forgave Billy surprisingly quickly — they even had dinner together that night — but never cast him in another movie.

11

In August 1966 I returned to Las Vegas again, but this time as the headline act at the opening of a brand-new resort casino, the seven-hundred-room Caesars Palace. Like the Flamingo and the Sands in their eras, Caesars Palace was now redefining the casino business in Vegas. It was by far the most extravagant and luxurious hotel ever built there, and it upped the ante for all its competitors. When Cliff Perlman owned it, he even installed a moving walkway (they called them people-movers back then) to transport people off the Strip and into the casino. Those who wanted to leave found that their exit was rather less glamorous. The walkways operated in only one direction, and the exit signs led people on a round-about route past virtually every slot machine and gaming table in the place. Those who still insisted on leaving rather than gambling eventually reached the door, but when they opened it, they found themselves not back on the Strip but in the parking lot at the back of the building.

Despite frantic last-minute work, Caesars Palace was still unfinished on opening night when scores of high rollers and Hollywood movie stars were flown in for its launch. Most of the rooms were not yet ready, and the lobby was full of movie stars milling around trying to get a key to their accommodations. I eventually pushed my way through to the front desk and said, "I'm opening tonight. I've got to have a room."

The desk clerk, showing a commendable sense of humor given the abuse he was taking from all sides, said, "I understand, Mr. Williams. I can probably get you a room if you don't mind making your own bed. I'll find you a hammer and some nails."

Those who did eventually get a room weren't necessarily the lucky ones; even the rooms that were supposedly finished had some alarming defects. One very high-profile guest inadvertently pulled his washbasin off the wall because the plaster around it was still wet, and the broken pipe flooded his room. In an effort to pacify the grumbling celebrities still camped in the lobby, the hotel started serving them cocktails, an amenity that went on for some considerable time. The show in the Circus Maximus Showroom was due to start at eight o'clock, and I didn't get onstage until eleven, by which time most of the audience, loaded with cocktails and with no dinner to soak them up, was roaring drunk.

Despite the problems on opening night, it was the start of my long association with Caesars Palace. I continued to headline there for the next twenty years and turned down offers from a number of other casino owners to switch venues, including one that came from Howard Hughes himself, though, like most people, I never actually met him face-to-face. A guy named Bob Mayhew was a senior employee of Hughes's for years and did everything Hughes told him, but in all the time he worked for him, he never met him once, either. Hughes would slip instructions under the door or talk to him on the phone, but the closest Bob ever got to him was the other side of a locked door. When Hughes was trying to get me to play at the Desert Inn, Bob acted as intermediary and was authorized by Hughes to cut me in on some of the property deals that the Hughes Corporation was doing in Vegas. That sounded a little too close for comfort so, like my brother Dick and his acre of desert dirt twenty years before, I just said, "No, thanks."

Although I was very handsomely paid at Caesars Palace, I really didn't like being in Vegas for the summer. The desert heat was too much for an Iowa boy, and it was such a rootless, restless town that I never really felt at home there. Most visitors stay only a couple of days, but I had to be there for eight weeks straight. It was much better when Claudine and the kids came along. We would go out on the lake in the Caesars Palace boat and come back all suntanned and happy, but while the kids went to bed, I had to go to work — and it was two shows a night. When my family wasn't in town, my main recreation was playing tennis. I used to get up early, before the day's heat became too stifling, and play a couple of games with a few regular partners. The tennis legend Pancho Gonzalez was the pro at Caesars Palace, and I can remember watching him knocking tennis balls around with a six-year-old kid he was coaching. The kid was pretty good; his name was André Agassi.

One evening Elvis Presley came to see my show at Caesars Palace and came backstage afterward. I was in my dressing room with a few friends and well-wishers when Elvis arrived with his entourage. It was the first time I'd met him, and we got on very well; he was very gracious and polite, a world away from the rock-and-roll rebel he had seemed in his "Elvis the Pelvis" days. We talked about music and a few other things, and after a few minutes I noticed that every time Elvis said something mildly funny, his entourage would burst out laughing as if it was the wittiest thing any of them had ever heard. Every time I said something halfway funny in response, my group would do the same thing. It was like two rival gangs meeting, and it was a reminder that if you started believing your own publicity, you could soon convince yourself that you were the wittiest, most wonderful person on the planet.

I think Elvis and I were both grounded enough to take the sycophantic laughter for what it was worth, and we just kept chatting, two country boys talking about music together. After a while Elvis asked me to come over to his hotel, where he had some music he wanted to play for me. We walked out into the small parking area behind Caesars, where his dark brown Mercedes 300SL limousine was waiting for him. His uniformed driver clicked his heels and saluted as we approached, and when we got in, the first thing I noticed was that all the upholstery was mink. The second was that a stunningly beautiful woman — actress, songwriter, and former beauty queen Linda Thompson —

was patiently waiting for him.

It was about 2:30 in the morning when we got back to Elvis's hotel, but as he opened the door of his suite, a wall of noise hit us. There must have been a hundred young kids in there, all partying like there was no tomorrow; apparently it was the same thing every night whether Elvis was there or not. Elvis ignored them and led me through to a quieter room and started playing some of his favorite music: gospel. Every now and then he disappeared into the bathroom and re-emerged a few minutes later, a little more red-eyed and red-faced each time.

About four in the morning I got up to go, but Elvis said, "Wait, I want to give you something." He went into the bedroom and came back with six or eight Navaho Indian belts with silver and turquoise buckles. "Pick one," he said. "I want you to have one." So I chose one, thanked him, and then headed back to my hotel while the party in Elvis's suite continued at full blast. It was an eye-opening insight into Elvis's life: a modest country boy caught up in a maelstrom of fame, money, and drugs. I hoped he had some true friends among the hangers-on. I still have the Navaho belt he gave me. It was not my taste, but I felt about it the way I did about those embarrassing things your kids sometimes give you: You keep and proudly display them not because of what they are but because of who has given them to you.

While I was appearing at Caesars Palace, the Rat Pack — Frank Sinatra, Sammy Davis Jr., and Dean Martin — were also in town, headlining at the Sands. The original Rat Pack, formed in the 1950s, had included Sinatra, Humphrey Bogart, Lauren Bacall, David Niven, Spencer Tracy, and Judy Garland. However, by the 1960s, when I knew him, Sinatra had assembled a new group around him, which also included Peter Lawford and Joey Bishop. It was still known as the Rat Pack by outsiders although Frank and his cronies referred to it as the Clan for a while — until Sammy took Frank aside. "Listen, Frank," he said. "Do you think we could find a name that didn't sound quite so much like the Ku Klux Klan?" Frank thought about it for a minute. "Okay," he said. "How about the Summit?" From then on that is what they called themselves.

The Rat Pack became hugely popular, and even when individual members were booked to appear alone, the other members would often turn up and stage an impromptu group show. It was such a regular occurrence that the billboards at the Sands or the other venues where they appeared often read: FRANK SINATRA ... MAYBE DEAN ... MAYBE SAMMY.

They were legendary as much for their offstage behavior as their onstage routines. All of them were drinkers and gamblers, and even the married ones tended to be single after sunset, and there was never a shortage of high rollers and beautiful women wanting to help them party. I was never a member of the Rat Pack, but I often saw Frank in the lounge at the Sands. I went there regularly after my evening show at Caesars because I loved its resident lounge act: Keely Smith and Louis Prima. She had a great voice but was almost expressionless, while Louis was just the opposite: very expressive, very raunchy.

I would be sitting there listening to them when Frank would come in with Sammy, Dean, and the rest of them. I sometimes joined them at the table that was cordoned off just for them and their friends, with a couple of guys standing around acting as a screen to make sure no fans or wannabes bothered them. Dean was always the first to leave. He wanted to get some sleep because he played golf every morning. I wouldn't be too far behind him. The rest would drink and gamble into the small hours and maybe take some company back to their suites, but if they hunted as a pack, there was never any doubt about who was the leader. Frank would sleep well into the afternoon, and when he eventually emerged, word would flash around the Sands — "He's up!" "Frank's up?" "Yeah, he's up" — and the rest of the Rat Pack would then head for the steam room to meet up with him. They would sweat out the previous night's excesses and start planning the next. There was always excitement at the Sands when they were there.

Otherwise, I never saw that much of Sinatra in Vegas. We were both working at the same time, and at least part of our leisure hours were spent at the casino that was paying our wages. Frank would often take over as dealer at one of the tables in the Sands, and I'd sometimes do the same at Caesars. The customers loved it, and the management didn't mind even when I let someone win a few hundred dollars. They liked a few winners; it made the suckers think they might finally be getting an even break.

Although I knew Frank pretty well socially, we never worked together. If Sinatra appeared on television, it was usually in his own specials where he could dictate his own terms and write his own ticket. He very rarely appeared as a guest on other shows, apart from Dean Martin's because he was very close to Dean. That was something few others could say. I first got to know Dean in the 1940s when we were both appearing in Chicago. Every night after Kay, my brothers, and I had finished our act at the Blackstone Hotel or the Palmer House, we would go over to a club on the near north side where Dean was appearing. He wasn't a particularly good singer in those early days and often a bit out of tune, but he would sit there singing songs all night with his pianist, Rosie. People would send drinks to him until he had them lined up on the grand piano from one end to the other, and he wouldn't finish his act until he had finished them all.

Later he got to be an excellent vocalist and a very spontaneous and relaxed performer. When he started his weekly TV show at NBC, I was working on mine in the studio next door. Dean never liked to rehearse. He would have the songs he was going to sing put on a cassette he'd play on the way to the golf course and on the way back. The kind of material he did — standards — meant that he knew all the words anyway. Then he would turn up at the studio a couple of hours before the show and say to his producer, Greg Garrison, "Walk me through it. What do you want me to do, and where do you want me to do it?" Allegedly that was as much preparation as he ever did, and although the entire script was on cue cards, he rarely ever used them as more than the vaguest of guides. If he had Nancy Sinatra on the show and the cue card read, "How are you feeling there, Nancy?" he'd likely say, "Hey, Nancy. What's up?" instead. She would suggest a song that they could sing, and if the cue card read, "That would be wonderful," he would probably come up with "I'm with you, baby," or something equally characteristic.

Dean's act played heavily on the suggestion that he was a bit of a lush, slurring his words and living the life implied by one of his signature tunes, "Little Old Wine Drinker Me," but his PR people managed to get the story widely accepted that Dean was actually a teetotaler and it was all an act. Anyone who really knew him was well aware that that was far from the truth. All of the Rat Pack were heavy drinkers, including Dean, although, like Sammy Davis, I never saw him really drunk.

While I had known Dean all those years, I never once got beyond the surface charm to the real person underneath. Very few people did because Dean wouldn't let anyone get close to him. He was a great performer with huge charisma, but he was always in character. He would hang out with you, wisecracking and joking, but I never saw him let the mask drop for an instant. I would see him and say, "Hi, Dean. How are you?" but even that sort of bland question would elicit the stock answer: "Compared to what?" And that would be the end of that line of inquiry.

Sinatra was twelve years older than me, and we had different circles of friends. We were neighbors for a while when he was married to Mia Farrow — I went to their wedding reception — and my relationship with him was always good, although it is doubtful things would have stayed that way if he had witnessed an incident with Mia one night. I was having a drink at The Daisy, a very popular disco at the time, when Mia walked over and said, "Andy, do you want to dance?" As soon as we started dancing, she put her arms around my neck. Fooling around with Frank's wife in the middle of a crowded dance floor wasn't the smartest move in the world, and I tried to ease away from her, saying, "Mia, this really isn't a good idea." She just laughed. A few seconds later two of Mia's friends, Ryan O'Neal and Barbara Parkins, came over, disentangled her arms from around my neck, and said, "Come on, Mia. Time to go home." I wasn't about to argue with them.

Sinatra was a Jekyll and Hyde character. He was in his fifties by the time I began headlining at Caesars Palace and was twenty years past the days when he had been the first teen idol in pop music history, but if his hair was thinning and the years of high living and heavy drinking and smoking could be read in his face, he showed little sign of slowing down. The procession of women leaving his suite in the early hours of the morning testified to his continued powers of attraction.

There were other sides to him, however. He had strong principles and did more than anyone to force the desegregation of Las Vegas by boycotting any establishment that discriminated against African Americans. He could be a loyal friend, too, but he had a petty and vindictive side to his character as well, as both Sammy Davis and Peter Lawford had reason to know. There were also always rumors swirling around Sinatra's possible involvement with the Mafia. Those rumors only strengthened after he abruptly cancelled his second show at the Sands one night to fly to Miami and sing at a gathering of the heads of all the Mafia families. Whether the rumors were true or not, I don't know, but Frank certainly had some heavy friends, and there was no shortage of incidents that showed his darker side.

The comedian Shecky Greene saw that side of Frank and was brave and unbowed enough to joke about it in his nightclub act. "People say a lot of bad stuff about Frank Sinatra," he'd begin a routine, "but I won't hear a word against him because he once saved my life. Three hoods were beating the crap out of me in the parking lot of the Fontainebleau Hotel in Miami one night when Sinatra walked past and said, 'Okay, boys, that's enough.' " That line always got a big laugh from the audience, but as he told me when we were chatting one night, the story was actually true.

The incident occurred after Sinatra took a fancy to Shecky's girlfriend one night and took her up to his suite. Shecky objected to this and started banging on the door, so Sinatra phoned down to the parking lot, which was run by Rocco Fischetti, one of the family who had taken over as Mob bosses of Chicago when Al Capone went to jail. Three hoods duly waited for Shecky in the parking lot and worked him over pretty good.

I also witnessed Frank's reaction one evening when I was having dinner at Ruby Dunes in Palm Springs with Frank and about eight other friends of his, including Lucille Ball and her new husband, Gary

Morton. Frank seemed very relaxed that night, wisecracking, exchanging gags with Lucy, and generally being the life and soul of the party, until a drunk at a neighboring table accidentally spilled a glass of red wine all over Gary Morton's beautiful new suede jacket. Frank's mood — and with it the atmosphere at the table — changed in an instant. Although the drunk apologized and offered to pay for cleaning the jacket, Frank fixed him with a look that would have frozen a martini. He then had a muttered word with his bodyguard and fixer, Jilly, who was never far from his side. Jilly took the guy outside and broke his nose. Any jokes and good humor after that were pretty forced, and the party broke up not long afterward. It was always a mystery to me how someone like Sinatra, who could sing with such heart-melting tenderness and sensitivity, could also act with the most coldhearted cruelty.

Sinatra was friendly with Jack Kennedy and even built a guest house on the grounds of his house as a discreet place for JFK to use when seeing one of his girlfriends. Among them, in addition to Marilyn Monroe, was Judith Campbell, who was also sleeping with Mafia boss Sam Giancana. Sinatra had made these introductions within two months of each other. When Bobby Kennedy, who as attorney general had fearlessly campaigned to bring organized crime figures to justice, heard about Campbell's links with Giancana, he persuaded Jack to cut his ties with the woman and with Sinatra.

When JFK next came to Los Angeles, he stayed with Bing Crosby even though Bing was a Republican supporter. That really hurt Frank, a lifelong Democrat. He was so infuriated that he promptly joined the Republican party and was an active campaigner and fund-raiser for them from then on. He took further revenge on the Kennedy clan by shutting Peter Lawford, JFK's brother-in-law, out of the Rat Pack and giving Lawford's role in the movie *Robin and the Seven Hoods* to Bing Crosby. So poisonous had the relationship become that when Sinatra heard Lawford and his wife, Pat, were in the audience at the Sands one night, he refused to go onstage until the casino security had escorted them out of the building. Lawford remained friendly with Sammy Davis, but he and Sinatra never spoke again.

In common with the members of the Rat Pack and a lot of other show business people, I had now become a regular and enthusiastic golfer. I didn't take up the game until about 1958 because I had been working so hard trying to get my career going. My brothers were all playing before then, but I never seemed to have the time. However, when I was working at the Copacabana in New York, Joey Bishop, who was opening for me, gave me a set of clubs. When I moved out to California, I started to play more regularly, and in 1961 I joined the Bel-Air Country Club. Clark Gable, Fred Astaire, and a lot of the movie colony played there, and Alfred Hitchcock's old house on Bellagio Road overlooks the course, one of the most beautiful and one of the toughest in the country. I could never play the eighth hole without recalling the time — a cherished part of Bel Air folklore — when Howard Hughes, running late for a game of golf with Katharine Hepburn, landed his private plane on the eighth fairway. Rather than pay the fine that the club's outraged officials imposed on him, Hughes resigned his membership.

I was good friends with Bob Newhart and Jack Lemmon, and I played regularly with them and Pierre Cossette, a television producer who over the years became one of my dearest friends. We still lunch together almost every day when we're both in Palm Springs. We were all reasonable golfers, though never in the top rank. Jack Lemmon was a more than useful golfer, a great actor, and a good friend, but he was also a major-league drinker. When he played in the Bing Crosby Pro-Am Pebble Beach Tournament, he would always finish up in the bar — as we all did. Jack's caddy, George, was always with him, and he would sit quietly at a table, eating and drinking on Jack's tab, while we were at the bar. Jack would eventually get so plastered that George's last job of the day was to pick him up, put him over his shoulder, carry him out to the car, and take him home. Jack would be dangling over George's shoulder, laughing fit to burst, and calling out to us, "No! No! No! Put me down, goddamn it! Boys, let's not go yet. Let's have another drink first." We all loved him, as he was never an unpleasant drinker and was always funny, but it was a relief several years later when he gave up drinking entirely.

Fred MacMurray was another regular golf partner, and he and his wife, June Haver, were very good friends of Claudine and me. Fred had a very successful television show called *My Three Sons,* and although it should have taken a full week to shoot each episode, he would go into the studio only one day a week, which left him plenty of time for golf. The crew would film all around him during the week, and then he would go in and do his lines. He would say, "Now listen to me, son . . ." Then the camera would cut away to the response. Everyone else had to turn up every day, but Fred didn't want to spend any more time there than he absolutely had to. Because he was a big star, the network indulged him.

Fred had made a lot of money from movies and real estate investments, and, boy, did he hate spending it. He would park his own car at the Bel-Air Country Club so that he didn't have to tip the valet. He took his golf bag home with him and then brought it back again the next day rather than pay $3 a week to store it. He would also carry his own bags in and out of hotels so he didn't have to tip a bellboy. He was also never the first man to the bar when there were drinks to be bought.

We did catch him once, though. We were playing golf at Bel-Air on a miserable rainy day and were so cold that we abandoned the round after nine holes and headed for the bar. When the waiter came over to our table to take our drink order, I said, "I'd like a hot buttered rum." Everybody else thought that was a pretty good idea and ordered one, too. There were seven of us, and the bill came to $56. Somebody suggested playing Ship, Captain, and Crew to see who would pay it. Fred didn't know that game, so we explained that we all threw dice in turn, and if you had a double six that made you a captain; if you threw a five and a four, you were an officer or a mate; and if you threw only a deuce and a three or something, you'd be the crew. The one who threw the lowest number would be the cabin boy and had to pay for the drinks.

We all threw the dice, and Fred lost. He went a bit pale but pulled out his wallet and paid for the drinks. He was clearly feeling generous because he added a $1 tip to the $56. When we finished our round, it was still raining, so we decided to have another one. "Well, I think I should be exempt this time because I got the first drinks," Fred said as I picked up the dice again.

"Ah, come on, Fred," I said. "Lightning doesn't strike twice. You'll be fine. Someone else will lose this time."

So we played again and once more Fred lost. His face was a picture as he reached again for his wallet. Ten or fifteen minutes later we decided to have one for the road. "Well, I'm definitely out of it this time," he said. "I already got the first two rounds." This time we all chorused, "Ah, come on, Fred. Live a little. No one's ever lost three in a row."

He hesitated, then gave a grudging nod,

and rolled the dice again: snake eyes, two ones. He didn't even wait for the rest of us to roll the dice, but just stood up, put $56 on the table — no tip this time — and walked out, leaving his drink untouched on the table. It might have been my imagination, but I thought I heard a muffled sob as the door closed behind him.

Sean Connery also had a reputation for having "short arms and deep pockets," but I never experienced that, and I certainly never had to play Ship, Captain, and Crew to get him to buy a round. I liked Sean very much; he was a delightful guy and played a lot of golf at Bel-Air, so we became friends. We both also used to play in a poker game every Sunday night — not an especially big game, but you could still lose a few dollars in the course of an evening. Sometimes Claudine would play, too, but she liked to stay in on every hand — not the smartest way to come out ahead at the end of the evening. The first time I joined the game I had to pinch myself at the thought that I was playing poker with James Bond. Sean didn't win quite as consistently as Bond did in the movies, but he did clean me out more than once.

My love of golf had become widely known, and in 1968 I took a call from the Century Club in San Diego asking if I'd be interested in an association with the San Diego Open. It had been part of the PGA Tour for several years, but because the prize money wasn't good enough to attract the top players, the San Diego officials were afraid they were going to lose their tournament. They wanted to use my name, calling it the Andy Williams San Diego Open, and they wanted me to invite some of my celebrity friends to play in the pro-am the day before the actual tournament. I was flattered; the only celebrities whose names were attached to golf tournaments at the time were Bing Crosby and Bob Hope, but the offer came with a price tag: They had raised the prize purse from $60,000 to $160,000, and they asked me if I would guarantee the extra $100,000 in case they had a rainout and didn't do any business at the gate. I told them I'd get back to them on that and later agreed to the proposal. I asked a few friends such as Jack Benny, Sonny and Cher, Henry Mancini, and the Osmond Brothers if they would help me put on a benefit show at the San Diego Civic Center on the eve of the tournament. We easily made $100,000, so the Century Club was happy and so was I.

It was agreed that I would always play in the pro-am with the previous year's tournament winner — my tournament, my rules

311

— and over the twenty years I was involved, I got to play with all the great names in the sport, including Jack Nicklaus, Tom Watson, Tom Weiskopf, Lee Trevino, and the first superstar of the sport, Arnold Palmer.

With all his success Arnold could have been forgiven for being a little swell-headed, but he was the most straightforward, approachable, and considerate of guys. He showed superhuman patience as we played our round of golf together, because despite my desperation not to let myself down in front of him, my tee shots were even more wayward than usual. We spent quite a bit of time visiting parts of the rough that I'm sure Arnold had never seen before in his entire career. He also cast a critical eye over my swing and my stance, and gave me a few tips on putting; in between we shared a few jokes and stories. He was also very generous with his time with the members of Arnie's Army who followed him around the course whenever he played. I came away from the eighteenth green still in awe of Arnold the golfer but more impressed with Arnold the man.

Unfortunately, despite letting my golf glove dangle from my hip pocket Arnie-style, the Arnold Palmer magic didn't rub off on my golf game. I had already turned thirty before

I took up the sport, and I never became more than an average player — either because I didn't start young enough or, more likely, because I just wasn't talented enough to get any better than that. I did get my handicap down to eleven, so I could play a round with anyone without embarrassing myself too much.

My worst moment probably came at Pebble Beach during the Bing Crosby tournament one year. On the eighteenth green I had a long putt, about thirty feet. I looked up at the announcers' booth at the tower on the eighteenth green and saw Bing wave to me and sitting next to him was Phil Harris. Then I noticed that all the cameramen were the same guys who did my show every week. Every camera, every eye was on me. I got so nervous that all the adrenaline drained from my body, and when I finally hit the putt, the putter grazed my toe and the ball ricocheted off at a right angle. There seemed to be about two hundred people in wheelchairs all around the green, and when I missed the shot, they all went "Ooohhhhhhh!" It sounded like a giant upchucking. I looked back up at the tower and saw that all the cameras had been turned away. Even on the biggest stage I've never felt quite so alone.

Robert Goulet had a similarly embarrassing moment in the same tournament. He had a big ego, always knowing where the cameras were and always being "on," as they say in Hollywood; whenever a camera was pointed at him, Bob would play to it. I was standing next to Bing while watching Bob come up the eighteenth fairway. He was in some heavy rough, and I saw him shoot a sideways glance at the camera (you could tell from the red light if it was live) and check that he was on before he took a swing at the ball. His club went underneath the ball and didn't move it at all. He gave a little laugh — as if to say, "Isn't that ridiculous? But, hey, I don't care" — tossed his head, and then swung again. The ball moved about two feet this time, still in the thick rough. Another laugh, another toss of the head, and then he hit it again. This time it traveled sideways about four feet onto the edge of the fairway.

Still playing to the camera, he went to jump over the rope that held the crowd back but accidentally caught his foot on it and fell flat on his face. He hid his embarrassment, bounced back up, gave another laugh and another toss of the head, and finally managed to get the ball on the green with his next shot. Bing had watched all this with a face like thunder. "I don't think Bob is taking this seriously enough," he said, and Bob

Goulet was never invited to play in his tournament again.

My name was attached to the San Diego Open for the next two decades, and celebrities such as Bob Hope, Jack Lemmon, the Smothers brothers, Glen Campbell, and Bob Newhart, and movie actors James Garner and Clint Eastwood would perform at the gala and play in the pro-am the next day. However, a financial company, Shearson Lehman, then began sponsoring the tournament, and the man running the sponsorship began badgering me constantly, even down to telling me what songs he wanted me to sing and which stars he wanted me to get. It was becoming a less and less enjoyable experience for me, and in the end I just said, "Okay, you do it from now on." The next year he couldn't get any celebrities to turn up and had to pay a performer to star in the gala.

Although many of the tournaments had celebrity names attached to them — the Sammy Davis Jr. Hartford Open, the Dean Martin Tucson Open, the Glen Campbell Los Angeles Open, and so on — the commercial sponsors all began flexing their muscles. If they were picking up the tab, Shearson Lehman didn't want to sponsor the Andy Williams San Diego Open; they wanted it to be the Shearson Lehman Open; they didn't even want it to say San Diego. So gradually all the tournaments were renamed for their commercial sponsors, and the only people who showed up to play in the pro-ams were their employees and customers. The pros hated it; they didn't like playing with amateurs in any case, but if they had to play a pro-am, they wanted to do so with Jack Lemmon or Bob Hope, not some regional sales manager. But in golf as in everything, money talks, and from then on that was the way it was and still is.

Bob Hope had been the second star to have his name linked to a tournament, and because we were good friends — I had known him since I was sixteen years old and sang in a group on his radio show during the war years — I always received an invitation to the Bob Hope Desert Classic, and he was always welcome at my tournament. He also performed in my galas, and I in his, and we both had homes in Palm Springs.

Bob had a little house out near the airport that he absolutely loved, but it wasn't anywhere near grand enough for his wife, Dolores. She insisted that they needed a larger place to accommodate the big dinner parties she loved to give. She commissioned an architect to build them a new house in

Palm Springs, well away from the airport. It was an extraordinary-looking building, perched high on a hill with a swooping roof like the wings of some vast bird of prey. Inside it had the feel and about the same proportions as an airport departure lounge. Bob used to call it the Flying Fortress. You could entertain three hundred people there at a sit-down dinner, and during the Bob Hope Classic they did exactly that. Dolores loved it, but Bob found it overblown and pretentious — as he did some of the people gathered around his dinner table. When we played golf together, he would get nostalgic about the old, unpretentious, but comfortable little house near the airport and the intimate dinner parties they used to hold with a few close friends. After his death the Flying Fortress was sold.

I had bought my own place in La Quinta, near Palm Springs, in 1965. I had already been thinking of having a second home in the area when a friend, Ed Crowley, who was president of the just-opened La Quinta Country Club, offered me a membership and a lot where I could build a small house, in return for the right to use my name in advertising the club. I chose a perfect lot between the ninth and eighteenth fairways, looking out over a pond full of water lilies. I became one of the first members of the La Quinta Country Club. There was no clubhouse at that stage, just a trailer and a stock of golf balls, clubs, shirts, and caps, but it was the beginning of what has turned out to be one of the great clubs in the desert, of which there are now many.

As well as running the country club, Ed was the manager of one of the big hotels in Los Angeles, the Sheraton West, and occasionally when a new Sheraton Hotel was opening somewhere in the world, he would invite some celebrity friends to attend the opening. Claudine and I went to two — one in Bogotá, Colombia, and the other in Munich, Germany. Bogotá wasn't the murderous drug- and crime-ridden place then that it became a decade later, and we had a great time there.

Munich was wonderful, too, and it was made all the better because Fred MacMurray and June Haver were also there. June was a celebrity in her own right, a singer and dancer who had starred in a series of musicals, including *The Dolly Sisters,* with Betty Grable. She also launched the song *"Give Me the Simple Life,"* which became a great standard. Her own life had its share of sorrow. Her parents divorced when she was a baby, and her first marriage to trumpet player

Jimmy Zito lasted just six weeks. She then rekindled a relationship with her former fiancé, studio dentist John Duzik, but he then died from complications after an operation.

After a pilgrimage to Rome and Jerusalem and an audience with the Pope, June stunned Hollywood by announcing that she was giving up her studio contract to enter the Sisters of Charity convent in Kansas, with the aim of becoming a nun. After a year or so, however, she left the convent and returned to Los Angeles. Several years afterward she met Fred, who had recently been widowed, and they were married six months later. They could not have children of their own but adopted twin girls.

As a rule, June did not drink, but she got a little carried away by the festivities at the opening of the Sheraton in Munich and had a few glasses of champagne. Not accustomed to liquor, it hit her hard; she got drunk for the first time in her life and decided to tell everybody a little bit about her past. June was one of the sweetest, kindest women you'd ever want to meet, but the mother superior at her former convent would definitely not have approved of one of her stories. "You know what?" June said, slurring her words. "Fred and I used to have a really big farm with a great big oak tree on it. Do you remember that tree, honey?" she asked as the color drained from Fred's face. He knew what was coming next.

"Yeah, I remember, honey, but —" he said, trying to steer her off the subject, but by now June was unstoppable. "And you know what?" she said. "Fred used to take me up there under that big oak tree and fuck the shit out of me, didn't you, honey? And he's hung like a horse, aren't you, honey?" She picked up the champagne bottle and, waving it around to emphasize the point, said, "It's as big as this, isn't it, honey?" Then, probably to Fred's relief, she passed out.

Fred just put her over his shoulder and carried her upstairs. She was sick all the next day and didn't want to see anybody. I don't think she ever had another drink in her life, and even years later she still blushed crimson if Munich or Sheraton hotels ever came up in conversation.

Over the years I made a lot of friends through golf, but the game almost got in the way of one of my greatest friendships. I never knew Jack Kennedy, but I met his brother Robert in 1966 when I was rehearsing my television show at the NBC studios in Burbank. While we were taking notes after a run-through, Bobby walked in and introduced himself.

He had been doing an interview for *Face the Nation* in another studio and heard I was rehearsing in Studio A. "We watch your show, and Ethel's crazy about you," he said. "I just thought I would stop by and tell you so."

It was the first time I had ever met Bobby, and I was immediately impressed by him. He had a disarming toothy grin, a very direct and penetrating gaze, and an honest way of speaking, quite unlike any other politician I had ever met. When I asked him what he was doing in L.A., he said that he and Ethel were on their way to Universal Studios for the fiftieth birthday party of Edie Wasserman, the wife of the studio head, Lew Wasserman. "Claudine and I are going to be out there, too," I said. "I'm singing 'Happy Birthday' to Edie." The party was held on the vast Universal soundstage, and after I had finished singing, Bobby invited us over to his table. I danced with Ethel, and Bobby danced with Claudine; then we sat and talked for a while before saying our good nights.

The next day I was playing golf at the Riviera Country Club with my friend Pierre Cossette. We had just finished the first nine holes and were passing the refreshment stand by the tenth tee when I was called to the phone. It was Claudine. "Bobby Kennedy just called," she said. "He wants us to go down to Palm Springs this afternoon and spend the weekend with them."

"I can't," I said. "I'm beating Pierre. I can't stop now."

When I told Pierre, he just stared at me incredulously. "Are you out of your fucking mind?" he said. "How can you even think of turning him down? We can play golf anytime. How often are you going to get an invitation from the next president of the United States?"

I took my time thinking about it, trying to decide if Pierre really meant it or had just found a new and even more devious way of avoiding defeat at golf. But finally he threw in the clincher: "Do you seriously think Bob Hope or Bing Crosby would pass up an invitation like that?"

I hurried home and threw some clothes in a bag, and we drove down to Palm Springs to meet the Kennedys. We had dinner that night and then sat around until three in the morning singing scores from Broadway shows. Ethel knew the lyrics to every single song, and although Bobby had a terrible voice, he loved to sing and more than made up in enthusiasm what he lacked in vocal talent. The next morning we played football with some friends, had a swim, and then played nine holes of golf — all before lunch. As I was to discover, the Kennedys were rarely still for a moment.

We had a great time that weekend, and over the next few months a close friendship developed between us. Claudine and I often had dinner with Bobby and Ethel, and nearly always we would finish up singing songs that Ethel loved at the tops of our voices, with Bobby always off-key. I liked Bobby enormously. He was great company, full of boyish enthusiasm, and he had a huge appetite for life, coupled with a very shrewd intelligence. I would see him many times in conversation, listening intently as others said their piece and then cutting through all the bullshit and striking right to the heart of the issue in a few incisive words.

Despite his own privileged background, he had a genuine empathy for the underdog, and when he talked about poverty or civil rights or the war in Vietnam, I could see the passion in his eyes. I felt that he took such issues personally; if someone was hurting, then Bobby felt their hurt, too. He was frank to the point of bluntness, relentless in pursuing what he felt was right (a quality that made him many powerful enemies over the years), but was also man enough to admit when he was wrong about something.

He was the first major political figure to concede that his initial support for the war in Vietnam had been a mistake. I had also never met anyone, in politics or show business, who had such charisma. It is a cliché to talk about someone's lighting up a room, but Bobby really was one of those rare people who could electrify a group of people just by his presence.

We went skiing with the Kennedys at Sun Valley, and I did a river trip with Bobby and quite a few of the Kennedy clan, paddling down the Colorado River through the Grand Canyon. Added to the Kennedys on the trip was quite a list of friends: the journalist and author George Plimpton, a friend of Bobby's since their Harvard days, and his wife, Freddy; the publisher of the *Los Angeles Times*, Otis Chandler, and his wife, Missy; the Pulitzer prize–winning humorist Art Buchwald; the former astronaut John Glenn and his wife, Annie; the ski coach Willie Schaeffler, who had been director of ski events at the 1960 Winter Olympics in Squaw Valley; and Jim Whitaker, a mountaineer and the first American ever to climb Everest, and his wife, Blanche.

I didn't quite get off on the right foot because when Bobby first mentioned the river trip to me, I thought he meant we'd be traveling the river on a luxury motor cruiser, a paddle steamer, or something similar. I turned up at the starting point wearing a suit and tie and carrying two Louis Vuitton suitcases, only to discover that it was a camping and rafting trip, and everyone else was in shorts and T-shirts. It certainly broke the ice because they all burst out laughing.

Once I had sorted out my wardrobe, it turned out to be a great trip, paddling downriver by day and sitting around a campfire in the evenings. On the first day we rode some big waves and roiling waters through a series of rapids and then heard a roaring thunder reverberating from the canyon walls. As we looked ahead, we could see that the line of smooth water ended abruptly in a wall of spray. It looked like the edge of a precipice. We weren't really going to go over that in a raft, were we? For a raft full of Kennedys there was going to be only one answer to that.

I hung onto the ropes as the raft accelerated toward that edge, and in the next moment there was a heart-stopping, stomach-churning plunge into the trough below the falls, with the raft standing vertically almost on its nose before righting itself with a lurch that nearly threw us all into the river. We hung on for dear life and, on our guides' shouted orders, began baling water out of the raft for all we were worth while they bent to the oars to haul us clear of the maelstrom of water below the falls. By the time we were back in calm water, we were soaked to the skin but on an unbelievable high.

As we drifted downstream I witnessed a few examples of the Kennedys' ferociously competitive spirit. If one did something, they all wanted to do it, and they all wanted to be the best at it. That striving for excellence had been drilled into them by their father, Joseph, who always told his kids, "We don't want losers in this family. Don't come second or third; that doesn't count. Win."

On one stretch of the river Bobby decided that a thirty-foot cliff above the water would be a perfect jumping-off place, so he leapt off the raft, swam to the other side, and began climbing up. A couple of minutes later he appeared at the top of the cliff and dove in with a huge splash. Before the water from the splash had settled to the surface, Ethel and the kids were in the river and heading for the cliff to give it a try.

A little later Ethel and Jim Whitaker, who were on the same raft, started a water fight. Both of them were drenched to the skin, but neither would give in first. Eventually Jim simply picked Ethel up and threw her into the river, right in the middle of a stretch of rapids. The water there was fairly shallow, so she just stood straight up and ran alongside the raft, still splashing water on Jim.

At another point we came to a section where the rapids looked too ferocious for novices. Our guides suggested that we take the trail that ran alongside the river and link up with them below the falls, after they brought the rafts down, but Bobby wanted to ride the rapids. He didn't ask the guides what they thought, or if he did, he didn't wait for their answer but just jumped on an air mattress and set off on it down the rapids. He had gone down four good-sized rapids before the guides caught up with him. I admired his courage, but I wondered why a man in his position, on the brink of the presidency, would risk such a thing. When I asked Ethel why he would take such a chance, she just said, "If he's going to become president of the United States, he doesn't want to be afraid to make decisions."

Between the rapids there were long stretches of calm water where we drifted between rock walls rising toward the rim of the Grand Canyon, a mile above us, and watched the ever-changing play of light and shadows on the rock formations, the stone shaped, swirled, and marked as if by a giant artist's brush. Around each bend breathtaking new vistas opened up: side canyons with waterfalls and natural swimming pools, ancient Native American ruins, abandoned mines, scrub, juniper, cactus, cottonwood trees, and jewel-like oases of shrubs and wildflowers, blooming in the heart of the desert.

As the shadows lengthened, we set up camp on sandy river beaches and ate dinner around a campfire. On the first night John Glenn sat down next to me and told me he had been a fan of mine long before we ever met. "When we were getting ready for some of the launches at Cape Canaveral, the other astronauts and I played 'Moon River' so often in our rest area that we damn near wore it out." He held me spellbound that night as he told me about his flight in *Friendship 7* in 1962 when he became the first American in space. With his crewcut hair, strong jaw, and blue eyes, he looked the archetypal, unemotional, even unimaginative career serviceman, but when he spoke about that flight, I could see his eyes shining at the memories he had unlocked.

He spoke about the strange sensation of a night that lasted only forty-five minutes, of the beauty of the lights of a city merged into a single brilliant white glow that gleamed like a jewel in the surrounding darkness, and of

looking downward to see stars below him —
a sensation no earthbound human had ever
experienced. There was the jaw-dropping
sight of a sunset viewed from space, and, as
the next day dawned, he saw literally thousands of brilliant little specks, like fireflies,
floating past the capsule. He thought at first
that he was looking into a starfield or that
the spacecraft was tumbling end over end,
but it was still holding its steady course as
the "fireflies" continued to stream past for a
few more seconds, then vanished as he flew
into brighter sunlight.

On some nights as we camped by the river,
Art Buchwald and I would read poetry to
entertain our captive audience, but often we
would just lie back, surrounded by the absolute peace and stillness of the canyon, and
watch the stars overhead, so many that the
whole sky seemed to glisten with them. And
each morning I'd wake to see the rock spires
and buttes high above us flaring into light as
the first rays of the sun struck them, and I'd
lie there watching the line of the sunrise inch-
ing down the canyon walls, bathing the rock
in a golden glow.

That river trip was one of the most memorable experiences of my life, although my
most vivid recollection is probably the time
that Ethel asked me to sing to them as we

were drifting along. I found a precarious perch on top of all the bags on the luggage raft and was singing "Happy Heart," eyes closed, when one of the kids snuck up behind me and pushed me into the river.

As we were drifting downriver one morning, one of the kids suddenly cried out, "There's a rat — a really big rat — on the rocks over there." As we all turned to look, another of the kids said, "That's not a rat, it's a dog!" We rowed over to the rocks, and the dog jumped straight onto the raft. There was no one in sight for miles, and the dog seemed lost or abandoned, so we took it with us as we carried on downriver. It was a dark brown Chihuahua, almost hairless, and its best friend would have struggled to describe it as beautiful, but Bobby's daughter Kerry adopted it, naming it Rocky because we had found it on the rocks. Kerry and the dog were inseparable the whole time we were on the river, but when we came out of the Grand Canyon into Lake Mead and beached the raft for the last time, a man waiting at the landing walked over to us and said, "That's my dog. We lost him coming down the river. I really love that dog, but you can have him for one hundred fifty dollars if you want him."

It was obvious he didn't care about the dog

at all, but Bobby wasn't going to be bamboozled out of $150, so he said, "If he's your dog and you love him so much, you'd better keep him," and he handed him Rocky.

Kerry didn't say anything at the time, but a few hours later, as we were flying back to Washington on the Kennedys' private plane, she burst into tears. When Bobby asked her what was the matter, she said, "It's Rocky. Why did we have to give him back to that horrible man?"

Bobby went straight to the pilot, who turned the plane around and flew back to Las Vegas. Bobby found the man, paid him $150, and took the dog. We all applauded when he came back to the airfield with Rocky. Kerry was so happy that she didn't know who to hug first, her dad or her new pet.

A few months later Claudine and I were having dinner with Bobby, Ethel, and John and Annie Glenn at the Lodge in Sun Valley. Partway through the meal I heard a little squeak coming from Ethel's purse. She took out the strangest-looking dog I've ever seen. He was the same height as a Chihuahua but had a long, thin body with a thick, curly black coat and white feet. Ethel handed the dog to me and said, "Here, Andy, I want you and Claudine to have this as your Christmas present from Bobby and me."

It turned out that Bobby and Ethel's backyard at Hyannisport connected with his elder brother's backyard, and one night Rocky had teamed up with a long-haired black cocker spaniel that had been given to JFK by the mayor of Dublin. I don't know quite how they managed it without the aid of a stepladder, but Rocky evidently had a good time with the spaniel that night; this little puppy was one of the results. Claudine and I called him Shoes because of his white feet, and we had him for many years.

As well as providing us with a family pet, Bobby did us a huge favor when Claudine's sister, Nicole, was in trouble. She lived in Paris and was trapped in a very unhappy marriage. We decided we had to do something to get Nicole and the children away from her husband and formed a plan to rescue them. Kirk Kerkorian, the head of MGM, was flying to Paris in his private 727 with Cary Grant, and he offered to fly Claudine there and then bring her and Nicole back to the States two days later.

At the end of her stay Claudine grabbed Nicole and her two children in the middle of the night and raced back to the airport where Kirk's aircraft was waiting, engines already running. They were airborne and on their way to the United States before Nicole's husband even realized they were gone, not that he would have particularly cared. Bobby had arranged for papers to be issued so that Nicole and her kids could pass the French passport control and board the aircraft, and clear American customs and immigration when they landed in the United States. They lived with us for a few months and then found their own house and never returned to France. The kids and their mom became part of our extended family and took part in several of the Christmas shows with us.

12

Our friendship with Bobby and Ethel Kennedy meant that whenever Claudine and I were in Washington, we'd stay with them at Hickory Hill, their Civil War–era home in McLean, Virginia, and we'd often see them in California, both in Los Angeles and in the desert. Sometimes Ethel would stay in Hyannisport with the children while Bobby flew out to California on political business, and she once called me in Los Angeles and said, "Why don't you give a dinner party for Bobby? Get some exciting people and find a really attractive girl to sit next to him. He's been working really hard, and a little dinner party will relax him."

Ethel wasn't trying to get him a date. She knew how much pressure he was under and just wanted him to have a night off and a relaxing time and really enjoy himself. A beautiful woman sitting next to him at dinner was just part of that, and I thought that the gesture showed her remarkable selflessness and generosity of spirit.

Claudine asked some of the younger Hollywood set, including Peter Fonda, and I invited Jack Lemmon and Bob Newhart and their wives, and people I didn't know particularly well, such as Kirk and Anne Douglas, Warren Beatty, and Barbra Streisand, who I thought Bobby would find interesting. As with all our dinner parties, we also made sure to invite Pierre Cossette and Phyllis Diller. Pierre was not only a great friend (he was Santa Claus to our kids every Christmas at our house) but was always affable and entertaining, while Phyllis was just plain funny; if she was included, everyone had a good time.

Bobby clearly enjoyed himself that night, and it was a pleasure to see him being able to relax and forget — even if only for a few hours — all the pressures he faced in his daily life. For that reason, whenever we were together, away from the gaze of the media and the public, I'd try to avoid talking politics unless Bobby wanted to. When he did, he'd fix me with that intense, urgent stare of his and push his hair back from his forehead with an almost impatient gesture, as if even that was too much of a distraction from the message he was trying to convey. He talked of his vision for a transformed America, healing the divisions over civil rights and Vietnam that were tearing the country apart, and harnessing the energy and idealism of the young to build a new and better society. Television had brought footage of the Vietnam War into every American home, and Bobby articulated the horror and the guilt that many Americans felt at what was being done in their names.

Sometimes, in a quiet moment, he would fall silent, staring off into space, and I'd get a strange, indefinable sense of sadness from him. But the next moment he would stir himself and be off again, talking and pacing to and fro as if his restless energy would not allow him to be still for more than a few seconds at a stretch.

It was a given for Bobby's supporters and opponents alike that he would run for the presidency one day, but I sometimes felt that he was almost a prisoner of the Kennedy name and the legacy of JFK. Joe Kennedy had never intended that Jack or Bobby should carry the weight of the family's political ambitions. Bobby's eldest brother, Joseph Jr., had been the chosen one, but he was killed during World War II, and Jack had then assumed the Kennedy mantle. Bobby had put his own career on hold to work tirelessly for his brother's elections, first as senator from Massachusetts and then as president, but now he in turn had to try to assume his dead brother's role. Both Bobby and Ethel knew the risks that running for president entailed: His relentless pursuit of racketeering and organized crime and his championing of civil rights legislation had made him a hated figure to some of the most extreme elements of American society. But he did not flinch from following in his brother's footsteps, even at the risk of his life.

At a dinner party in New York just after Bobby announced his candidacy for the presidency, Jacqueline Kennedy remarked to another guest, "Do you know what I think will happen to Bobby? The same thing that happened to Jack." It was a fear that many shared; the poet Robert Lowell said that Bobby had "doom woven into his nerves." Once, as we sat together outside the house in Malibu on a warm California evening, with the sound of Claudine and the children's voices drifting through the open doors and the waves breaking on the beach in front of us, I asked Bobby whether the fear of another assassin preyed on his mind. His answer was, as ever, direct and to the point. "How could it not? I'd be a fool not to be aware of the risk, but you can't live your life in fear. I've got to do what I believe to be right. I know what must be done, and I'm obliged to do all I can to achieve it, whatever the cost might be." His eyes were shining as he spoke, and his voice revealed the passion he felt, speaking about his country and his vision — yet the word "obliged" sounded curious to me, suggesting how much he was bound by the Kennedy name. Perhaps he was acting as much out of a sense of obligation to his family, his destiny, and his country as of his own free will.

Neither fear of assassins nor the grubby deals and compromises of "politics as usual" could sway Bobby from the course he had chosen and the policies in which he believed. I had a vivid demonstration of that one evening in Palm Springs. We were going into a restaurant for dinner just as three men in expensive suits were coming out. Bobby told me afterward that they were very senior executives in the tobacco industry and had already crossed swords with him over his plans to push through tough new anti-smoking laws. As soon as they caught sight of him, one of them said, "Hey, Bobby! You'd better cut out that anti-smoking rhetoric of yours. You keep campaigning against tobacco, and you're not going to win any of the southern states."

"Then I'll just have to lose them," Bobby

said, "because I'm not changing my policy. This thing is too important. You're advertising to kids, telling them that smoking's not addictive. You're getting too many of our kids hooked on tobacco, and you'll kill them many years before their time. I'm not going to let that happen even if I lose every single southern state." It was a statement of principle, irrespective of the political cost, that I could not imagine a "machine" politician such as Hubert Humphrey or Richard Nixon ever uttering, and it was one of the reasons that so many Americans — and young Americans in particular — were flocking to support Bobby.

With Lyndon Johnson as the incumbent Democratic president, Bobby had been focusing on a probable run in 1972, but as opposition to the Vietnam War grew ever more bitter, he began to rethink his plans. His name was not on the ballot when Senator Eugene McCarthy stood against Johnson in the New Hampshire primary in January 1968. Although defeated, McCarthy had gotten a 42 percent share of the vote — only 7 percent behind Johnson — which demonstrated the depth of the divisions in the Democratic Party. Pressure on Bobby to stand now became overwhelming, and on March 16, 1968, he announced his candidacy. A fortnight later Johnson, with his standing in the opinion polls in freefall, made his famous "I shall not seek, and I will not accept, the nomination of my party for another term as your president" speech.

Bobby now began a battle with Eugene McCarthy for the popular vote in the Democratic primaries, while Hubert Humphrey — LBJ's vice president and a politician steeped in the Democratic Party machine, whose name was not on any of the primary ballots — ran a largely invisible campaign, making deals in smoke-filled rooms with party bosses who could deliver their state's delegates to him, whatever the popular vote might be.

When Bobby began his run for the presidency, I immediately volunteered to campaign for him and sing at a couple of fundraisers. He then asked me if I would be one of the California delegates to the Democratic convention: "Shirley MacLaine is going to be one of my delegates, and I'd like you to be one, too." I told him I'd love to do it, but a couple of weeks later a thought suddenly struck me, and I called Bobby and said, "I hope I haven't screwed this up, but it's just occurred to me: I'm a Republican." He just laughed. "That doesn't really matter. If you'd still like to do it for me, just go down and register as a Democrat."

On June 4, 1968, Bobby won the California primary, a huge stride toward the Democratic nomination. We had been having a drink in his hotel suite while we waited for the result to be declared. When it came through, we were all euphoric at the result, but there was also an almost electric charge in the atmosphere, a feeling that what had seemed beyond reach only a few weeks before was now within his grasp. "It's really going to happen, Bobby," I said as he put on his jacket. He grinned. "Don't jinx it, Andy. There's still a very long road to travel before we can start thinking about that." As he and Ethel left to go downstairs for him to give his victory speech, Bobby said, "Watch it on television up here, and I'll give a little hand signal like this" — he mimed it for me — "to let you know I'm almost at the end of the speech. It'll give you time to finish getting ready and come down. We'll meet at the cars and go and have a late dinner at The Factory." They were the last words he ever spoke to me.

While Bobby gave the speech in the Embassy Room of the Ambassador Hotel, Claudine and I remained in the Kennedys' suite, chatting with John and Annie Glenn. We were watching on television as Bobby gave the little hand signal he had mentioned and then ended his speech with the words "My thanks to all of you, and now it's on to Chicago, and let's win there." He gave a thumbs-up and a V for Victory sign and pushed his hair back from his forehead in that characteristic gesture. I had already put on my jacket, and we were walking out the door with the Glenns as Bobby stepped down from the podium and began moving through the press of people toward the service exit through the hotel kitchen, out of sight of the television cameras.

We were in the elevator for perhaps thirty seconds. As the doors opened and we stepped out into the lobby, there were still a few seconds of normality. I could hear Bobby's supporters in the ballroom on the ground floor still applauding and chanting, "RFK! RFK!" but as I looked around, I felt a growing unease. A wild-eyed woman and then another suddenly burst out of the Embassy Room and ran across the lobby. Before the doors swung shut again, I heard cries and a couple of screams. I looked at John; the concern was as evident on his face as it must have been on mine. "What's happening?" he asked.

The noise grew louder, swelling into a pandemonium of shouts and hurrying feet.

My thoughts were racing. Looking back, I think I already knew what had happened, but I tried to deny it to myself, conjuring a series of explanations: someone had fainted in the crush of supporters; a car backfiring or fireworks going off outside had caused a small panic. I stood for another moment, irresolute, staring at the doors of the Embassy Room. Then they burst open, and a torrent of people poured out, stumbling, jostling, fearful. Above the hubbub of noise I heard a woman's voice cry out, "They've shot him! They've shot him!"

We began struggling against the tide as we tried to push our way through the mass of people streaming out of the room. Above the shouts and screams I could hear a rising chorus of sirens, and through the darkened glass of the lobby windows I saw the flicker and flash of blue and red lights.

We at last fought our way into the Embassy Room. Someone on the platform at the front of the room was shouting, "Doctors, we need doctors!" Beyond the chaos of overturned chairs and abandoned paper flags and banners, a dense knot of people was clustered before the service doors in the north wall of the room, held back by a semicircle of stone-faced police and Secret Service men. As we pushed our way forward, I passed close to a well-known television reporter. All trace of his normal urbanity had vanished, and his voice was shaking as he said — whether to a colleague or a television audience I could not tell — "They're saying he's been shot. Kennedy's been shot." There was no room left for denial. The thing that I — that all of us — had privately dreaded had happened. Like his brother before him, Bobby had been gunned down.

A Kennedy aide stumbled past me, his cheeks wet with tears. "Is he . . . ?" I couldn't bring myself to say the word.

He stared at me, unseeing. "I don't know."

As we pressed forward through the crowd, word rippled back, passed from person to person: "He's in an ambulance." "They're taking him to a hospital." All but extinguished a few seconds before, hope flared up in me again.

We turned and pushed our way back out of the room. The confusion and rising panic had now spread to the main ballroom on the floor below. The chants of "RFK" had faded and died, replaced by more screams, shouts, and a rush for the exits. The hotel lobby was in bedlam. Stunned Kennedy supporters were milling everywhere, and police and emergency vehicles were still arriving outside. Reporters and television crews were scrambling to exchange information and interview anyone who could offer any details on the shooting, but no one seemed to have more than a fragmentary picture of what had happened. Slowly the facts emerged: Bobby had been shot twice in the back and once in the head at point-blank range.

My concern was now to find out where Bobby had been taken and to get there as soon as I could, but for long, agonizing minutes, although John and I accosted every Kennedy staffer we could find, no one had any definite information. Finally, one of Bobby's campaign staff shouted to me across the lobby: "They've taken him to the Good Samaritan Hospital."

Claudine and I rushed for our car. Neither of us said a word the whole journey. We stared into the darkness outside as we made the top-speed drive across the darkened city to the Good Samaritan Hospital. Four cops blocked access to the wing of the hospital where Bobby had been taken. They recognized both of us but radioed someone for authorization before allowing us through. We walked down a long corridor and sat down to wait outside the closed door of what I thought was the room where Bobby lay. All I could think was that on the other side of that door my friend was dying.

We sat there the rest of the night. Finally, in the early morning, I decided to knock on the door. I knocked several times, but there was no answer, and when I quietly opened the door, I found not Bobby's room but a deserted hallway. We walked quietly along it and at the far end was a dimly lit room. No one barred our way. There were no cops or even medical staff in the room, just Ethel and Bobby alone.

Ethel, carrying the child that would now never know its father, was passed out on a cot next to his bed; the doctors must have sedated her. The last time I had seen Bobby, he was a smiling, vital young man, surrounded by hordes of admirers and well-wishers, and about to grasp his destiny. The figure lying on that hospital bed was almost unrecognizable. Bobby lay flat with tubes coming out of his head, and his face was a vivid red color. Even his hair was red. He didn't move or make a sound; I think he was already gone then, his brain dead, his body functions taken over by hospital machines.

I took a last look at my friend and went back into the corridor to sit and wait for the inevitable. Bobby used to tell his kids and his nephews, "Kennedys don't cry," but the Kennedys shed tears that black day. Like the nation as a whole, I was numb with grief. I had lost a friend, and the country had lost someone who was dedicated to doing good and who I believe would have made a great president.

Later, Ethel came out to see us in the hospital corridor. Haggard and pale, and still in the same sleeveless white dress she had been wearing at the victory celebration at the hotel, she seemed to have aged ten years in twenty-four hours. She made a visible effort to hold back her tears as, speaking in a hoarse monotone, her voice barely recognizable, she thanked us for being there.

Bobby's clothes, covered in blood, had been cut away by the medics when they began treating his wounds. John Glenn and I went back to the hotel to pick up one of Bobby's suits and a clean shirt. The traffic was terrible, and it seemed to take hours to make the journey. We had the radio on, tuned to a news station — not with the intention of keeping up with any new developments but with the absurd, superstitious hope that we might suddenly hear Bobby's voice and wake to discover it had all been a nightmare. Instead, hearing the constant repetition of the horrific events of the previous day darkened our mood even more. John and I couldn't find anything to say to each other and sat staring out through the windshield at the barely moving traffic while a succession of radio voices recounted the grisly details of Bobby's wounds and speculated on the motives of his killer.

When we at last reached the hotel, Bobby and Ethel's room had not been touched, and a half-finished drink still stood on the table. We opened the closet, and hesitated over the choice. I caught John's eye, and we both shook our heads in disbelief at the surreal situation we found ourselves in: trying to select a suitable outfit to clothe the body of a murdered friend.

We eventually chose a suit and a shirt and then hurried back to the hospital. We handed the clothing to the funeral director. Then we realized that neither of us had remembered to bring one of Bobby's ties, so I took off my own tie, a black one, and handed it to the man. Bobby was dressed in his suit and shirt, and my tie, before being flown to New York for the funeral.

John, Annie, Claudine, and I headed straight for the airport; we had no spare clothes with us, no luggage, nothing. When we arrived, hundreds of silent people, many in tears, were crowded behind a chain-link fence; we were hurried through the terminal and out to Air Force Two.

Ethel spent much of that long, miserable flight discussing the way she wanted the funeral to be conducted. Bobby had run for president as a candidate for ordinary Americans, and she was determined that his funeral reflect that. There was to be a minimum of military and state rituals: no lying in state in the Capitol, no vast military parades and marching bands. With the exception of four Green Berets (included at Teddy's request) the guard of honor at Bobby's funeral would be an entirely civilian one. Ethel then asked me if I would sing at the service. Ever since Buddy's death, when my brothers and I had had to sing to pay off the family debt to the funeral parlor, I had always refused to sing at funerals, but I couldn't turn down Ethel now; I agreed at once.

We arrived at La Guardia just before nine o'clock in the evening. Governor Nelson Rockefeller, Senator Jacob Javits, and New York City's mayor John Lindsay were among the party who greeted Ethel as she stepped from the plane, watched by a crowd of several thousand people. We stood in silence as the casket of African mahogany was taken from the aircraft, and Archbishop Terence J. Cooke said a prayer. We then drove in procession behind the gray hearse to Saint Patrick's Cathedral, where we filed through the great bronze doors for a short, private service conducted by the archbishop for Ethel, the family, and close friends.

Still struggling to come to terms with what had happened, I barely slept that night; I doubt if any of us did. The next morning, a stifling June day, we returned to Saint Patrick's. As we drove along Fifth Avenue, every flag on every building in the city hung limply at half-mast, and an endless line of silent mourners — stretching eight abreast for as many as twenty-five blocks — waited their turn to enter the cathedral and file past Bobby's casket to pay their last respects as he lay in state.

The lines of mourners had been there all night and continued all day and all through the next night. Over one hundred thousand people had filed past by the time the cathedral was closed to prepare for the funeral mass. The New York Times reported, "World statesmen in formal dark suits stood next to Harlem schoolboys in torn Levis and sneakers; Wall Street stockbrokers with morocco briefcases under their arms walked behind flower children with daisy chains wound in their hair; and suburban housewives in trim, fashionable suits waited side by side with young Puerto Rican girls who fingered worn rosary beads."

The diversity of people Bobby had drawn to his campaign was reflected, too, in those who took their turn in the six-person honor guard keeping vigil around his casket: World Bank President Robert McNamara, long-time Kennedy adviser Robert Schlesinger, Ed Sullivan, Sidney Poitier, Sugar Ray Robinson, and Ralph Abernethy of the Southern Christian Leadership Conference, wearing dungaree trousers and jacket for the Poor People's March. Tom Hayden, one of the founders of Students for a Democratic Society, also stood there, alongside civil rights leader Charles Evers (brother of Medgar Evers, the 1963 victim of the notorious racist killing), former Olympic decathlete Rafer Johnson, and Chuck McDowell, a former Peace Corps volunteer who ran a city poverty program. I took my turn at the foot of the casket, in the flickering light of the tall amber candles that surrounded the bier, and Kennedy aides also chose people at random from the crowds of mourners, including a fourteen-year-old schoolboy from Washington Heights, Kenneth Roberts, who stood motionless by the bier as the lines of mourners slowly filed past.

The only sounds in that vast echoing space were stifled sobs and the scuff and shuffle of feet. Some mourners could not contain their grief, and several women in hysterics had to be gently led away by police. On the sidewalks outside more than one hundred people needed medical treatment after collapsing from a combination of the heat and the emotion of the occasion.

When Ethel discussed the funeral arrangements with Monsignor Duffy, she told him that Bobby would have wanted me to sing at the funeral. He said that was fine and suggested "Panis Angelicus."

"I'm not a Catholic," I explained. "I'm afraid I don't know that one." He named another hymn, and I said, "I'm afraid I don't know that one, either." The silence was broken by an FBI agent, Bill Barry, who had been with Bobby every step of the way on the campaign trail. He reminded us that when they were out campaigning, Bobby's favorite song had been "The Battle Hymn of the Republic." I can still picture him belting it out, off-key, his eyes shining with passion. Ethel then asked me if I could sing that, and I said I could. Monsignor Duffy's expression showed that he didn't think much of the idea, and Leonard Bernstein, who was also there to discuss his contribution to the funeral mass, was no more enthusiastic. But Ethel felt that it was what Bobby would have wanted, and she got her way. That night we had dinner at Bobby's sister Jean's apartment, and after dinner John Glenn and I looked up "The Battle Hymn of the Republic" in the *Encyclopaedia Britannica*. I wrote down the verses that I thought I would sing. There were six in all, but in the end I chose just three:

Mine eyes have seen the glory of the coming of the Lord:
He is trampling out the vintage where the grapes of wrath are stored;
He hath loosed the fateful lightning of His terrible swift sword:
His truth is marching on.
Glory, glory, hallelujah!
Glory, glory, hallelujah!
Glory, glory, hallelujah!
His truth is marching on.

He has sounded forth the trumpet that shall never call retreat;
He is sifting out the hearts of men before His judgment-seat:
Oh, be swift, my soul, to answer Him! be jubilant, my feet!
Our God is marching on.
Glory, glory, hallelujah!
Glory, glory, hallelujah!

Glory, glory, hallelujah!
Our God is marching on.

In the beauty of the lilies Christ was born
* across the sea,*
With a glory in His bosom that transfigures
* you and me:*
As He died to make men holy, let us die to
* make men free,*
While God is marching on.
Glory, glory, hallelujah!
Glory, glory, hallelujah!
Glory, glory, hallelujah!
While God is marching on.

The funeral mass was held at Saint Patrick's on Saturday, June 8, 1968. One hundred friends, Kennedy aides, and interns had labored to reduce the guest list to the twenty-three hundred the cathedral could hold. Alongside the Kennedy family were scores of heads of state, political leaders, and diplomats representing every major nation on earth. President Johnson led the American mourners, who included Harry Belafonte, John Kenneth Galbraith, Lauren Bacall, Cary Grant, John Glenn, Averell Harriman, Princess Grace of Monaco, and Coretta Scott King, widow of Martin Luther King Jr. who had also been assassinated that year, just three months before Bobby.

I felt pulled and pushed by conflicting emotions: nervousness and an overwhelming sorrow, coupled with a grim determination not to let Ethel — and Bobby — down. Before I took my seat, I stood for a moment behind one of the pillars, trying to calm myself. I took some deep breaths, resting my hand on the cold white marble of the pillar while I let my gaze travel around the cathedral, from the delicate wooden tracery and the ranks of silvered pipes of the great organ, up past the stained glass of the rose window to where those towering pillars merged with the fan vaulting overhead. I took my seat moments before the funeral mass began.

The air was heady with the scent of incense, and as they proceeded along the aisle behind the great gold cross, the robes of the clergy — bishops in long violet robes, archbishops in purple, and cardinals in bright scarlet — made vivid splashes of color among the ranks of black- and gray-clad mourners. When Leonard Bernstein conducted thirty members of the New York Philharmonic as they played the Adagietto from Mahler's Fifth Symphony, the grandeur of the setting seemed matched by the majesty of the music soaring and swirling around the great stone arches high overhead.

Archbishop Cooke's address spoke of Americans "together in our bewilderment and grief. Our sense of shame and discouragement, tears alone will not wash away." Teddy delivered the funeral oration — the youngest brother now taking up the Kennedy mantle, just as Jack and Bobby had done before him on the deaths of their elder brothers. Hearing his voice breaking with emotion brought tears to my eyes and those of everyone there: "My brother need not be idealized or enlarged in death beyond what he was in life. He should be remembered simply as a good and decent man who saw wrong and tried to right it, saw suffering and tried to heal it, saw war and tried to stop it."

When I rose to my feet to sing, I wasn't at all sure I could do it because it was such an emotional, heart-wrenching occasion — everybody was crying, including me. But I knew how important it was to Ethel, and I tried to pull myself together. I told myself, *This is my job. I can't let emotion get in the way of the song,* and I concentrated on not thinking about Bobby. I sang it not as a fierce old war song but as a sad and tender lament. It was the hardest performance I've ever given, but I managed to complete it without breaking down.

I sang it unaccompanied, my voice echoing alone at first in the vast stillness of that great cathedral, but as I sang, everyone in the congregation gradually joined in. Then the huge crowds outside on Fifth Avenue and Madison Avenue, listening to a live relay of the service, began singing it, too. It was the most moving thing I ever heard. I was reminded of it years later while watching Elton John singing "Candle in the Wind" at Princess Diana's funeral. The hairs on the back of my neck stood on end, but I forced myself to shut out everything but the song. At last it reached its crescendo, and as the echoes of the last note faded away, the emotions of the occasion overwhelmed me and I fell apart. I have never sung "The Battle Hymn of the Republic" since then; I can't even bear to listen to the song. There are too many memories and too many sorrows swirling around it.

After the service, Bobby's friends and family accompanied his casket on his last journey, by special train from Pennsylvania Station to Washington. The coffin was placed at first on a low bier in the observation car, but because it was not visible from outside, the pallbearers lifted it up and balanced it on chairs so that it could easily be seen by the huge numbers of people who had gathered at the stations the train passed through and who also lined the trackside in between. At several places they sang the song of the civil rights movement, "We Shall Overcome." Wherever the railroad tracks ran near state highways, traffic on them came to a standstill as the train passed slowly by.

Ethel spent part of the journey alone with Bobby's casket. It was the only time in that harrowing day that she allowed her self-control to slip and shed tears for the husband she had lost. A rosary in her hands, her forehead resting against the cold surface of the casket, she sat on a plain straight-backed chair, so still she might have been carved from stone. Then she straightened up, squared her shoulders, and, with her eldest son, sixteen-year-old Joe, she walked the entire twenty-car length of the train and thanked every one of the mourners for being there and for sharing a part of Bobby's life.

As we made our slow way south through Newark, Trenton, Philadelphia, and Baltimore, to Washington, D.C., Teddy spent much of the journey out on the rear platform of the train, thanking the people who had come to honor his brother. There was a tragedy at Elizabeth, New Jersey, however, when a crowd of people spilling onto the track as the funeral train passed by were hit by the northbound New York express. Several people were injured and two of them killed. An eighteen-year-old boy was also critically burned at Trenton after touching a live wire while trying to get a better view of the railroad track.

The speed of the funeral train was reduced in the hope of preventing further tragedies, and this, combined with the crowds and the stops for ceremonies along the route, meant that we arrived at Union Station in Washington almost five hours late. President Johnson was waiting at the head of a guard of honor one hundred strong and was the first to greet Ethel when she stepped down from the train. As the casket was being taken from the train, the crowds began singing "The Battle Hymn of the Republic." With those majestic words still so fresh in my mind, I was in tears once more. We transferred to a motorcade for Bobby's final journey down Constitution Avenue to the Lincoln Memorial, and then across the bridge over the Potomac where a full moon was reflecting from the dark waters. In an apparently spontaneous and deeply moving gesture, thousands of the mourners lining the route from the Virginia shore through Arlington National Cemetery lit candles as the cortege approached, lighting the way to Bobby's grave.

The interment at Arlington — beneath a magnolia tree, a few yards from the eternal flame marking the grave of another Kennedy whose life had also been cut short by an assassin's bullet — took place after dark. It seemed a fitting ending to a chain of events that had cast a pall of darkness and sadness over the whole country.

The grave at Arlington now carries two inscriptions taken from Robert Kennedy's speeches, embodying the ideals with which he had begun to galvanize the nation. The first, from a speech he delivered in South Africa, celebrated the unquenchable human spirit that would one day sweep away the apartheid regime and bring Nelson Mandela to power:

It is from numberless diverse acts of courage and belief that human history is shaped. Each time a man stands up for an ideal or acts to improve the lot of others or strikes out against injustice, he sends forth a tiny ripple of hope, and crossing each other from a million different centers of energy and daring, those ripples build a current that can sweep down the mightiest wall of oppression and resistance.

The second was taken from a speech he

made on the campaign trail in America that fateful year:

Some men see things as they are and ask, "Why?"
I dream things that never were and ask, "Why not?"

It was a message of hope that was cruelly extinguished that June night in Los Angeles.

13

I had one more duty to perform for Bobby. Although he had died, I still had to attend the Democratic Party Convention in Chicago as one of his delegates from California. I voted for George McGovern — probably the only Republican who ever did — believing that he was the candidate Bobby would have preferred. Shirley MacLaine followed her own preferences and voted for Hubert Humphrey, who was eventually nominated after a convention as bitter and divisive as American politics has ever witnessed. After the horror of the slayings of Martin Luther King Jr. and Robert Kennedy earlier in the year, the poisonous atmosphere at the convention and the brutality on the streets of Chicago and in Grant Park, where demonstrators and police in riot gear clashed violently and repeatedly, were enough to sour me on politics for years.

Only one good thing came out of that bitter experience for me. I was being driven down Michigan Avenue on my way to the airport. It was a day as gray and grim as my mood, but as we passed the Richard Gray Gallery, I caught a glimpse of a painting hanging in the window. The vivid hot colors were like a burst of sunshine piercing the drizzle and murk. I asked my driver to stop and back up, and then I went into the gallery for a closer look. I had never heard of the artist, Hans Hofmann, but I fell in love with the painting, *Beatae Memoriale,* an abstract with broad slabs of bright color that had caught my eye. I bought it for the asking price; however, I had learned enough of my dad's negotiating tactics to get a drawing by Egon Schiele and a large oil by Bob Thompson (whom I'd never heard of, either) thrown in as part of the deal. The Hofmann was recently valued at over $1 million, but I would never sell it. Forty years later I still love it, and if the house was burning down, it would be the first painting I'd try to save.

A Palestinian, Sirhan Sirhan, was eventually convicted of Bobby Kennedy's murder. He was sentenced to death, later commuted to life imprisonment. He is still behind bars in the California state prison in Corcoran. As with the death of JFK, a raft of conspiracy theories have been floated in the years since

Bobby's death, suggesting that more than one gunman may have been involved. Years later I asked Teddy whether he believed the theories about either of his brothers' deaths, and he said no, but I got the feeling from both Teddy and Ethel that whether there was one assassin or two or twenty made no real difference in the one undeniable fact: Like JFK before him, Bobby was dead, and no amount of conspiracy theories and nothing anyone could say or do would ever bring him back.

I grieved for Bobby for a long time. I had liked and admired him so much that, when Claudine told me a few months later that she was pregnant and we discovered the baby would be a boy, neither of us hesitated over the choice of name; it had to be Bobby in memory of our friend.

Jackie Kennedy was now married to Aristotle Onassis, and in the wake of Bobby's death, Ari phoned Ethel and offered her the use of his yacht *Christina* if she wanted to get away for a few days. She took him up on it and invited Claudine and me, John and Annie Glenn, Bobby's sister Pat Kennedy Lawford, and Jim and Blanche Whitaker to join her. Ethel decided to sail down to the Bahamas. When we all arrived, we found that Ari and Jackie were also onboard, which none of us had expected. I had not met Ari before, and like most of the world, I'd been baffled about what Jackie saw in him, but I found him to be a very affable man. He spent a lot of time up on the bridge talking on the radio telephone to business associates all over the world, but when he was with us, he was an absolutely perfect host.

The word "yacht" doesn't really begin to describe the boat. It was big enough to carry a seaplane that was lowered into the water every morning to fly off for a fresh supply of Ari's favorite caviar. It came from Iran, and the grains were so big that they looked like kernels of corn. There was a swimming pool, a dozen staterooms and suites, and so many terraces and dining areas that we ate lunch in a different place every day. It was a really relaxing trip for us all, and I think it did Ethel a world of good to get away from the photographers and the well-wishers, and just spend a few days recuperating.

After the pain of Bobby's death had begun to ease a little, I flew from Hyannisport to Chicago with Ethel, Teddy, and a few of their friends to view a film about Bobby, *RFK Remembered,* made by Charles Guggenheim. It was a very emotional evening, and when we got back to Ethel's house at Hyannisport later that night, we all drank a little too much — in my case a lot too much. As a result, I fell down a flight of steps leading to the beach and crashed into a boulder at the bottom. When I got up the next morning, along with a major-league hangover I had a very swollen, black and purple, broken big toe. Feeling like death, I staggered down to the breakfast room where Teddy and a few of the others were sitting and talking.

"Andy, you were pretty out of it last night," Teddy said. "You took your clothes off and tossed them everywhere: your shirt over the couch, your pants behind the television. You were really beautiful! You finished up stark naked. It gave a whole new meaning to Moon River!" Taking their cue from Teddy, the rest of them joined in, and for twenty minutes or so they had me convinced. Finally, Teddy let me off the hook. "I was just kidding," he said. "Now you haven't forgotten the game, have you?"

"Game?" I said, my mind a blank.

"The tennis match. You and Ethel are playing me and Jim Whitaker."

"Well, I don't know, Teddy. I've broken my toe." I showed him my foot, but Teddy just said, "Great. Now we all have a handicap. Ten minutes?"

Well aware that they didn't take no for an answer to anything, I hobbled upstairs and changed into my tennis clothes. I had to cut away the front part of my left tennis shoe so I could get it over my bulbous toe, and then I limped back downstairs.

When I got to the tennis court, I burst out laughing. I was hobbling around on one leg; Ethel was six months' pregnant and could only play by holding the racket in one hand and supporting her bump in the other; Teddy had back trouble and was wearing a brace; and Jim Whitaker had just had some varicose veins removed from his leg, so he was wrapped in bandages from ankle to groin and could barely bend his leg at all. We looked as if we were playing in the hospital mixed doubles championship, and we could hardly play for laughing. It was the first time any of us had really seen Ethel laugh since Bobby was killed. When I left Hyannisport the next day, I got my driver to stop at a shoe store, and I bought two pairs of velvet slippers, one size 8½ and one size 9½, and flew home with my broken toe encased in an oversized slipper.

My friendship with Ethel Kennedy has endured through the years; we're still good friends today. I sometimes served as her escort during the 1970s when I visited her and took her to dinner or an opening at an art gallery, and to the first Ali-Frazier fight at

Madison Square Garden, prompting speculation that we were an item, but there was no truth in the rumors. No one could ever take the place of Bobby in Ethel's heart, and I never even harbored the thought of trying to do so. I was always more than happy to be with her — it was a pleasure, not a duty, to take her out — but in this case the old show business cliché was true: We really were "just good friends."

With everything that had been going on, I hadn't seen Billy Pearson in quite a while when one day, out of the blue, he called me in a state of great excitement and said, "Andy, I can get us a Sheldon Peck."

"Great," I said. "What's a Sheldon Peck?"

"What's a Sheldon Peck? Are you kidding? Sheldon Peck is only one of the greatest American folk artists, that's all. The painting is in Chicago, and I think I can get it for twelve thousand dollars."

"Is Sheldon Peck really that big a deal?" I asked. "Well, good for you, Billy. Why don't you go ahead and buy it then?"

"Well, the problem is, I don't have any money. I can get six thousand dollars from my mother, and if you came in with the other six thousand dollars, we could buy it together."

I said that would be okay, and he called me again a couple of days later. "I got it!" he said. "And I got it for less — only ten thousand dollars — because it had a hole in it."

"Wait a minute," I said. "You paid ten thousand dollars for a painting with a hole in it?"

"Yeah, yeah, but that's easily fixed. I can get it repaired for five hundred dollars, and you won't even be able to see where it was."

A few weeks later he turned up with the painting. True to his word, it had been invisibly restored, but I discovered it was also one of the ugliest things I had ever seen, a painting of a grandmother in a black dress with a white lace collar. She was sitting in a chair, and her equally unattractive granddaughter was at her side.

"Isn't it great, Andy?" Billy said, bubbling with enthusiasm. "You can have it for six months, and then I'll have it for six months. It's great, isn't it?"

"What do you mean 'have it for six months'? I thought we were buying it as an investment to sell it. Do you think you can sell it?"

"Well, yes, I could, but I thought we would keep it and enjoy it."

"Billy," I said, "sell it."

About three months later he called and said, "Well, I've sold it."

"That's great, Billy. What did you get for it?"

"Twenty-six thousand dollars from a guy in Connecticut."

By now I was feeling sorry that I had been so hard on Billy. I was delighted he had sold it — I certainly didn't want to live with it for six months or even six days — but I also felt a bit guilty that I had made such easy money by making him sell something he loved so much. I said to him, "Tell you what: Give me the six thousand dollars back, and I'll buy some other things from you with the rest of my share."

A while later, while I was staying at Bobby and Ethel's house in Hyannisport, I noticed that Ethel, Teddy, and Jean all had these beautiful little carved wooden shorebirds and ducks. I asked where they had bought them, and then I called Billy and said, "There's this auction house up here, Bourne, and they're having an auction of Americana. I'd really like to buy some shorebirds and duck decoys, but I don't know anything about them or what prices they go for. Do you know anyone in this area who could advise me?"

"Sure," he said. "There's a dealer in Americana I know, Peter Tillou."

I called Tillou, who agreed to come up and

advise me. I went to the viewing at the auction house and picked out some shorebirds and decoy ducks that I particularly liked and then met Peter for lunch on the day of the sale.

"So you know Billy Pearson," I said by way of breaking the ice.

"Yes, I know Billy, all right," he replied. "He's quite a character, but he has a great eye for a painting."

"He's a good salesman, too," I said. "I bought a Sheldon Peck with him a few months ago. It was horrible, but Billy sold that piece of junk to some asshole in Connecticut for twenty-six thousand dollars."

Peter burst out laughing. "I know," he said. "I'm the asshole who bought it." He had the last laugh because he later sold it for over $600,000, and it is featured in all the books on American folk painting. It is considered the greatest folk painting of a grandmother and granddaughter ever painted, but I still think it's ugly.

Once that little misunderstanding had been cleared up, we got down to business. I told him about the lots I was interested in, and he said, "Listen, I do this all the time. Let me do the bidding for you. Tell me the price you're willing to go to and then leave it to me because if you do it, you may get caught up in it, go crazy, and find you've bid about five times as much as you wanted to pay."

It sounded like good advice to me. When we got to the auction house, I pointed out the lots I liked, including a pair of pintail ducks by the Ward brothers, Steve and Lemuel, that I was especially keen on.

"How much do you want to pay for them?" Peter said.

"I have no idea," I said. "I don't know how much these things go for."

"Well, I wouldn't go above six thousand dollars for the pair, but as I said, I do this for a living, so let me do the bidding."

We bought a few other lots for a few hundred dollars apiece, but when the Ward brothers lot came up, there was a buzz of anticipation around the room. "See," Peter said. "You have a good eye. They're good, all right. Now leave it to me."

The bidding started at $2,000, went to $4,000, and then Peter bid $6,000. The next bid was $8,000, and I was just sitting back thinking, *Oh, well . . . ,* when I heard Peter bid $10,000. He kept bidding and bidding — ignoring my increasingly frantic attempts to get his attention — all the way up to $29,000, the price at which they were knocked down to him and therefore to me.

"What the hell were you doing?" I asked
when I had recovered the power of speech.
"I thought we had a ceiling of six thousand
dollars. What was all this bullshit about
'I know what I'm doing' and 'Leave it to
me'?"

"Well, Andy," he said, "sometimes you just
have to step up and take a shot."

I could have told him to keep them himself at that cost, but I still really liked those
ducks, so I shrugged and paid the price.
They turned out not to be a bad buy. When
I sold them a few years later, they fetched
more than twice that, and I still have another pair of ducks that I bought at that sale.
Peter and I stayed in touch with each other
and have become very good friends.

Not all my purchases worked out quite so
well. I bought a lot of things from Billy and
other dealers over the years, but one lot of
six Navaho blankets that Billy sold me were
spectacularly good. "You've got to see these,"
he told me. "I've never seen such beautiful
blankets in such incredible condition. They
could have been made yesterday."

"And were they?" I asked.

"Hell, no. These are the real deal."

When he showed them to me, I had to
agree. They were fabulous: six superb blankets from the late nineteenth century and

in absolutely pristine condition. I couldn't believe it. I bought them all, but a week later Billy came back to the house and said, "You know what, Andy? I have a feeling these blankets might have been stolen from the Los Angeles County Museum. It's been bothering me because I had the feeling I'd seen these somewhere before." Billy remembered everything he ever saw. "I think these are ones I once saw at the museum."

I'm not sure he was acting out of the highest of moral principles. He just might not have wanted all the problems he would get from the police, not to mention the grief I'd give him, but he called the museum and got through to the curator in that department. "I have reason to believe," he said, "that some blankets which have come into my possession were stolen from your collection."

"You're mistaken," the curator said. "There are no blankets missing from our collections."

"Are you sure?"

"Of course I'm sure. I'm the curator." The conversation ended rather abruptly.

The more Billy thought about it, the more convinced he became that they had come from the museum, so he called back a couple of days later. The curator brushed him off again, but Billy called him right back and practically begged him to go into the museum storage room and check. Grudgingly, the curator agreed and within half an hour he called back. "You were right. We've been robbed!"

They turned out to have been part of the collection given to the museum by Fred Harvey, who had made a fortune in the nineteenth century by setting up restaurants alongside the new railroads and selling food to the hungry men building them. He hired good-looking women to serve in them — the *Harvey Girls* sound track I'd sung on in the 1940s was inspired by them — and some of them made a little extra money on the side by selling the railroad workers a lot more than food. Harvey used some of his money to start a collection of American Indian blankets, and since many of the railroads passed through American Indian lands, there were plenty of opportunities to buy them.

In later life he donated them to the museum, and someone had now stolen some of them. They had clearly passed through several pairs of hands before Billy bought them. I don't think they ever traced the original thief, but obviously we had to give them back and swallow the loss of the money.

Years later my own collection of American Indian blankets was being shown in a big show at the St. Louis Art Museum. After Monet, it was the most successful exhibit they ever put on there. While it was running, I received a call from a former curator at the Los Angeles County Museum. "I've just been to see your exhibit in St. Louis," she said, "and I think two of the blankets there came from the museum's collection."

"I don't think so," I replied, "because I gave back the six blankets I'd bought that turned out to be stolen."

"Well, I think you still have a few more."

She was right, and once again I had to give them back — just one of the pitfalls of collecting.

If the 1960s had brought me some of the happiest and most successful times of my life — a wife and three beautiful children, a smash television series, sell-out concerts around the world, and a series of gold and platinum albums — they ended for me in sadness, first with Bobby Kennedy's death and then when Claudine and I began to drift apart. It was such a subtle process that I don't think either of us realized it at first. We had come to have different circles of friends and different interests, and if I had been less preoccupied with my career, I might have seen the warning signs and done something about them.

I was still working constantly, either in the television studios or recording, and in every gap between shows and during the summer break I was on the road touring, with all the pressures, tensions, and temptations that entails. I had worked so hard to get where I was in my career, and now that the rewards were there, I wanted to seize them with both hands, but in doing so I had been neglecting my family and especially Claudine. Even when I did manage to be at home, I didn't give her the attention I should have, and there was a price to pay for that.

When we went to parties at friends' houses, Claudine would often disappear, and I'd find her later just walking on the beach on her own. That should have made me aware that there was a problem we needed to solve, but I preferred to ignore it and hope that it would go away. It didn't.

When I got home early one evening, after being away on tour for two weeks, Claudine was waiting for me in the kitchen. Bobby was asleep upstairs, and the other two kids were playing on the beach with Lula. I was pouring us glasses of wine when Claudine said, "Andy, I need to talk to you." Something in her voice told me this was not going to be a normal conversation, and there was a hollow feeling inside me as I turned to face her.

"I can't go on living like this, Andy," she said. "The kids and I hardly ever see you, and when we do, you're preoccupied or on the phone with your manager or the studios. And . . ." She paused for a moment. "And things aren't the same between us."

I started to argue with that, but she held up her hand. "You know it's true."

I knew that the thrill I used to get when I saw her walking toward me had faded and that the private, intimate looks we used to exchange, as all lovers do, were less frequent, but until that moment I had not realized how far down that path we had traveled. Now one thing was all too clear: Claudine had fallen out of love with me.

We talked far into the night, more than we had done in years, and the bitter irony of that did not escape me. We were both often in tears. We knew what we were losing, or what we had already lost, but we couldn't turn back the clock and undo what had already been done. I think it broke both our hearts, but in the end we agreed that we should split up.

My marriage was over, and I had to live with the knowledge that I bore the full responsibility for that. The decision made, there seemed no point in delaying it any longer. I packed a bag and moved out. By now the kids were all in bed and asleep. I went into each of their rooms, kissed them, and whispered, "I love you." Bobby slept peacefully on, Christian just stirred and muttered something in his sleep, but Noelle, still half-asleep, slipped her warm little arm around my neck and held me tight for a moment. I was crying as I closed the bedroom door and walked downstairs. I didn't say a final good-bye to Claudine — I'd be seeing her every time I came to see the kids — but instead said, "I'm sorry."

"I'm sorry, too, Andy," she replied. She was still standing in the doorway, staring after me as I drove out of the driveway. I went back to the little house on Bobolink, which may not have been the wisest move. It had been the first home we shared and was full of now-painful memories.

For weeks after that I couldn't sleep and lay awake night after night, going over and over the events that led to the breakup, torturing myself over every incident, major and minor, that had led us to this point. Often I gave up the struggle to sleep, got up at two or three in the morning, and paced through the empty house or walked for miles through the deserted streets. We were still friends and still saw each other because of the kids, but the spark, the love, had gone.

It is a sad fact, I think, and probably true for a lot of men, that we learn from the mistakes we made in our first marriages, which makes us better husbands the second time around, but that must be doubly wounding to our first wives, who had to bear the brunt of the inattentiveness, selfishness, and career obsession that eventually drove us apart.

At the same time that Claudine and I were splitting up, I also parted company with my manager, Alan Bernard. He was great in some ways and was a tough negotiator, but there were drawbacks. He wasn't a very likable guy and tended to rub some important people the wrong way. When NBC, which was airing my television series, contacted him to arrange for me to sing at its annual convention, he asked, "How much are you paying?"

"We're not paying anybody, but we'll give Andy a top-of-the-line television."

"Make that two," said Alan, "one for Andy and one for me." He irritated a lot of people, and I was getting a bad reputation as "a difficult performer" because of him. He knew he had the power, so he just stuck it to people, but that sort of thing can come back to bite you in the ass. I was loyal to him much longer than I should have been or than was good for my career. Friends had told me to get rid of him more than once, but I stuck with him . . . and then he got into cocaine.

He would have been the last person on earth who I'd have thought would let anything get between him and business, but he did. The situation got so bad that he simply couldn't function, and I had to let him go. He cleaned himself up — or said he had — and tried to get work with other organizations, but he had made enemies in a lot of them, and they turned their backs on him. Finally, Pierre Cossette said, "Okay, Alan, if you really aren't using now, I'll give you a job. You can work in this office, and we'll see what happens." Within a week Pierre found Alan snorting coke off his desk. He had to fire him, and Alan's downward spiral never stopped. He was hospitalized and eventually died from his drug abuse.

I had a number of agents and managers over the years, but the most impressive of all — both as an agent and as a man — was Jerry Perenchio. I've known him for more than fifty years, and he remains my favorite friend long after he ceased to be my agent and moved on to much bigger and better things. He was an agent when I first met him, and he took over my little "railroad "carriage" apartment near Central Park when I moved to California.

We became close after he moved to California, and over the years we spent a lot of time together. He started his show business career at UCLA, where he booked bands for concerts and private parties. After he graduated, he joined the Air Force and became a flight instructor, but in 1958 he was hired by Lew Wasserman's Music Corporation of America as an agent. He was in the agency business for years; by the late 1960s, he owned one of Hollywood's top talent agencies, with such headliners as Glen Campbell, the Righteous Brothers, Sergio Mendez, Richard Burton, and Elizabeth Taylor. He was also my agent. He was an entrepreneur and deal maker as well; one of the deals he made was to acquire the rights to promote the first Muhammad Ali–Joe Frazier fight.

Jerry also masterminded the tennis match between Billie Jean King and Bobby Riggs on September 18, 1973. King was a great women's tennis champion and Bobby, who was an out-and-out male chauvinist, had been a world champion himself. At first Jerry struggled to sell the television rights to the networks, but then he came up with the brilliant idea of billing the match as "The Battle of the Sexes." It was no longer just a tennis match; it became a cultural milestone and was the talk of the country. Then the networks all started bidding against each other to get the TV rights. As a curtain raiser to the big match, Jerry asked Claudine and me to play a celebrity mixed doubles set against Merv Griffin and Sandra Giles — we killed them!

Starting from that tiny $130-a-month apartment in New York City, Jerry made himself into a billionaire. It was a pleasure to watch him build this empire because he was such a gifted entrepreneur and deal maker.

I knew Jerry during his first two marriages, but then he finally married Margie, a terrific person who has a will and mind of her own. She is a very talented painter, a great golfer, has her own set of male friends, and plays golf with them almost every day at the Bel-Air Country Club. She is a perfect hostess for Jerry, and they share many friends and entertain lavishly in their gorgeous château-like mansion, the Arnold Kirkeby house in Los Angeles, where *The Beverly Hillbillies* was filmed and where Kay Thompson and the Williams Brothers first auditioned their act. He has completely remodeled the house and filled it with fantastic art, and he has seventeen acres of beautiful gardens in Bel Air that are manicured by a team of thirteen full-time gardeners.

Jerry asked me if I would sing at his wedding ceremony at the house, and I sang "Ave Maria" from the balcony on the second floor, overlooking the gardens, where he had a symphony orchestra to accompany me. He had eighteen violinists playing on the stairway leading from the second floor to the lobby of the first floor. Many of the older violinists were bald and normally wore toupees, but Jerry hated violinists who had hairpieces that looked as if they were put on backward. He issued strict instructions that none of the violinists could wear them. So there were many bald-headed violinists playing on the stairway.

I was often at Jerry and Margie's beach house in Malibu, and we played tennis almost every weekend. Margie's father had been a tennis pro at one time, and until she took up golf, she was a really top-notch tennis player. Pavarotti often stayed in their guesthouse at the beach, and we played tennis a couple of times with him. For obvious reasons it wasn't easy to pass him at the net, and for such a big man, he was also amazingly fast on his feet. Pavarotti also sang "Moon River" to me one afternoon, very softly in a pop singer kind of way, and it was absolutely beautiful. I've always hated hearing opera singers doing pop songs, but he was great.

Despite all the upheavals I had been experiencing in my personal and business lives, the show had to go on. I was about to make a tour of Europe, performing in concert halls with a full orchestra. I had hired an English composer and arranger, Ken Thorne, to work with me, orchestrating some of the arrangements I'd previously been using with my regular band. My big mistake was to introduce him to Billy Pearson. We were going to be staying in San Francisco for a few days. I was recently divorced. Ken was married, but his wife was back in England. When Billy said with characteristic if occasionally misplaced generosity, "Tell you what, Ken. I'm going to find great dates for you and Andy," I didn't hear any objections from Ken. The woman Billy found for him was a young, very beautiful Japanese American named Linda. They obviously got along because I didn't see much of Ken for the next few days, and when I did, he didn't look as if he was getting much sleep.

He was due to fly up to Lake Tahoe with me, where I had a week-long booking at Harrah's; the idea was that he could work on the orchestral arrangements during the day.

Ken clearly had something on his mind, however, and eventually said, "Andy, would you mind terribly if Linda came up to Lake Tahoe with me?"

"Well, I don't know, Ken," I replied. "We're supposed to be working, remember. But I guess as long as you get the arrangements done . . ."

"Oh, don't worry about that, Andy. I'll get them done."

So Linda flew up with us. I didn't see much of her while we were there, but, come to think of it, I again didn't see much of Ken, either, and when I did, the only things he had apparently been working on were the black shadows under his eyes, which were now even deeper and darker.

I next had a booking in Chicago. Once more the plan was for Ken to accompany me, and once more he took me aside before we headed for the airport. "Andy, I wonder if you'd mind if Linda came with me again."

"But Ken, you've been here for three weeks, and you haven't written a note yet. When are you going to get those orchestrations done?"

"Don't worry, Andy. I swear I'll get them done in Chicago."

He didn't, of course, but at least he made a start. We then flew on to New Jersey, the last

386

stop before we headed for Europe and the opening show of the tour. Yet again Linda accompanied us, but this time Ken at least did enough work to complete the orchestrations.

The first stop in Europe was to be London, and once more Ken approached me to ask if Linda could come with him. "For God's sake, Ken," I said. "You're a married man. Your wife lives in London."

"I know, I know," he responded, "but Linda will meet us in Munich after London. Don't worry, I'll handle everything. It'll all be fine."

If that was so, I'd have hated to be there if it *hadn't* all been fine because as we came out into the arrivals hall at Heathrow, the first person we saw was Ken's wife, who had come to meet him. Ken immediately blurted out everything to her. When he said, "I've fallen in love with a Japanese girl, and I want a divorce," the look in his wife's eyes was one of the most terrifying things I've ever seen. I thought she was going to kill him right then and there. There must have been a more sensitive way to break such news.

And when we played London's Royal Albert Hall, I was still afraid that his wife would take her revenge by shooting him dead while he was onstage conducting the orchestra. I didn't want to be in the way if that happened, so for that show I worked well over to one side of the stage, a safe distance from Ken. In any event, both of us survived unscathed. Ken eventually divorced his wife and married Linda, and they're still together, living in Los Angeles with three beautiful daughters, and they are still in love after thirty-seven years.

As well as doing the orchestrations Ken was also conducting the large orchestra at each concert. It was made up of British musicians supplemented by my American rhythm section of piano, bass, and drums. The drummer, Larry Brown, always felt that it was his job to "drive" the band. Many of the British musicians normally played in symphony orchestras, which do not have rhythm drummers like pop and rock bands do. Larry's drum setup — snares, bass, and crash cymbals — was center stage, directly behind the string section, and from the very first concert Larry's high-energy drumming irritated the string players. His "driving the band" was driving them crazy.

Half a dozen dates into the tour we were playing in Newcastle-upon-Tyne. Midway through the concert, Larry got so carried away during an upbeat song that his drumsticks flew out of his hands. They landed in the string section, one hitting a viola player on the head and the other bouncing off a cello. The viola player stopped playing, picked up the drumstick, and hurled it back at Larry, hitting him on the ear and provoking fresh volleys of drumsticks back and forth between Larry and the string section.

Ken stared at this in disbelief but somehow managed to keep the rest of the orchestra playing while I, facing the audience with my back to the feuding musicians, just kept on singing, completely unaware of the turmoil behind me. When the audience began to laugh at the mayhem in the orchestra, my first reaction, not knowing what was going on, was to check if my fly was unzipped.

Ken continued to wave his baton, the remainder of the orchestra played on, and the drumstick throwing died down before the end of the song, although tempers were high throughout the remainder of the show. The entire British contingent of musicians was ready to attack Larry as soon as the audience left the concert hall.

After taking my bows, I returned to my dressing room, still unaware of what had been going on behind me and puzzling over what had made the audience laugh halfway through a song. Back onstage Ken rapped his baton on his music stand to get the orchestra's attention and then ordered all the musicians to remain in their seats until the house had been cleared, like a class of naughty children made to stay late after school. He said to them, "I have never seen such unprofessional behavior in my entire career. I'm embarrassed. You were appallingly disrespectful to the audience and to an artist who is a guest in this country." He turned on his heel and strode into the wings, leaving them all still sitting there. Although Larry was known behind his back as "Drumsticks" for the rest of the tour, there were no further outbreaks of hostilities between him and the British musicians.

During that tour I was also booked to perform at an amusement park, Belle Vue, in Manchester. The driver who picked us up at the train station said, "Can I give you some advice, Mr. Williams? The place you're playing tonight is where we have a small circus in the summer. There's an elephant who does tricks in it, and everyone loves the elephant. Well, sir, Shirley Bassey gave a concert in the tent last weekend, and when she finished her first song, she sniffed the air, wrinkled her nose, and said, 'It smells like elephants in here.' The audience was so offended that they booed her."

"Thanks for the warning," I said.

That night after singing my first number, I wrinkled my nose and said, "It smells like Shirley Bassey in here." The audience went wild. I owe Shirley a thank-you for an opening line that really bonded me with the audience.

While we were in Manchester, I did an interview on a radio station. When we arrived, the receptionist asked me if she could have an autograph for her mother. "You know, you saved her life," she said.

"Really?" I asked.

"Yes, you really did. Last December she was in hospital in a coma for two weeks. She loved your music, so we played your *Greatest Hits* album for her over and over, day after day. After two weeks in a coma, she at last opened her eyes. The first words out of her mouth were 'Will you turn that damned thing off! I'm sick of it!'" I guess you can get too much of a good thing.

Billy Pearson flew in to join me while I was in England. We had been traveling the world together for years — he accompanied me on many of my overseas tours — and I picked up the tab for everything even though with Billy it was always Dom Perignon, not sparkling wine. I never begrudged a penny of it because I never laughed so much or enjoyed life so much as when Billy was around. If he used me, I also used him. I learned a huge amount about art and antiquities from him, and I also learned a lot about how to relax and enjoy myself. There was almost nothing he wouldn't do, no risks he wouldn't take. It made for an edge-of-the-seat ride whenever you were in his company, but life was certainly never dull.

When we went to one of the best restaurants in London for dinner after my show, he had all the diners abandoning their tables and lining up to play "shuffleboard," tossing their rolls toward the wall. "Closest to the wall wins a bottle of Dom Perignon," he said, "but if it hits the wall, you're out." While the maitre d' and waiters gave us their iciest stares, captains of industry, lords, and ladies were taking turns tossing rolls like kids pitching pebbles into a pond.

Peter Sellers was there that night with a party of eight, and I invited them back to the house we were renting for a drink. Billy had arranged our wine supplies as soon as we reached London. The people whose house we were renting were obviously very keen on glass models of animals because every shelf and windowsill was full of them. When Peter Sellers and his friends arrived, we started arranging these models into curious and often downright lewd tableaux. Eventually, after Peter and his friends left, we stumbled off to bed. When I heard the housekeeper, Mrs. Ludbrook, a gray-haired and very respectable Englishwoman, arrive the next morning, I groaned aloud at the thought of her seeing the scenario we had forgotten to dismantle. Nothing was said, however, and when we finally went downstairs, order had been restored and all the animals were back in their places.

The next night, after drinking too much wine, Billy and I continued our little artistic game of arranging these glass animals into ever more bizarre couplings before stumbling off to bed, and Mrs. Ludbrook would replace them the next morning. On the third night Billy and I excelled ourselves, if that's really the word, with the most bizarre and pornographic tableau involving virtually every animal in the entire glass menagerie.

Once more we stumbled off to bed, and once more I woke with a pounding head, as I heard Mrs. Ludbrook's key in the lock. I froze when I heard her footsteps cross the hall and then stop in the doorway to the living room, where our latest creation was prominently displayed in the middle of the table. I got out of bed, croaking, "Mrs. Ludbrook? Mrs. Ludbrook?"

There was a long silence. "Oh, Mr. Williams," she said, "I think this is the best one you've ever done." I gave her a very generous tip at the end of our stay.

One of the dates on that tour was in Norway, and we stayed at a hotel in Oslo. I had a day off between shows, so Vic Lewis, the agent who had set up the European tour, told me he had arranged for us and three other people to see a show. Thinking no more about it, we jumped into the limousine and set off for the venue. It was an unusual one, not in a theater but in a large private house. When we got inside, we found a couple of dozen chairs arranged in four rows facing the grand sweeping staircase.

"Just what sort of show is this?" I said to Vic.

"It's a live sex show. Trust me, you'll love it."

Always up for whatever new experiences life could offer him, Billy was already taking his seat in the front row, but whatever curiosity I felt was tempered by the feeling that if the press ever found out about this, Andy Williams's career as a family entertainer would be over in ten seconds flat. So I wasn't exactly thrilled when I saw that the six seats in the front row were all labeled "Reserved for Mr. Williams." Even more alarming, among the audience were a couple from Iowa and four or five other Americans. I didn't know any of them, and they gave no sign of recognizing me, but it added to my feeling of unease. That increased even more when some music started playing: my record of the theme from *Love Story*.

A naked couple came down the stairs and then proceeded to have sex right in front of us. After the climax — in every sense — of the act, I got to my feet and was trying to hurry Vic and Billy out the door when a voice came over the loudspeaker asking in a Norwegian accent, "How'dja like dat, Andy?"

I bolted for the exit without even glancing in the direction of the couple from Iowa. I checked the tabloid newspapers with trepidation for a few weeks after that, but nothing ever appeared, and my secret has remained safe until now.

Being on tour was a way of hiding from my problems for a while, but they were all still waiting for me when I finally returned home. Whether because of the parting from Claudine or for other, less tangible reasons, my life was now in complete turmoil. I couldn't figure anything out: Why had I gotten a divorce? Why wasn't I happier with my life? Why wasn't I feeling well physically?

I decided to get a full examination of my physical and mental condition at the Scripps Clinic near San Diego. The last person I saw there was the psychiatrist.

Lying on the black leather couch in the psychiatrist's book-lined consulting room while he sat behind me in a straight-backed chair with a notebook on his knee was a truly surreal moment. It was such a clichéd scene — I'd seen it on movies and TV a hundred times — that it was all I could do not to laugh, even though my reason for being there was entirely serious.

After I told him my life story, he said, "You might be helped by taking LSD treatments. You could see a shrink for years trying to find out why you're not happy, but with LSD you might do that in just a few sessions." LSD (lysergic dyethylamide) was then seen as something of a miracle drug, and doubts about it were only just beginning to surface.

I talked to Claudine and persuaded her to give LSD a try with me. I wonder now if I had really accepted that we'd split up for good or whether I still clung to the hope that somehow it might be all right again. I had friends who had split up with their wives but kept finding excuses to see them, only prolonging the agony, and perhaps I was doing the same thing. Whatever the reasons, our first session was all set up when the psychiatrist called and said, "I'm sorry. We can't do these treatments anymore." Timothy Leary's "turn on, tune in, drop out" rhetoric was drawing a lot of unfavorable press and causing such problems for the Scripps Clinic that they had decided to cease LSD treatments. Having told me all this, the psychiatrist paused for a few seconds and then said, "However, if you're still interested, I do know a place in Hollywood, Canada, where it's still allowed."

Claudine decided that if it wasn't at Scripps, she didn't want to do it, but having gone this far, I felt I had nothing to lose, so I went ahead and flew up to Canada alone. I stayed for a couple of weeks at the clinic while a doctor named Ross MacLean administered LSD and mescaline to me in different doses and supervised my "trips." They took place in an antiseptic-looking room, watched over by Dr. MacLean and his assistants. The LSD was in liquid form — dripped onto a sugar cube or a tiny square of blotting paper — and was odorless, colorless, and tasteless. The mescaline was solid and had a bitter, musty taste; the first time I took it, I threw up.

For my first LSD experience I waited for minutes on end, but nothing seemed to be happening. "I don't think it's working," I said, but Dr. MacLean just smiled and said, "Give it time." Then things did start to happen: Shapes began shifting and changing, colors and sounds intensified. I became absorbed in one object or sensation, totally unaware of anything else around me, but then I'd snap back to reality, spiraling in and out of awareness of my surroundings. I fought it at first, feeling a wave of panic at the loss of self-control, but as the drug really took hold, I relaxed and was completely engulfed. When, hours later, I began to come down again, I could not have told you if minutes, hours, or even days had passed.

Dr. MacLean gave me different visual stimuli and played different kinds of music, from very soft and sensual sounds to marching bands, and noted the reactions. I experienced the things that most people did when taking psychedelic drugs: the intensely heightened senses, the beauty of colors and sounds, the contrasting phases of feeling, from being a lord of the cosmos one moment to becoming totally focused on some microscopic detail the next — a colored thread fluttering in the breeze, dust motes hanging in the air.

LSD gave me some powerful feelings of euphoria — some sex-related — but also feelings of fear and despair. During one session

I was even born again, not in the evangelical sense but in believing I was experiencing the very painful physical sensations of birth.

I'm not sure if the LSD experience ultimately did me any real good overall, but one thing certainly did come out of my stay at the clinic: It was probably the first time in many years that I had taken even a few days away from my career. In between the LSD sessions in Canada I had time to reflect on the direction my life had been taking and to examine my priorities. I finally came to realize that my children and my relationship with my family were the things that really counted; nothing else was that important.

Sadly, that realization had come too late to save my marriage to Claudine; it was already fractured beyond repair. That had been entirely my fault, and I had to face up to life without her. Although Claudine and I had separated, there was no personal animosity between us, just sadness that our relationship had come to this. Even after we divorced, we remained on good terms. It was such an amicable separation that we used the same lawyer to represent both of us. I made a financial settlement that would support her and the kids, and she kept our beach-front house in Malibu. We also kept doing the Christmas shows together. We had done them for so many years, we still got on well, and the ties remained so strong that we just couldn't stop getting together for Christmas; it was a natural part of our lives.

With Claudine's having kept the house at Malibu, I was still living on Bobolink, and despite what had happened, I was determined to remain a good friend to Claudine, if she ever needed me, and be a good father to our children. Even when I was at my busiest, I found ways to spend time with them, and it was really important to me that I play an active part in their lives. I always told them, "If I'm not with you guys for a while, I still want to know what you're doing, and I want you to tell me what you're thinking and feeling." I tried to fit family life around my work as much as possible, and sometimes I would take the children on tour with me so they got to travel and see different places around the world — but they also had to deal with the drawbacks of being the children of a celebrity. Noelle once told me, "I loved being with you, Papa, and always wanted to be with you; the only problem was that everybody else in the world did, too."

In one way the breakup of our marriage may have been less traumatic for our children than for other kids whose parents were separating because I was away on tour so often that they were already pretty much living with Claudine and seeing me only on weekends and holidays, an arrangement that continued in much the same way after we split up. Claudine didn't criticize me in front of the children or try to influence them against me, nor did I act in that way when the kids were with me. Life went on for them as normally as we could make it.

Years later my son Bobby admitted to me that for years he hadn't even realized that Claudine and I were divorced. In my less self-aware moments, I might almost have taken that as a compliment, but what it really revealed was how distant and inattentive I must already have been in the years before we separated and how much love and time Claudine had devoted — with only the most minimal help from me — to making our children's home life a loving, happy, and normal one.

It has been said that the only inscription you never see in a graveyard is "Wish I'd spent more time at the office," and my greatest regret is that I didn't spend more time with my children when they were young. Although, once again, Claudine must take the lion's share of the credit. One of the things of which I'm most proud is that despite growing up with every material advantage, my children haven't become spoiled rich kids, celebrity fodder for the pages of trashy magazines. They are all very different from one another, have done well as a result of their own efforts, and remain grounded, normal, everyday people.

Noelle married her childhood sweetheart, Keii Johnston, and they settled down in L.A., where she chose to devote herself to her family and raised three children, RJ, Cody, and Keri. Christian fell in love with Costa Rica after vacationing there, and he now lives there with his wife, Cassie, and their children, Sarah and Rachelle. They are very happy, and he is still the same laid-back character he was as a child. He makes his living from teak plantations and once said to me, "You know what the great thing about teak planting is, Dad? Once you've planted the trees, you just lay on the beach for the next twenty years and watch them grow!" He is also in land development.

From the time he was just a little boy, Bobby always wanted to be in the army. He enlisted when he was just eighteen and over time became a Green Beret, a member of the Special Forces, which he served with great distinction. He was assigned to Haiti in 1994 when the United States intervened to remove a brutal dictatorship. He remained there for several months, until he became disgusted with the way we were handling the intervention and disenchanted with the strategy and tactics we were following. He subsequently resigned from the military and built a new career. He is now a very successful producer of television documentaries and recently married a beautiful Sri Lankan–American girl named Mystica.

14

By 1969, the year in which Claudine and I split up, *The Andy Williams Show* had been running for seven years. We felt it was showing its age a little, so we decided to revamp it, making it a different kind of program. It had been scheduled to air earlier in the evening, at a time when children were watching TV, and my aim was to make a series that my own kids would enjoy. If they liked it, then so might other children. We designed a special cartoon-like set using bright primary colors. My clothes were almost as vivid as the set, and we used more comedy along with more contemporary music.

It became quite an off-the-wall show and very popular, but I had to accept the fact that as far as kids were concerned, I was no longer the star of the show. We had a talking bear who was obsessed with cookies. He would saunter down the hallway and say, "Hi there, Andy. Hi there, snappy dresser, old buddy, old pal. I wonder if you could spare a cookie."

I'd scream, "No. You are not getting any cookies from me — not now, not *ever! Never!*" He would always fall over backward — *bam!* — on the ground. Kids loved it. We received literally thousands of letters every week, and not all of them from children; adults also found the routines funny.

The bear came about one day when the writers and I were sitting in my office in L.A. trying to decide what we could do with our guest star that week, Flip Wilson. Flip was a very funny up-and-coming young black comedian who was gaining in popularity with viewers because of his guest appearances on various television shows. While we were trying to come up with an idea for a spot for Flip, a man walked into the office dressed like a big rock, moving in a very slow and ponderous way. We didn't know who this man was. It turned out he was a stuntman named Janos Prohaska looking for a job as one of the weird and wonderful menagerie of background characters we already had in the show, which included a walking suitcase and a large bumblebee. He then left the room and returned as a big black bear. This gave one of the writers a great idea for a sketch for Flip. Civil rights legislation had made it illegal for landlords to refuse to rent rooms to African Americans, and racist landlords had to find different excuses when a prospective black tenant turned up on their doorstep wanting a room. So we had Flip knocking on a succession of doors that had signs advertising rooms to let. At each one the landlord would do a double take when he saw Flip, scratch his head, and then catch sight of the bear and say, "Sorry, no pets allowed," and slam the door in Flip's face. The sketch was funny and the bear became a permanent fixture on our show.

The new *Andy Williams Show* ran for two years, but in the spring of 1971, believing the variety format was dying, NBC network executives cancelled four shows, including mine. Although I continued to make occasional specials for television, my days of hosting a regular series were over. The show had been on the air for nine years, a long stretch in the fast-changing world of television. We had racked up a total of twenty-three Emmy nominations and three Emmy awards, but although the public still liked it, there was a general feeling that it had run its course and it was time for a change.

Although my own series had been cancelled, I soon had an offer to host a different type of program. It was the thirteenth year of the annual Grammy Awards show, but as bizarre as it now seems, it had never been televised. My old friend Pierre Cossette had recently bought the TV rights from the Record Academy and was attempting to bring the Grammys to television. The networks weren't convinced, however, that a music awards show would draw a sizable television audience, and he was rejected by three of them. His last hope was NBC, and he pestered the life out of the network executives about it until in the end they told him, "All right. If you can get Frank Sinatra, Dean Martin, or Andy Williams to host it, we'll put the show on. Otherwise, forget it."

Half an hour later Pierre was on my doorstep. He related the conversation with NBC to me and then said, "So forget about Sinatra and Dean Martin. You're my buddy, right?"

"I'm your buddy, Pierre," I said. "I know how much this means to you, but I'm not sure I want to do it."

He looked at me for a long moment and then said, "You've got to be kidding. You're crazy."

When I wanted time to think about it, he absolutely drove me nuts over the next couple of days. Every time the phone or the doorbell rang, it was Pierre. There was no escape, even on the golf course. I was playing a round at Bel-Air with another friend when Pierre rode up on his electric golf cart and started lobbying me again. "I'm not trying to persuade you, Andy. I'm absolutely begging you. You've got to save my life here. Please do the show."

Finally I cracked. "All right," I said. "I'll do your goddamn show. Now will you please leave me alone for five minutes?"

Despite my initial reluctance, once Pierre had won me over, I could see the possibilities. The movie business had the Oscars, television had the Emmys, and the recording industry really needed a televised show of its own. The first one aired on NBC on March 16, 1971, and, helped by the presence of stars such as John Lennon and Paul Simon, it was a big ratings success. I went on to host the Grammys for the next seven years.

John Lennon didn't typically do television, but he agreed to this appearance; it may have been because it took his fancy or because he was returning a favor I'd done him a couple of years earlier. The Nixon administration had attempted to deport him, and I spoke up on his behalf. It seemed to me the grossest hypocrisy to attempt to deport a great musician and a man who at least had been honest about his own past drug use, when cocaine and grass were so widespread in the American music, movie, and entertainment communities that it was almost impossible to go to a showbiz party without being offered drugs or seeing them being taken. I was glad when the public outcry forced the administration to backpedal and allow John to remain in the United States.

Whatever his reasons, he enjoyed himself, and afterward at the Grammy party we shared a table with David Bowie and David Essex. We had a great evening, and at one point, like a pair of kids, John and I were even blowing bubbles together using one of those plastic hoops. However, I was less comfortable with David Bowie, who was in his Ziggy Stardust period at the time, heavily made up and dressed in glittery androgynous clothes.

John was wisecracking a lot, and some of his comments, especially about Paul McCartney, were quite barbed. The *Imagine* album, including the track "How Do You Sleep?" that was a public rebuke to Paul, was released later that year. But John also showed glimpses of a much gentler, more vulnerable soul, and I liked him immensely. The next day I received a hand-delivered letter from him.

March 9 or 10? 1975

Dear andy,

I enjoyed meeting you at Discogrammy, we both did. Hope you got home OK. A couple of as got to talking about you the next day and we ended up thinking what a great job you would do on my song Bless You. So i thought, what the hell, i'll tell you! i've never written a letter like this before, i'm worried in case i come off like some kind of 'promo' man. anyway i've done it now, all the best to you,

love John.
p.s the typings mine all mine!

I still have the letter framed in my office. I did listen to the song John was suggesting, but to be honest, I didn't really think it was right for me. Feeling rather like the man at Decca Records who turned down the Beatles, I never took John up on his suggestion.

After doing the Grammys show together, Pierre Cossette and I also became fifty-fifty partners in a series of television specials, but while Pierre was always happy to pay top dollar for things that would improve the quality of the show, he was much less enthusiastic about spending money — half of which was his — on anything he regarded as unessential. This could have unfortunate consequences. When we were filming the special *Easter in Rome,* Pierre refused to pay the customary bribes and sweeteners to the Italian officials and fixers who appeared, as if by magic, as soon as we hit town. "It's a waste of money," he said. "We don't need those guys. It's not as if they're the Mafia or anything."

"Pierre," I said, "this is the country that invented the Mafia." Late the following night, as we and our bleary-eyed and exhausted crew were trying to complete a nighttime shoot by the Trevi Fountain, I was halfway through "Three Coins in the Fountain" when, without warning, all our lights went out and the water in the fountain was turned off. One of the officials and fixers we didn't need had pulled the plug on us. To cure that little misunderstanding took several hours and twice as much money in bribes as Pierre had refused to pay the day before.

Another of his economies was to do without a trailer for me. When I complained, he said, "Look, it's your money, too." That meant I had to change clothes in the back of a small Fiat car, parked in Saint Peter's Square, while hordes of tourists were wandering past. Some of the crew had to hold up towels and anything else at hand to screen

411

the car from view while I struggled in and out of my trousers.

Another show, *Search for Santa Claus,* was filmed in Finnish Lapland, well above the Arctic Circle, at the place where all the letters addressed to "Santa Claus, The North Pole," end up. We were still shooting late one night, trying to wrap up a crucial sequence. Everything was going perfectly, and I was three-quarters of the way through my song when the director, Walter Miller, came bursting out of the control room, tearing off his headphones and turning the air blue. "Cut! Cut! Cut!" he yelled. "Which idiot" — although that's not the word he used — "is snoring? It's all over the goddamn sound track." A search revealed that the culprit was Pierre, stretched out on a bench, fast asleep, and snoring louder than a jumbo jet. Despite these little mishaps, we had a ball in Rome, Lapland, and everywhere else we went. We were being given an all-expenses-paid tour of some of the great sights of the world, such as the Colosseum, the Trevi Fountain, and the Spanish Steps in Rome, and the awe-inspiring majesty of the Northern Lights in Lapland. I stayed up one entire night watching those astonishing, shimmering veils of light sweeping across the heavens above me. I was well aware of how privileged and lucky

I was, and it was only in the silence of my hotel room, struggling for sleep, that a small voice inside me reminded me how much more wonderful these experiences would have been if I were sharing them with my wife and children.

Pierre and I have remained very close friends over the years. The best word to describe him is "lovable," and when you're as lovable as he is, you can get away with murder. In all the time I have known him, I have done more shows, more work, and more favors more times and for less money for him than for anyone else I know. And any time I complained, I only got more love in return. One day I received a call from him about his tribute for multiple sclerosis. I knew from the way he said hello that I was in for an especially large dose of love.

My accountant had already warned me that if I got any more love from Pierre that year, he would have to put me in a lower tax bracket, so before Pierre had a chance to ask, I said, "I can't."

"But you have to," he insisted.

"But I did it for you last year."

"No," Pierre said. "Last year you did it for you — it was *your* tribute for MS."

"Well, who is MS paying tribute to this time?"

"Me."

"Then it's for you," I said.

"No, it's really for you. It's your chance to thank MS for last year."

"Well, next year when you thank MS for this year," I said, "will you be calling me to thank them for you?" And he gave me a big lovable laugh. Pierre is the only one who can do that when he knows that you know that you've been had. He then went into one of his long jokes to change the subject, and by the time I hung up, I vowed to myself that I would not give in the next time, but deep down I knew that I would.

Pierre also threw a fiftieth birthday party for me, which would have been great but for one small detail: I had been lying about my age for years. It had started when I was twenty-nine and had a few hit records selling to kids, and the PR person who was handling all the fan magazines said to me, "Kids won't buy records if they think you're thirty. That's really old to them. I suggest you stay twenty-nine."

Like a dummy, I took her advice, with the result that when I hit fifty, all my PR material was still claiming that I was only forty-seven. I decided to age three years overnight, and ever since then my real and professional ages have been the same.

Pierre booked the Bel-Air Country Club for the party and invited everyone who had ever been on my show and every celebrity he knew, and that was plenty. Harry James and his band played for the evening, friends flew in from all over the place — Ethel Kennedy came from Washington — and it was the biggest party I'd ever seen.

Pierre told me afterward that he had had only one problem. For reasons now lost in the mists of time, Pierre always calls me "Pussy," and all our friends know that is his nickname for me. When he was organizing the party, a new secretary had just started working for him, and before Pierre left for lunch one day, he handed her a list of things to do while he was at lunch.

When he returned, she was in tears. "What's the matter?" he asked.

"It's this list," she said. "I can't do it."

"What do you mean you can't do it?"

She passed him the tear-stained document. Every task had been crossed off except the one reading: *Get Pussy for party*. "I just can't do it," she wailed. "I don't know anyone like that. I don't even know any airline steward-esses."

Although I enjoyed doing occasional television specials with Pierre, they did not compensate for the loss of my own series.

Coupled with the breakup of my marriage, the cancellation of the show left a void in my life and contributed to my feelings of frustration and lack of direction that the LSD sessions did nothing to alleviate. I had been used to heading to the studio virtually daily, but now I had no particular place to go and no family to go home to at the end of the working day.

I tried to fill the hole by throwing myself even deeper into touring and performing, but I wasn't happy with what I was doing and still missed the TV show. I was lost for a while, rootless, restless, and often unhappy, feeling like an outsider everywhere I went, just drifting with no real destination in mind. I was successful, famous, and had enough money, but work was really all I knew. I didn't like to burden my friends with my personal problems — and, anyway, like a lot of men, I've never found it easy to open up to them about such personal things — but I was almost as unhappy as in those grim days when I was singing in near-deserted nightclubs and eating dog food to survive.

After Claudine and I separated, I dated a lot at first, avoiding any longer-term commitments, but in the summer of 1976 I met a girl in Hawaii, and there was enough electricity between us to power a small town.

Laurie Wright was twenty years old and on a baton-twirling scholarship at the University of Hawaii. I never even knew such things as baton-twirling scholarships existed. She herself didn't take it too seriously, but it put her through college, paying her bills and tuition fees. She was glorious-looking, but as we talked I discovered that she was also intelligent and funny, and had a great appetite for life; she was fun to be around. It was also the most intensely sensual relationship I'd ever had: I had a "hard-on in every pocket" for months.

A couple of days after we met, I had to fly back to Vegas, but I begged Laurie to come along. She hesitated and then agreed. We were on our final approach to McCarran Airport in Las Vegas when we realized something was wrong. We heard the roar of the engines as the pilot pulled the aircraft out of its descent and exchanged a few of those nervous smiles people do when they think they're about to die in an aircraft but don't want to lose face in front of a planeload of strangers by mentioning the fact. Then the pilot announced that we couldn't land because the landing gear wouldn't come down. "We're turning around and going back to L.A. because they have better equipment for planes that are in trouble."

He tried to sound reassuring but only succeeded in scaring us all to death. Those feelings intensified when the stewardesses came down the aisle holding the four corners of a blanket and told us all to drop our watches, glasses, and any false teeth into it.

By now Laurie was absolutely terrified and said out loud, "Dear God, if I come out of this alive, I will never drink or smoke again."

Jack Carter, a well-known Vegas comedian, was sitting across the aisle from us and heard what Laurie said. "To hell with that," he said. "If I end up alive, I'm going to drink like a fish, smoke like a chimney, and lay every girl I can get my hands on!"

Once more the landing gear did not appear to have come down, but after the pilot flew past the tower at LAX, the air traffic controllers told him that despite what the indicators in his cockpit were telling him, the landing gear appeared to be down and locked. As we came in, we saw a posse of firetrucks and ambulances flanking the runway, their lights flashing, and they roared off in hot pursuit as we swept in to touch down. The landing gear held, and we were safely down with no more than a bump and a few muffled prayers. Sorting out the jumble of teeth, glasses, and watches took quite a while, but everybody was so relieved to be on the ground in one piece that for once there were no complaints about the ensuing delays. Laurie quickly broke her pledge — we both had a stiff drink at the airport's bar — but from what I heard, Jack Carter stuck to his promise.

Laurie and I were in Las Vegas together for a couple of weeks, and then she accompanied me to my next concert in Washington, D.C.; by then I was ready to ask her to come back to Los Angeles and live with me. It was the start of a nine-year relationship.

When her twenty-first birthday came around, I suggested she give a little birthday luncheon at St. Germain, a really fine restaurant in Hollywood. That wasn't easy for her because all her friends were in her hometown of Oswego, New York, or in Hawaii, and she didn't know too many people around town. She ended up inviting an unusual assortment of people: a few friends of mine; Marsha Diamond (Neil's wife); my mother and some of her friends; my sister, Janey; and a few other people, most of whom didn't know one another.

Billy Pearson and his third wife, Myra, were staying with me at the time. I received a panic phone call from Myra, who had been added to the guest list for the lunch. "Andy, it's a complete bust," she said. "No one is talking to anybody. It's going to be a disaster. Andy, you and Billy have got to come here and turn this party around."

I remembered a chance meeting I once had with Jack Lemmon in the lobby of the Beverly Hills Hilton. He was carrying a pile of hatboxes, and I asked him what he was doing there. "It's my mother's birthday," Jack said, "and she's invited some friends of hers to lunch here at the hotel. I thought I'd surprise them with a little show." Jack put on one hat and was one character, and then he put on a different hat and was another character, just to liven up the party and make her laugh.

That memory gave me my inspiration, and when I told Billy what was happening — or not happening — at the luncheon and what I had in mind, it took us five minutes to get changed. Billy put on one of Myra's dresses, one of her wigs, and a pair of her high-heeled shoes (they had the same-size feet), but his mustache was a bit of a giveaway. I wore one of Laurie's Hawaiian muu-muus and borrowed Myra's long cigarette holder. Then we set off for the restaurant. As we were driving along, we passed a police car. Cops were used to unusual sights around town — West Hollywood was a gay mecca — but their facial expressions as we cruised past suggested that they had never seen anything quite like this before. I could imagine the dialogue: "Tell you what, bud. Those have got to be the two ugliest drag queens I've ever seen."

We managed to reach the restaurant without getting arrested and left the car with a smirking valet. The maitre d', a consummate professional, didn't even raise an eyebrow at our attire, as if fifty-year-old drag queens with hairy legs and no makeup were always popping in for lunch or a drink. We got him to steer us by a discreet route to a table near where Laurie and her guests were sitting in painful semi-silence and then sat back to await recognition. My mom was the first to spot us. There were many things she could have said when confronted for the first time with the sight of her youngest son dressed in women's clothes, waving a long cigarette holder around like a poor man's Noel Coward, and accompanied by another transvestite with a mustache, but she managed to surprise me: "Why, that's Andy," I heard her say. "Oh my word, I hope he hasn't started smoking again."

Our entrance broke the ice. Everybody started laughing, and suddenly the conversation started flowing like the wine. By the time they all headed home, the luncheon had turned out to be a fun time for all of them.

Later that evening I gave Laurie a dinner party at Le Bistro, a lovely restaurant in Beverly Hills, and invited some of my friends who soon became hers: Jerry Perenchio and his girl, Connie; Charlie Blaylock and his wife, Bonnie; Pierre Cossette and his wife, "Foopie"; and Billy and Myra. Right before dessert the five guys went into the kitchen, borrowed five servers' jackets and hats, and then came out singing "Happy Birthday" and carrying a large chocolate cake with twenty-one sparklers as candles. The whole restaurant joined in singing "Happy Birthday" to Laurie, and although one of the sparklers set a lady's blue-rinsed hair on fire, it was soon doused by pouring a glass of wine over her head. It made for a memorable end to an unusual twenty-first birthday for Laurie.

When we went to the Super Bowl Game in Los Angeles later that year, Laurie and I met up with Dwight Hemion, whom I'd known since he was directing *The Tonight Show* with Steve Allen. His wife, Kit, was there as well, and she and Laurie became fast friends. Dwight and Kit were living in Montecino, California, and we used to go there quite a bit to see them. Nick Vanoff, the producer of *The Tonight Show,* and his wife, Felicia, and

Steve Martin also had places near there.

The year that Pierre's wife, Foopie, died, Laurie and I took him with us when we went up to Dwight and Kit's for Thanksgiving. We were having drinks at Steve Martin's place when Pierre decided that he would take us all out for Thanksgiving dinner. The restaurant was elegant and the dinner was great, but as he usually did, Dwight was smoking during dinner. He noticed Steve glaring at him, so he turned to him and said, "Do you mind if I smoke?" and Steve said, "Do you mind if I fart?" Dwight put out his cigarette without another word, and we then had a smoke-free dinner.

We had great times in Montecino and also shared a Thanksgiving at my house in Palm Springs with them all. Billy Pearson was a regular visitor as well, but although we were great friends, there was a period in our relationship when we fell out and didn't speak for quite a while. I did try to patch things up, without success, but when I heard that he was seriously ill in the hospital, I went to see him. "Billy," I said, "this is ridiculous." "You're right," he said, and from then on we were fine again. His health never really recovered, and he died a few years later. But Billy had lived his life to the fullest, and if there is such a thing as the perfect way to go, he found it. He was in the hospital on life support and knew he was on his way out, so one afternoon he gathered all his wives and his children around him. His current wife, Maggie, had hung his favorite paintings around the hospital room, and a tape machine was playing the music that he loved.

Then Billy threw one last party — and there had been plenty of them in the course of his life. His guests had champagne, and he drank gin and beer; he loved a gin with a beer chaser. They called me during the afternoon and put Billy on the phone, and I said good-bye to him. "I love you, Billy," I said. Then I heard his voice, weak but still with a spark of the old Billy, answer, "And I love you, too, Andy." About half an hour later, after he had kissed and hugged all his wives and children one last time, the doctors switched off his life-support machine, and he died. He could be quirky, temperamental, and even mean at times, but he loved life and living it. He made me laugh more than anybody I ever met, and I never had a dull moment in his company. I still miss him.

Soon after Claudine and I had split up, she moved to Aspen. We had skied there often when we were married, and she'd always loved the place. I used to go up there skiing, too, and because I owned the Aspen Ski

Lodge with Cliff Perlman (who also owned Caesars Palace), I was up there reasonably often. After a while, however, Claudine asked me not to come there anymore. "This is my hometown now," she said, "and it would make it a lot easier for me if you didn't come up because it's a small town and people talk. You know what I mean." I understood that, and from then on I respected her wishes.

Soon after she moved to Aspen, she met and fell in love with Vladimir "Spider" Sabich, a blond, blue-eyed ski champion, reportedly the real-life model for Robert Redford's character in *Downhill Racer*. Aspen was the most famous ski resort in America, but not all the white powder there was found on the ski slopes. An official of the Federal Drug Enforcement Agency called Aspen "the cocaine capital" of the country, and *Newsweek* described it as the home of "rich recluses, hip hedonists, mellow cowboys and cocaine-snorting vegetarians." It was certainly a place where a man with good looks and the glamour of being a champion skier would not lack for party invitations. About a year after they met, Spider asked Claudine and the children to move into his stone-and-glass A-frame house in the Starwood district of Aspen, a gated community that included Jack Nicholson and John Denver.

It was a mercurial relationship: Claudine and Spider were both strong characters, and with their head-turning looks, they were never short of admirers. But I spoke often on the telephone with Claudine, and she sounded very happy. I suppose I wouldn't have been human if I hadn't felt a twinge of jealousy, but I was also genuinely glad for her. I had had my chance and blown it, and she deserved some happiness with someone.

On the afternoon of March 21, 1976, however, I received a phone call from a friend, Bob Biatti. "Turn on the radio, Andy," he said. "Claudine's been arrested in Aspen. They're saying she shot Spider."

My immediate reaction was that I had to be in Aspen, both to make sure the kids were okay and to support Claudine. We might have divorced, but she was the mother of my children and we had never stopped being friends. The weather that day was terrible — snow and high winds — but I managed to get a flight on a private jet. By the time I arrived, a pack of press and television reporters had already gathered. I had to push my way through them, ignoring a barrage of questions like "Do you think she did it, Andy?"

Claudine had already been interrogated

by the police and released on bail, but the house that she had shared with Spider was now a crime scene, sealed off with police "incident tape," and she and the kids had nowhere to go until John and Annie Denver, neighbors and good friends, took them in for the night.

When I saw Claudine, she was pale and still shaking with shock and cold. I called her doctor, who gave her a sedative to ensure that she at least got some rest before her ordeal began again in the morning. The kids, too, were pale and unusually quiet, trying to come to terms with what had happened. I hugged them, and we sat on the sofa and talked for quite a while before we all settled down to sleep.

After breakfast the next morning, Claudine told me what had happened. She had seen the children off to school and then got ready to go skiing, but not liking the look of the weather, she changed her plans and went shopping instead. She had lunch with a couple of glasses of white wine in the Center Bar downtown and was back at home by half past three when the children got home from school.

Spider, who had been skiing, got home half an hour later. He was getting ready to take a shower before going to a party that night when Claudine found a pistol in a closet while putting away some sweaters. It was an imitation German Luger that Spider's father, Vladimir Sabich Sr., had bought in France while watching his son at the 1968 Winter Olympics. He had given the gun to his other son, Steve, but it was kept at Spider's house.

Claudine told me that Spider had shown her the gun before, in case she needed it for her protection when he was away, and she now walked into the bathroom with it, saying, "Spider, I want to know more about this gun. When the lever is on the red spot, it is safe? It won't fire?"

"You've got it," he said, but at that instant the gun went off. Tears coursed down Claudine's cheeks as she told me that Spider fell against the wall, clutching his stomach. "He called my name three times," she said, "and he sort of slid down. I told him I would call an ambulance and not to move."

When she turned around, Claudine saw to her horror that Noelle was standing behind her and had witnessed the entire incident. There was no time to console her then, and Claudine ran to call for an ambulance, but when she got back to the bathroom, she found the other children, who had heard the shot and came to see what happened.

All three of them were now staring at Spider as a pool of blood spread around him. The bullet had pierced his side and severed an artery. To save the children any further trauma, Claudine sent them outside to watch for the ambulance. Then she cradled Spider's head in her lap. "I told him to try to make it," she said, "to talk to me. He was fainting. I tried to give him mouth-to-mouth resuscitation, but I didn't know how." Spider had lost a huge amount of blood by the time the ambulance arrived, and he died on the way to the hospital with Claudine still at his side.

It was a terrible tragedy, but it had clearly been an accident, though that view was not shared by everyone in Aspen. Spider had been a local hero, a party animal and a very popular guy, and some of his friends came to the opinion that it had been cold-blooded murder. False rumors began circulating about jealous arguments and drink- and drug-fueled rows. There were wild and untrue claims that Spider had tired of Claudine and was trying to dump her, that police blood tests on her had shown traces of cocaine, and that her diary, which the police had confiscated, told of a series of arguments and rows.

The story had every ingredient — celebrity, wealth, sex, drugs, and bloodshed — to fuel a full-scale media feeding frenzy, and the story became front-page news around the world. Aspen was besieged by reporters and camera crews, interviewing every passerby and airing speculative reports based on little more than gossip and innuendo, that all but accused Claudine of murder and made it increasingly unlikely that she could ever get a fair trial in the town. The atmosphere was poisonous, like the Salem witch trials. It seemed as if the whole world was lining up against her. Something like that can shatter a family, but it had the opposite effect on us: We stuck together, supporting and standing by one another. But much earlier than children should ever have to, my kids learned how tough and cruel the world can be.

They had to put up with taunts from their schoolmates. A lot of people in Aspen were spreading such gossip as "I heard them arguing in a bar the other week. That French bitch shot Spider, and it was no accident." Their children would then repeat what their parents had told them or what they had overheard, as kids will, and my kids bore the brunt of it. The boys managed to shrug it off, but Noelle, who was older, took the taunts and comments to heart. Already traumatized by witnessing the shooting, she was now in such a fragile state that I decided to get her out of Aspen altogether for a while. Fortunately, although it was already clear that Claudine would be put on trial, Noelle was not required as a witness by either the prosecution or the defense. Had she been subjected to a bruising cross-examination on top of everything she had already been through, I would have had serious concerns for her long-term mental health. We certainly weren't trying to conceal evidence; her recollection of events was no different from that of her mother, and she would have testified as much, but it was a further ordeal that I was anxious for her to avoid if at all possible.

I flew to Los Angeles with her and drove to Malibu. Bill and Peggy Traylor, our neighbors from when we had the beach house, were still living in the area. They were lovely people with two daughters of their own about Noelle's age. When I asked them if she could stay with them for a while until things calmed down in Aspen, they were happy for her to do so. They really loved Noelle, and she and their daughters, Stephanie and Susan, had always been good friends. So, not without a few tears on both sides, I left her there. I took the boys down to see her on a few weekends, but she stayed in Malibu for several months. I can never thank Bill and Peggy enough for what they did for us then.

Back in Aspen, I tried to persuade Claudine not to go to the memorial service for Spider, but she wanted to say her last good-byes to her lover. She also felt that not to make an appearance would be taken as a sign of guilt by the Aspen rumor mill. She stood alone in the middle of the front row of mourners, holding a single flower, her eyes downcast, and tears trickling down her cheeks. Spider's family avoided any contact with her.

On April 8, 1976, I accompanied Claudine to the Pitkin County Courthouse, a handsome redbrick Victorian building on Main Street, where she was formally arraigned and charged with manslaughter. If convicted, she faced up to ten years in prison, and the district attorney, Frank Tucker, made it clear to reporters that he had deliberately decided not to opt for the lesser charge of negligent homicide.

As soon as it was inevitable that Claudine would face charges, I called my lawyer in Los Angeles, Larry Kartiganer, and asked him to recommend a trial lawyer to defend Claudine. He suggested a top attorney in L.A., Charles Weedman. We discussed applying to move the trial out of Aspen on the entirely reasonable grounds that a fair trial would be impossible to obtain in a town that had been so drenched in adverse publicity, speculation, and rumor, often fueled by leaks and off-the-record comments. However, Weedman felt that to seek a change of venue might be seen as a tacit admission of guilt and could sway a jury in a different town against Claudine. We resolved to stay and fight the case in Aspen. Given the strength of local feelings, Weedman also thought it would be unwise to risk hostility to a lawyer from out of town. While he would still orchestrate the strategy, he recommended that we hire a local attorney, Ron Austin, to lead Claudine's defense in court.

The preliminary hearing was held on June 10, 1976, and the case had generated so much publicity that the presiding district court judge, George Lohr, at first imposed a gag order on all the attorneys and barred the press and the public from the courtroom altogether for the first day of the hearing. The most significant and contentious part of the day's proceedings centered on the police seizure of Claudine's diary and the blood sample taken from her on the day of the shooting. After listening to legal arguments from both sets of attorneys, Judge Lohr ruled that the diary and the blood test results were inadmissible as evidence because both had been obtained by the police without a warrant.

The trial was originally scheduled for August but was postponed for several months after District Attorney Tucker, who had bragged to reporters that the diary would "play a big part in the trial," appealed to the Colorado Supreme Court to review Judge Lohr's ruling. The appeal was unsuccessful; Judge Lohr's ruling was unanimously upheld. When the diary was eventually returned to Claudine, she burned it to prevent any more intrusions into her private life.

Jury selection began on January 3, 1977, and the most difficult part of the whole process was finding twelve Aspen citizens who had not already made up their minds about the events leading up to Spider's death. A near endless line of potential jurors was ruled out one by one as each admitted to having prejudged Claudine's guilt or innocence. It took five days to select a jury of seven men and five women, ranging in age from twenty-seven to sixty-two. Even then some of the jurors and alternates admitted to being friends or acquaintances of Spider and expressed reservations about Claudine's innocence. Despite this, they promised to reach "a fair and objective verdict." It was hardly an encouraging start, but nothing more could be done.

The trial opened on Monday, January 10, 1977. I again walked with Claudine to the courthouse, running the gauntlet of jostling reporters, strobe-lit by the barrage of photographers' flashes. Once safely inside I took my seat in the public area while Claudine sat at the defense table with her attorneys. The prosecution then laid out its case, including an autopsy report describing the massive internal bleeding from a gunshot wound to the left side that had caused Spider's death. Roy Griffith, the head of security in the gated community where Spider and Claudine lived, who had gone into the house after the ambulance call, claimed that he found Claudine "confused and upset." When he asked her, "Who shot who?" she replied, "I shot Spider." Only under cross-examination did he admit that she had also immediately added, "In here! In here! Help him!"

A police detective's claim that Claudine had initially told him she had "raised the gun, pointed it at Spider, jokingly went 'bang, bang,' and the gun went off," provoked a furious outburst from Claudine, protesting that it was a lie. Our confidence in the competence of the Aspen police was scarcely strengthened by the revelation that the policeman who had retrieved the gun from the bathroom had then wrapped it in a towel, put it in the glove compartment of his car, and forgotten about it for three days. Robert E. Nicoletti, a Denver police firearms expert who examined the gun for the defense, testified that its safety catch was broken and its firing pin was too heavily greased, so it could easily have been fired accidentally. A second expert, Lama S. Martin, testified that the gun could have gone off without the trigger even being pulled.

On the second day of the trial I was called to the witness stand after neighbors of Claudine's were quoted as saying that I had told them she was "a crazy-type gal who likes to drive fast, ski fast, and take chances." It was potentially very damaging to Claudine, suggesting a degree of recklessness that the prosecution did not hesitate to link to the shooting, but as I testified in court, it simply wasn't true. I had made a different, completely innocent remark to them, which they had chosen to interpret in an entirely different way.

That afternoon the prosecution rested its case, and the next morning Claudine took the stand and gave her account of events, just as she had told it to me, and was then cross-examined. She was clearly nervous, speaking so softly that sometimes I had to strain to hear her words. I kept studying the faces of the jurors, trying to detect Claudine's likely fate in their expressions. One or two seemed to show some overt hostility, but most were impassive and impossible to read.

The prosecution went to some length to try to prove that Spider was intent on throwing Claudine out of his house, even trying to introduce into evidence a claim that an unnamed witness had a $100 bet with Spider that Claudine "would be gone by April 1." With the jury excluded, the judge ruled the claim too flimsy to be admissible. After an hour and a half Claudine's ordeal was over, and she returned to the defense table. I was then recalled to the stand to testify that Claudine had no knowledge of guns. I had never owned a gun, and while we were together, Claudine never handled one.

The defense wrapped up its case the next morning, and the prosecution, either confident of its case or lacking the ability to refute the defense evidence, declined the opportunity to offer a rebuttal. Judge Lohr then scheduled the closing arguments for the following morning and sent the jurors home. It meant another day of agonizing suspense and tension before the verdict would be known.

On January 14, 1977, I again walked to the courthouse with Claudine through crowds of media that had grown even more dense since the trial began. The legal arguments presented before the jury was sent out centered mainly on the prosecution's attempts to allow the jury the possibility of finding Claudine guilty of criminally negligent homicide — the charge that District Attorney Tucker had specifically rejected before the trial. It was a lesser charge than reckless manslaughter — a misdemeanor rather than a felony — but it still carried a possible two-year sentence.

Ron Austin and Charles Weedman argued furiously against that. They believed the prosecuting attorneys, sensing that the tide of the case was running against them, were now hedging their bets and hoping the jury would settle on a compromise verdict that would at least see a conviction, albeit on the lesser charge, rather than the acquittal that had seemed likely. On this occasion, however, Judge Lohr sided with the prosecution, and the jurors were sent out to consider their verdict.

For three hours and forty minutes we waited in a back room while they deliberated. Then, early in the afternoon, we were called back into court. The foreman of the jury handed the verdict to the clerk of the court, and the judge read out the findings: "We the jury find the defendant, Claudine Longet Williams, guilty of criminally negligent homicide." The judge then announced that sentencing would not take place until January 31, a further seventeen days of terrible uncertainty for Claudine to endure.

We drew some consolation from the comments of one of the jurors, Daniel de Wolfe, who was reported in the press as saying that he hoped Claudine would not be given a prison sentence. "By no means is she the type of person who should be in jail," he said. "I don't think she's a threat to society." He went on to describe the trial as a waste of taxpayers' money and observed, "She would never have faced a trial if she had not been a celebrity." There were others in Aspen who took the opposite view, however, and were claiming that the judge had been starstruck and that Claudine's celebrity had saved her from conviction on the more serious charge of manslaughter.

On January 31 we returned to the courthouse one last time to hear the judge pass sentence. Claudine first made a plea in mitigation, begging him to show mercy on her for the sake of her three young children. "They are beautiful, they are happy, they are very gentle and open. With all my heart I would like them to stay that way." Close to tears, she begged the judge to save the children from the stigma of having their mother jailed, which might make them resentful of "a system that would send to jail the mother they trust and believe in."

Judge Lohr then said that he felt putting her on probation without imposing any jail time "might undermine respect for the law," and he announced a sentence of thirty days. I felt tears well in my eyes. I had hoped against hope that it would not come to that. The decision makes no more sense to me now than it did then, and I can only assume the judge was trying to placate the hostile Aspen residents who felt that even though Claudine "had gotten away with it," she should still "get something." The judge then sugared the pill a little by announcing that Claudine could serve the sentence "at a time of her own choosing," to ensure that the children would be properly looked after. He went on to say that he had had "considerable mail" from people claiming that Claudine was guilty of murder, and he savaged "the hostile attitude" of many Aspen residents toward her, saying, "The defendant will have to live with that for a long time."

Claudine duly served her thirty days in the

Pitkin County jail, and to the fury of some in Aspen, she was allowed to have meals sent in from a restaurant. She, Christian, and Bobby even painted her cell pale blue. By the time she was released, I was in Las Vegas, working my fourteenth year at Caesars Palace. By now even though I was very well paid for it, I hated appearing in Vegas. Although people flocked there in the millions from all over the world, it seemed to me to have become the most soulless and dispiriting place, a world turned upside down, where the human virtues — truth, honesty, and fidelity — were treated as vices, while the vices — greed, lies, cheating, swindling, and excess of every kind — were hailed as virtues. A season at Caesars Palace put a lot of money in the bank, but it was something to be endured rather than enjoyed. I was always glad to have company there, and I thought it would do Claudine good to get away from Aspen for a spell. As the judge had indicated, not everyone in town was willing to accept the court's verdict. Some charming Aspen residents had filled Claudine's convertible with horse manure one night, and there were a lot of dark looks and muttered comments whenever she went into town.

The trial had also put an end to Claudine's career as a singer and actress; she never released another record or appeared in any films or television shows. Given the continuing hostility to her in Aspen, I felt that Claudine showed enormous courage in resolving to continue living in the town and face down those mounting a whispering campaign against her. She has done so and still lives there now, and one good thing did come out of the trial: She is now happily married to Ron Austin, the Aspen attorney who led her defense.

More than thirty years have passed since the court case, but my view has not changed one iota: I still believe what the jury believed — that the shooting of Spider Sabich was a tragic accident.

After the dust had settled and Claudine and I had picked up the threads of our separate lives again, I bumped into Bing Crosby's wife, Kathy, at a party. She told me that she was amazed I had gone to so much trouble to support Claudine when we were already divorced. "Anybody would have done the same thing," I said.

She shook her head. "Bing wouldn't have." She didn't elaborate and changed the subject, but I'm sure that, under similar circumstances, divorced or not, most husbands and fathers would have done exactly what I did.

15

I had hoped that the trial would be the last bleak event in the least happy period of my life, but not long afterward I faced fresh heartbreak: My parents died, first my dad and then my mom. Dad had suffered poor health for years with the breathing problems and emphysema that had dogged him since his days working on the railroad. Late one afternoon I sat by his bed, with the sunlight streaming through the window. We were alone together for an hour or so since Mom, who had been constantly at Dad's side, had seized the chance to take a little rest. There were two bright spots of color on his cheeks and a faint sheen of sweat on his brow. His breathing was rasping and irregular, and he often had to pause to use an oxygen mask. But words poured out of him in torrents as if he were afraid that if he stopped he might never speak again. We talked nonstop of old days and past times, of Wall Lake, Des

Moines, Chicago, and Cincinnati, and of the long, happy years in California. "I did right to move us out of Wall Lake, didn't I?" he said with a smile. "I got a few things wrong over the years, but I sure as heck got that right."

It was as close as he or I came to acknowledging in words that this would be the last conversation we would ever share, but it was the subtext to everything we said that afternoon, unspoken but still understood by us both. If there were farewells to be made, they were expressed only in a look, a squeeze of the hand, and a hug. As we heard Mom's footsteps in the corridor, he spoke his last words to me: "Take care of your mom." A moment later she came back into the room, and I left them alone together, sitting hand in hand as they had done all their adult lives. He died that night, peacefully in his sleep.

I wouldn't have had a career as a singer if it hadn't been for my dad. I might never have gotten farther than a karaoke bar in Des Moines. I owed him everything, but he was much more than the driving force and motivator for me and my brothers. He was also a very warm and loving father to us all. He was devoted to my mom, and she to him, and I really think she lost the will to live after my father had gone. They had been together since childhood, and life without him was too empty for her. Two years later she followed him to the grave. She was a wonderful person, an old-fashioned mother, devoted to her family above all else. They had a great life together, and they were in love until the day they died. It was lovely to see.

I drew a little consolation from the thought that they were now together in death as they had been in life, but my parents had meant everything to me, and I was heartbroken that they were gone. A friend of mine had once said to me, "When your parents die, for the first time in your life you realize that you're truly alone." I now knew what he meant; I still miss them today.

To cap what had been a miserable decade for me, my record sales also began declining. I was primarily an album artist, and by 1973 I had eighteen gold albums to my name — at that time only Frank Sinatra, Johnny Mathis, and Elvis Presley had ever had more — but that was then, and this was now. Changing tastes and fashions in music — Beatlemania, psychedelia, and progressive rock — had apparently left my style of music beached like a piece of driftwood left by a receding wave. After fifteen years with Columbia Records, I was dropped by the label, and I now had to face the real possibility that I might be finished as a recording artist.

It was partly my own fault. I had felt for a while that Columbia really didn't know what to do with me, so I tended to go off on my own, make an album, and then deliver it to them, rather than involving them in the process. Some of the records I did weren't commercial enough and didn't sell particularly well. Also, there were a lot of newer, younger people working at Columbia, many of whom were into music that was much different from mine. Whatever the reasons, Columbia called my lawyer one day, and announced, "We're not going to pick up Andy's contract."

It was a psychological blow more than anything. I just couldn't imagine not recording anymore; it had become so large a part of my life. I began to put even more time into touring, but that in turn further damaged my personal life. The lesson I should have learned from my breakup with Claudine still hadn't sunk in.

Laurie often toured with me when I went on the road. I was traveling a lot in Europe, Asia, and Australia and also doing Caesars Palace in Las Vegas, Harrah's in Lake Tahoe, and other gambling meccas. Laurie was never bored coming to rehearsals or sound checks or anything to do with the theater. She had majored in theater arts at the University of Hawaii and was fascinated by every aspect of show business.

While I was doing a few shows in Manila, we were staying in the penthouse suite at the Manila Hotel, which had its own swimming pool. While we were there, Manila was struck by a tremendous earthquake. The whole building shook violently, pitching us out of bed. Water was splashing over the sides of the pool, and the chandelier overhead was swaying wildly back and forth. We were both frightened, of course, and when it was all over, Laurie refused to stay in the rooms; we settled for less luxurious but safer-feeling accommodations on the first floor instead.

Imelda Marcos came to one of the shows and insisted on driving me around Manila. I had already done two shows that night, and there had been a cocktail party after the latter. I had had a couple glasses of wine and was understandably sleepy, but she insisted on showing me her city. I think what she really wanted me to do was go back and tell Teddy Kennedy, a fierce critic of the Marcos regime, about all the progress they were making in the Philippines and that the city was not under martial law. After we had been driving for a while, she asked, "Would you like me to show you some of the hospitals and other things we are doing?"

"If you don't mind, Imelda," I responded, "I'll have to pass on that," at which point, still cruising around Manila in the presidential limousine, I fell fast asleep. Laurie had to make polite conversation with a furious Imelda Marcos while I dozed peacefully between them.

Back in Vegas, ready for my next season at Caesars Palace, I had been casting around for a different opening act for a while when I thought of Edgar Bergen, the greatest ventriloquist in America, and his sidekicks, Charlie McCarthy and Mortimer Snerd. Edgar had not performed for a while, but after much coaxing he agreed to come out of retirement and was soon talking excitedly about it. He was going to do the show, make a farewell tour, and then retire permanently and donate his trademark monocled partner, Charlie McCarthy, to the Smithsonian.

The audiences loved him; they hadn't seen him for years, since his huge success on radio and television. Unfortunately, after the third night of the show, he went to bed and died in his sleep. I flew his body back to Los Angeles, and Laurie and I went to pay our respects and sympathy to his wife, Frances, and their actress daughter, Candice.

The Bergens had a little shih tzu dog with which Laurie fell in love, so on her next birthday I gave her a shih tzu in the same colors, black and white. When we showed the dog to Dwight Hemion and Kit, Dwight named him Bushy, and the name stuck.

After I had finished my summer season in Vegas, Laurie and I would often meet up with Jerry Perenchio at the Hôtel du Cap in the south of France and dine in some of the great restaurants on the Côte d'Azur, although nothing could really top the food at the Hôtel du Cap. We had great times on the water, too, both in Lake Tahoe and Las Vegas, the casinos giving me the use of the company yacht. We also had wonderful times in New York, London, Paris, and Rome. When we visited New York, I took Laurie to the Guggenheim, the first museum she had ever been to. We looked at some of the French Impressionist painters, and I taught her the song that Kay Thompson had taught my brothers and me so that she, too, would be able to remember their names. That visit got her interested in art and art history, and from then on she enjoyed visiting museums as much as I did.

Although we had been very happy together for years, problems now began to arise. The hard-partying lifestyle we had been living was taking its toll on both of us. I was drinking more than was good for me until I put the brakes on that. Laurie, however, became hooked on alcohol, and although she twice went into rehab, she twice drifted back into her old habit. Her drinking was causing problems between us and blighting her life, but only she could rescue herself from it. To her enormous credit, that is exactly what she did. The third time she went into rehab was the charm. She got herself straightened out, turned her life around, and began putting that experience to good use by becoming a counselor at the Betty Ford Clinic in Palm Springs and at St. John's in Santa Monica, helping others to kick their habit. Since then, and to this day, she is in recovery.

Things had changed irrevocably between us, however, and as I had already discovered with Claudine, once a damaged relationship slips beyond a certain point, it is almost impossible to repair it. There was no one else involved, but we both knew that we had reached the end of the road. We parted on amicable terms — we still speak regularly — and we both felt much sadness that things had come to this. I bought her a house and helped her financially; it was the least I could do after nine years together. She is now a successful interior decorator and into construction property management in L.A.

Once more I had no one in my life, no plan to follow. I felt rudderless, directionless, and rootless. Fueled by my personal unhappiness, my dislike of performing grew even more pronounced. I was asked to take part in a program of readings and songs from Americana at the reopening of the Ford Theatre in Washington, D.C. — the theater where Abraham Lincoln was shot — and found myself waiting in the dressing room with the actor Richard Crenna and two show business legends: Henry Fonda and Harry Belafonte. My assistant, Keats Tyler, was also present, having flown with me from Los Angeles. When the stage manager called for us to go onstage, the other performers all got up at once and hurried out of the dressing room. "See?" I said to Keats. "They can hardly wait to get on, while I can hardly wait to get off." I really didn't like performing. I was burnt out!

At this low ebb there was the first sign of an upturn in my mood and fortunes. My good friend and former press agent Jim Mahoney, who was now living a few doors from me in La Quinta, said to me one day, "I know a girl who'd be great for you. Her name is Debbie Haas. She's beautiful, intelligent, funny, and plays golf like a professional. What's not to like?"

"Okay," I said. "I could certainly use a little company, but let's not do that whole blind date thing. Let's just play some golf together. If Debbie and I get on, that's great, but if not, at least we'll have had a round of golf out of it."

As soon as I met Debbie, I felt there was an instant connection between us. We began talking as if we'd known each other for years, and by the time we'd played the first hole, I was barely aware that the other two in the foursome were still with us. Originally from Buffalo, Minnesota, she was a lot younger than I, and as Jim had said, she was certainly beautiful. She was also sharp, sassy, very funny, and very organized. We had dinner together that night; she came home with me afterward, and she has never left since. That was how instantaneous it was for both of us and it was twenty-two years ago, so it certainly wasn't just an infatuation. I knew at once that Debbie was the one for me, the love of my life, and from the start we were meant to be.

Like me, Debbie had been married before, but her divorce was quite bruising. Apart from the emotional scars, she came out of the marriage with nothing other than the clothes she wore and a membership at the

La Quinta Hotel golf club. After her divorce she stayed at the club for weeks and did practically nothing but play golf every day for six or eight hours at a stretch on the practice range. As a result she became a very good golfer; she got down to a six handicap. But the rest of her life was pretty much on hold when we met.

We dated for five years, and when it came, the marriage proposal wasn't the most romantic or carefully planned. We were standing in the kitchen of the house at La Quinta, and I just found myself saying, "So, okay, what do you think? Do you want to?"

"What?" she said.

"Well, do you want to?"

"Do I want to *what*?"

"You know, get married."

She stared at me for a moment and then said, "Oh, that's a nice proposal. But . . . well . . . since you're asking, yes." Then she started crying.

We were married on May 3, 1991, in my New York apartment at the Museum Tower. I had bought it two or three years earlier when Jerry Perenchio and Pierre Cossette were purchasing apartments there, and it seemed like a very good idea. I loved the building, and it was a great location, near the theaters in the heart of the city and only a block from 21. I thought, *Why not?* and bought an apartment on the twenty-eighth floor of the tower.

I got my architect friend, Ted Grenzback, to design the interior for me. I didn't want a space that was all on the same level, so he designed it at different elevations with a couple of steps to create more intimate areas within it. It had white walls with recessed downlighting, which gave a soft, beautiful illumination, pure white carpets and rugs, and a raised dining area floored with gleaming black tiles. That and the white walls made even the larger paintings seem almost jewel-like. My Hans Hofmann painting is vibrantly colored, but in that setting it looked luminous. I also set a fabulous Robert Graham life-size sculpture of a girl and a horse, *Stephanie and Spy,* near the vast windows, as if they were admiring the view from twenty-eight floors up. A writer from *Architectural Digest* remarked in July 1989 that "they seem to float, suspended, in the heart of a high-rise forest."

It was a beautiful apartment and an ideal setting for the small, intimate wedding that both Debbie and I wanted. We both had had the big church wedding the first time around and decided to keep it simple this time with just a few very close friends. A justice of the peace conducted the ceremony, and we took our vows looking out over the Manhattan skyline. As I kissed my bride, a pianist struck up with ". . . two drifters, off to see the world" from "Moon River." After the ceremony we drank a glass of champagne and then went to 21 for a celebration dinner.

It was a magical day that I'll never forget, and it had only one minor flaw. As we were getting ready for the wedding, the doorman called to say there was a photographer at the entrance. I told the doorman to send him up and called out to Debbie, who was in the bedroom, "The photographer's here." As soon as he came in, he started shooting pictures of everyone and everything, and as I was mentally congratulating Debbie on choosing such an enthusiastic individual, she walked into the room, took one look at him, and said, "He's not the photographer I hired."

He turned out to be a member of the paparazzi, who had somehow gotten wind of the wedding and turned up to try to get a picture of us on our wedding day. When the doorman asked him what he was doing there, he had replied — quite truthfully — that he had come to photograph Andy Williams's wedding. He couldn't believe his luck when he was invited into our apartment and was making the most of his opportunity. Once he was ejected and the real wedding photographer arrived, the service could begin. In retrospect, we should have let the paparazzi guy stay and take the wedding photographs, because the ones we got from the photographer we had hired were a big disappointment.

16

Newly married, I was now sixty-three years old, an age when many people are considering retirement, but I not only had no intention of slowing down or stopping, I was about to take a huge step into the unknown. Just after the wedding my brother Don called me. "I'm in a great place called Branson, Missouri," he said. "Ray Stevens has just built a theater down here and is doing incredible business. You belong down here too, Andy."

I just said, "In Missouri? You've got to be kidding me." But after I thought about it for a while, I decided that I had nothing to lose by taking a look. I could have flown, but I chose to drive there instead. I was in no hurry. I could take my time, enjoy the drive, and break my journey whenever and wherever I wanted. So I took three days to travel there from New York, and it seemed like a trip back in time, too, leaving the urban hustle and bustle of New York for a journey into the heart of a simpler and maybe purer rural America. It had been a very long time since I had driven the highways and backroads of the American heartland, and it felt a bit like going home.

Way back in the 1920s, Branson had been just a tiny, sleepy town in a beautiful setting, surrounded by lakes and rivers, at the foot of the Ozark Mountains. People used to go there to hunt and fish, hike, or camp by the lake. Then a local mountain family decided to put on a show for these campers and built a little place where they could sing and play. It was a homespun building, more of a barn than a theater, but it was a big success. Soon more country musicians began coming to Branson, and people were going to Branson just to listen to country music.

At about the same time, Silver Dollar City started up in an old silver mine. At first people just paid to go down into the old mine, and when they came out again, they'd buy a lemonade or a T-shirt from the concessions stand by the entrance, but over time it steadily expanded until it had become a turn-of-the-century theme park with shops, glassblowers, wood-carvers, blacksmiths, and many other craftspeople, with everyone wearing period clothes. It is now a major

Branson attraction, with a roller coaster and all kinds of rides.

Theaters also began springing up. A country singer, Roy Clarke, was one of the first to open his own small auditorium, and when he wasn't working himself, he imported other country stars to play there. Some of them soon began to wonder why they were playing at Roy Clarke's instead of opening their own place, and new theaters and attractions began to spring up and spread farther and farther down Highway 76, soon to be renamed Country Music Boulevard.

When I first visited Branson, on a beautiful afternoon with the leaves on the trees still the fresh green of spring and the sunlight shimmering on the water of the lake, the town was still little more than one street wide and a couple of miles long, but I couldn't believe what was happening there. Most of its twenty or so theaters were packed every day for both the afternoon and evening shows. When I did some research, I discovered that 4 million people were already visiting Branson every year, yet the majority of Americans, and particularly those living on the East and West coasts, had never even heard of the place. The few who had tended to dismiss it as sort of a elephant's graveyard — "the place where old singers go to die" —

but if I was going to stake a claim there, I certainly didn't intend to fade away.

The night I arrived I went to see the Ray Stevens show, and Ray introduced me to the audience. When the show ended, I was surrounded by about a hundred people who were all asking, "Why don't you come and sing here, Andy? We don't get to places like Vegas and Los Angeles. Why don't you come here and do a show?"

It certainly got me thinking. Rather than traveling all over the world to give concerts, moving on every couple of days to another airport, another town, another hotel, I could settle down in Branson, build my own theater, and let the audiences come to me. Just the same, I knew it would be a huge gamble. In some ways, basing myself in Branson would be like getting out of the business altogether. The people I knew in New York and California hadn't even heard of Branson, and they always think that if it isn't happening where they are, it's not happening at all. In Branson I'd be out of the loop, not appearing on television or in the media or the theaters. I feared that within a short time I'd be forgotten.

Branson was also a country music town, which meant I would be the only pop singer there, but the more I thought about it, the more attractive that idea became. I could see that Branson had the potential to really expand, and I was strangely comfortable there. It felt like my sort of place, a midwestern country town rather than a big city and only one state away from Iowa.

So I returned to our apartment in New York and said to Debbie, "What would you think about moving to Branson, Missouri?" Like all my friends, none of whom had ever been to Branson or could even find it on a map, she thought I was crazy. "What are you doing?" she asked. "Why would you want to live in a little country town like Branson? We have a great life: a beautiful apartment in New York City, a house in Beverly Hills, and our home in La Quinta. We have some great friends; we go to shows, museums, and art galleries; we eat in wonderful restaurants. We're living a life that most people would kill for; why would we want to give all that up — and kill your career?"

Considered logically, her objections were entirely right, but logic no longer seemed to be playing a part in my thought processes. I listened carefully to all the arguments that Debbie and my friends put forward and then carried on doing exactly what I had already made up my mind to do. Soon afterward we moved to Branson. Debbie came with me only with the greatest reluctance, but if she was a fish out of water at first, she has now grown to love it as much as I do. We've established a life that is a good one for both of us.

I was so keen to make the move that I didn't even play a trial concert in Branson to see what kind of audience I would draw. I just went ahead and did it. Even Don balked at that, and said, "Why don't you at least try it out first?"

"No," I said. "If I do that and I like it, and it works, I'll have wasted a year because the season will be over. I'm too impatient to wait around. If I start now, we can be up and running by the spring of next year. So I'm going to do it, starting right now."

I felt a great wave of exhilaration. For the first time in years I had a challenge. I knew exactly what I wanted to do: to build a theater and a home in Branson, live and work there, put down some roots, and feel part of a community again. More than anything I had ever done, I wanted to start a new life with Debbie in Branson, and I threw myself into it heart and soul.

If I was going to carry out my plan, I was going to need money, so the first things I did were sell the apartment in New York, the house in L.A., and some citrus groves

I owned. Then I went back to Branson and found an architect I liked, Warren Bates, senior partner of Bates and Associates of Springfield, Missouri, who was a disciple of Frank Lloyd Wright. I needed his help because while I knew exactly what I wanted my theater to be like and what it should contain, I didn't know how to build it.

It is fair to say that the facilities and infrastructure in Branson then weren't exactly top of the line. There were some basic hotels and motels, and some thrown-together music theaters, but I had decided that my theater had to be absolutely state-of-the-art. Whatever I've done throughout my life has always had to be the absolute best I can make it. There are four things every singer wants: great sound, great lighting, a great band, and a great dressing room. I was determined that my theater would have the very best in all those categories, just as I wanted the audiences to feel they had seen the best show ever, in the most beautiful theater in Branson.

I wanted the whole place to have a feeling of spaciousness, with a two-story lobby and a roomy, airy auditorium. It had to be very different from all the other theaters in town. I wanted it to look like an art museum with a theater attached, and I wanted to hang many paintings from my collection there.

However, I had been around the block enough to know that there is no substitute for specialized knowledge. I took advice from people I knew who had expertise in every key area — sound, lighting, stage sets, and the backstage layout, from points as basic as how big the doors needed to be to get the scenery in and out, and the amount of space needed backstage, through to the specifications of the equipment we needed. The only requirement I placed on everyone was a simple one: "Get me the best there is."

We found a perfect site, an empty sixteen-acre lot on Country Music Boulevard. It was a steep-sloping parcel of land, but everything in Branson is on a hill; there's hardly a patch of level ground in the whole town. I bought it from Pete and Jack Herschend, the owners of Silver Dollar City; they sold it to me on the condition that I would build a hotel of at least two hundred bedrooms on part of the site. If I didn't find a way around that provision, it looked as if I'd be going into the hotel business as well as the theater business, but as it turned out, we struck a deal with Holiday Inn, which constructed a five-hundred-room hotel (now operated by Radisson Hotels) on a six-acre section at the bottom of the property. That more than satisfied the terms of my agreement with the Herschends and was very good for me as well since all those guests had to pass the theater every time they went in or out of the hotel.

We worked closely with the architect as he drew up the plans for the theater. Covering an area of 48,000 square feet and adapting to the contours of the site, the building would spread over three levels and have a lobby on each one. People arriving on tour buses would enter through the lower lobby; the main lobby would be on the next level; and the third, on the top level, was for people in wheelchairs and those whose seats were in the upper part of the auditorium. When everything had been costed, the budget was eye-watering; if it wasn't quite all the money I had at the time, it was certainly a big chunk of it.

I wanted everything about the theater to be beautiful, and that extended even to the parking lot. All the other theaters in Branson had lots that were blank expanses of black asphalt. I wanted mine to be much less intrusive, so we planted hundreds of trees throughout it. The rest of the grounds around the theater were also landscaped with trees and shrubs, rock formations, waterfalls, and even a Moon River running around the theater with pools full of ornamental fish.

I was driving through the hills near Branson one day, admiring the beauty of the rock formations, when it came to me that what we needed around the theater were some of those rock faces, beautiful in themselves and also typical of the area. We obviously couldn't steal the formations from the mountains, and when we tried to get large blocks cut from a quarry, we discovered that the rock crumbled much too easily. Then I remembered a golf course I had played in Palm Springs that had rocks and waterfalls so natural-looking that I couldn't believe it when I discovered they were made from concrete.

I got in touch with Larson Construction of Tucson, Arizona, got them to send a contractor to Branson, drove him to that spot in the mountains, and said, "That's what I want." After we had negotiated a permit from the Highways Department, his men went out there, cleaned the rock surface with air compressors and brooms, and applied five layers of latex, stiffened with cheesecloth. They made twenty huge molds that way and used them to cast the concrete rock faces that now surround the theater.

The concrete was stained with acrylic latex

paint to resist fading by the powerful Missouri sun, and it was distressed with drilling scars, mineral stains, lichen and fungus, and fragments of feldpsar, quartz, and mica until it was indistinguishable from the real thing; I would defy anyone to spot the difference from even a few feet away.

The building and the landscaping were completed on time and on budget in eight months, and I was immensely proud of what we had achieved. I have played theaters in great cities on five continents, and there is not one that can match the Moon River Theatre's seating, sound, lighting, sets, backstage facilities, dressing rooms, lobby, souvenir shop, and outside grounds. Everything is as perfect as we could make it.

We've used a lot of natural materials in the interior, and everything is of the highest quality, from the oak floors to the striped mahogany ceilings. Even now I'm still looking for slight improvements we can make. Debbie says that out of the tens of thousands of miniature white lights that illuminate the grounds in winter, I can spot a missing bulb at five hundred yards. I'm still as proud of the Moon River Theatre as I was the day we opened — May 1, 1992 — and the day not long afterward when it became the only theater ever to be featured in *Architectural Digest.*

In all the years since then I've also taken great pride in putting on the best possible show I can, and from the day we opened, for the first time in my entire adult life I've actually enjoyed going onstage and singing. My brother Don was quick to notice the change in me. "What happened?" he said to me one day. "You're more relaxed, confident, and self-assured." I was finally enjoying performing again.

My move to Branson marked the end of a long-lasting relationship. My assistant, Keats Tyler, had been with me for about twenty years. I had originally hired him as a result of a conversation with Janet Leigh when she was guesting on my television show back in the 1960s. We were talking during a break in rehearsal one day, and I mentioned that I was looking for a secretary and asked her if she knew anyone who might be good for me.

"Tony [Curtis] used to have a male secretary named Keats Tyler," she said. "Tony thought he was terrific and said there were a lot of advantages to having a male secretary. They could do things for you that you couldn't really ask a female to do, such as go on the road with you, so you'd always have a secretary with you."

So I got in touch with Keats, and when we met, I liked him immediately. He was a gentle guy, somewhat quiet, and an elegant dresser. He could take shorthand and type quite well, and he was also very organized. I had to mention a thing only once and I knew that it would be done — and very discreetly. All in all he was the perfect secretary; I hired him on the spot, and he became my assistant. It turned out that he had another talent, too: He was a very fine photographer, and over the years he took many pictures during rehearsals of all the stars on my show — great pictures, many of which I still have today. We also used his photos of me on many of my album covers.

I wanted him to join me in Branson and continue working for me, but he just didn't want to leave L.A. With regrets on both sides we ended our working relationship, but we're still friends and keep in regular touch. In the first few years in Branson I had a couple of assistants who didn't stay with me too long, but then I hired a woman named Judy Donohue. I didn't need a male secretary to go on the road with me any longer because I had pretty much stopped touring. Hiring Judy was the best move I could have made because she's every bit as efficient and organized as Keats and a lovely person as well, and she has been with me now for seven years.

Two years after we opened the Moon River Theatre, I was playing a concert in North Carolina and, wanting some dinner afterward, I saw a restaurant called McGuffy's. When I went inside, I liked everything about the place. They served good, healthy food, using top-quality fresh ingredients; it was all well cooked, well presented, and not expensive. I arranged a meeting with the owners and said, "If I build a restaurant in Branson, will you come and run it for me?" They said they would, so we built one across from the theater. When it opened, it was a huge success because there wasn't anything else around Branson like it. After a few very lucrative years, they sold the restaurant to an out-of-state owner, and it ran down to the point where he couldn't make the rent any longer. I didn't want to be a restaurateur, but I didn't want the place to close, either. Finally I took it over and completely redesigned it, and it was reborn in 2006 as Andy Williams' Moon River Grill. The menu includes many of my mother's recipes, and we have good chefs and managers to run it. It is packed each night for dinner before the show, and many people come in afterward for dinner or just to have a drink in the beautiful long bar. I have pop art from my collection on the walls, and I'm as proud of the grill as I am of the theater. I eat there every day because the food is great and it's *free!*

In my shows at the theater, I try to find something a little bit different to do with my co-stars. Ann-Margret, who appeared with me in 2008, is a singer and dancer, but more than that she's a great personality and a big movie star. Years before, I had done a screen test and shared a passionate kiss with Barbara Eden, so we lowered a movie screen onto the stage and showed me kissing Barbara and a scene of Ann-Margret kissing Pat Boone in *State Fair,* a movie they had made together. Then I asked her who she thought was the best kisser, Pat or me. "There's only one way to find out," she said, and as the orchestra played "Love Story," we rushed into each other's arms and kissed while the screen showed fireworks exploding. It was corny but very funny, and audiences loved it.

Our choreographer, costumer, and lighting designer all have their input, and then we work two weeks with the dancers and one week with the orchestra before each new show. I have a great team working with me. About eighty-five people work at the Moon River Theatre in one capacity or another, and every one of them, from the parking lot attendants to the theater manager, goes out of his or her way to make the audience's experience an enjoyable one from the moment they are greeted by the parking lot attendant to the final curtain of the show.

The only real problem I've ever experienced in Branson was a health concern. For years I had been following a dietary regimen that I'd been introduced to at the Pritikin Longevity Center in Santa Monica, California. Its founder, Nathan Pritikin, became interested in nutrition when, still very young, he was diagnosed with arteriosclerosis. His arteries were over 90 percent blocked, and he was not given long to live. He began reading about the parts of the world where people tended to live to a ripe old age — all of them Third World countries — and he came up with the theory that a diet of grains, fruits, and vegetables and very little if any fat would prolong life. He cured himself with that diet and was able to clear his arteries completely of all the built-up plaque. With that success he set up the Pritikin Longevity Center to spread his message.

I started going to the Longevity Center in Santa Monica, and on my first visit I remained a month. It was an almost monastic existence, staying in a very plain and simple room and eating a very basic diet of grains, legumes, vegetables, and fruits, with no alcohol or coffee. There were also daily classes to learn about what you should and shouldn't eat. By the end of those four weeks, I was practically brainwashed. I wouldn't dream of eating a piece of meat, eggs, any dairy products, or anything containing fat.

For six or seven years I followed that regimen religiously; I would even take my own food with me when I went on tour. All was well until one day in Branson when I couldn't get out of my chair because I was so weak. I had bleeding ulcers and was so anemic that my doctors thought I might die. I hardly had a red corpuscle in my body. They couldn't even go into my stomach to deal with the ulcers because they were afraid I wouldn't make it through the anesthetic. I had a series of blood transfusions that kept me alive, and then my doctor told me, "You've got to start eating some meat. Eat plenty of spinach and beets and anything else with iron in it, but you've got to eat some red meat."

So I started eating meat again, and I've continued ever since — and so far I'm still here. Later we found that my ulcers were the kind that resulted from bacteria, and powerful antibiotics have cleared them up for good. So now the ulcers are gone and should never come back. Lucky me.

17

With my diet and my health back to normal, I've continued to perform onstage well past the age at which most other singers have hung up their microphones. I'm sure every performer has a different way of preparing himself for a show, but the way I do hasn't changed in decades. I don't know if it's still a faint echo of my dad's "work harder; you're not as good as them" mantra, but I can't walk straight off the golf course and onto the stage and start performing. Glen Campbell can turn up a few minutes before the curtain goes up, go onstage, and do a great show, but I have to get mentally ready.

I do that by spending some time alone, going through my act in my mind, and visualizing it, just like top golfers visualize a shot before they play it, and I get psyched up by that.

I always take a nap before a show, even if only for twenty minutes. Then I take a shower, and all that time I'm visualizing the show. I don't warm up my voice very much. When I'm in the shower — everyone sings in the shower, don't they? — I'll do some high notes and low notes, just to make sure they're all there, and I'll do some moos like a cow, because that really gets the vocal chords warmed up. The vocal chords are muscles, so they need that sort of preparation, like an athlete stretching before a race.

My dresser, Billie, comes in five minutes before the show. I get into my show clothes, pick up a hand microphone that the sound engineer leaves in its place next to the dressing room door, and I'm ready.

I don't have any superstitions — odd socks, lucky mascots, or any of those kinds of things — but I do have one ritual: The last thing I do before I go onstage is check my fly. There are few things more embarrassing than realizing halfway through your act that your fly is open. By the time I've done all this, I'm raring to go out there and perform.

Some audiences are more responsive than others. A really good audience always has a few people who start all the whooping and hollering, and then everyone else feels able to join in. I've known performers who have even "seeded" the audience with a few exhibition laughers and clappers to get things going, though I've never done that myself. Audiences don't owe you anything, and even if a particular audience is very quiet, experience has taught me not to let it bother me. I just try to enjoy the show as much as I can, and I know that even if there's no shouting or cheering, when you talk to people afterward, you often find that they had just as good a time as the people the night before who were going crazy. They just have a different, more restrained way of showing it.

If you want a standing ovation every night, you can get one. Play "God Bless America" and unfurl a giant Stars and Stripes, and the audience is on its feet. That isn't the way that I want to go; I prefer to take my standing ovations when they occur naturally. When everything clicks and the audience has had a great evening, there's a surge of pure pleasure in seeing them spontaneously rise to their feet to salute the people who have given them such a good time — and the Andy Williams Show is very far from a one-man show. There is a ten-piece orchestra, a co-star, and a dozen dancers and singers before we even start counting the stage crew.

I used to see Frank Sinatra often at the Sands, and at times he was brilliant. He would pick out individuals in the audience and sing to them, and they gave him the sort of feedback that helped him, and when he was "on" he was terrific. However, I don't visualize and plan the show to the point where I know I'm going to move to a particular point on the stage and pick out someone in row one and sing a song to her. The stage lights allow one to see only the people in the front few rows, but I try not to play to them all the time because there are an awful lot of people farther back who want to feel part of the show, too. I have a song list that I have to follow, but I'm out there to have fun, so in and around that I'll just do whatever seems right at that particular moment. If I'm having a good time, I figure that the audience is having a good time, too.

Sometimes you'll get a bit of friendly banter going with an audience member, but at others you'll encounter someone — and he's inevitably right in the front row — who clearly doesn't like you at all and is sitting there sullenly, as if to say, "So you think you're so great. Show me what you've got." Why such people bother to come to the show at all is beyond me, but it does bother me; it shouldn't, but it does. As Bill Cosby once said to me as he came offstage, "That guy in the front row who didn't clap and never even cracked a smile. That guy's driving me crazy."

"But what about the other two thousand?"

"I know, I know," he said. "But that guy's the one I think about."

When the show is over, I take off my makeup immediately and change clothes, and then I'll either go across to the Moon River Grill and have dinner or I'll head directly home. I'll have a glass of wine with Debbie and something light to eat, and by the time we've done that, Debbie is usually more tired than I am because she's been out at her ranch all day. So we'll usually just go to bed and talk and watch television for a while before going to sleep.

I'm not a good sleeper, but however badly I sleep, I'm always up very early — 5:30 or 6:00. I love it at that time of day, so quiet and still and with the dew on the ground and the fog still hanging over the lake. I take a half-hour walk, and when I get back, I have breakfast with Debbie. By 9:00 I'll be in my office at the theater, ready for another day.

Debbie and I lived in a condo while we were building the theater, but once that was finished, we started planning a house. I used Ted Grenzback, who had done some remodeling of my home in La Quinta and also designed my apartment in New York. He designed a home for us in Country French style on a beautiful tree-fringed site we had found that had a golf course on one side and Lake Taneycomo on the other. The façade of the house is clad in Aspen river rock. I asked Claudine to source some Colorado water-rounded stones, and she had them trucked down for me. The fireplace in the living room is also faced with the same material. The living room is light and airy, with high ceilings and floor-to-ceiling windows looking out over the lake. We have some of our favorite art in the house — including the Hans Hofmann painting that I bought in Chicago forty years ago and still love as much now — and part of my collection of Americana, including some beautiful old weather vanes.

I had a craftsman carpenter, Stanley Rose, make a white pine fireplace mantel and bookshelves in the library, and I hung my favorite Jean Dubuffet painting, *Affaires et Loisirs,* over the fireplace. It's the last thing I look at every night before I go to bed, and on a neighboring wall is a small jewel-like Picasso. Debbie has her office on the lower level, and there's a state-of-the-art gym that she equipped.

We don't encourage too many visitors to the house, and we don't even have a guest bedroom. Friends and family stay in a nearby condo so that they have their privacy and we have ours. During the day they are at our house, but they sleep in their own quarters, and it really works out better that way for them and for us. Because I live a very public life the rest of the time, the house has become my refuge where I can kick off my shoes, relax, and unwind. The house is completely private, and its rear windows and terraces look out across the lake to a beautiful tree-clad hillside that is so steep it could never be built on. In the fall it's a gorgeous sight as all the leaves on the trees turn yellow, orange, and red. There is a sheltered sculpture garden at one side of the house and grounds big enough to let our dogs run free — we have three, all rescued from animal refuges. We can play golf, fish for trout in the lake, or just stroll around, breathing that sweet mountain air. It's heaven.

Debbie has always loved horses and the outdoor life and we've bought a ranch a few miles out of town, which she is in the process of renovating. She raises cattle and horses and is building a caretaker's house, a barn, and a cutting pen where the horses practice herding cattle and cutting one out of the herd. Debbie loves it and is out there practically every day when we're in Branson.

We live in Branson in the summer and autumn, and in winter and spring we're in our house in La Quinta near Palm Springs. I remembered how Bob Hope felt after he built his big house and moved out of the little one that he loved by the airport. Rather than move to a larger, grander place, we still live in our modest little house, but it now has floor-to-ceiling windows that look out over the terrace, surrounded by orange, lemon, and palm trees, and across the lake between the ninth and eighteenth fairways of the golf course, to the wall of the mountains rising sheer from the desert floor. I never tire of the view. The mountains seem to change constantly as the light shifts, strengthens, and fades in the course of the day. At times, just after dawn when the rising sun reddens the rock, they seem close enough to touch; at others, shimmering in the heat haze, they seem to fade into blue-tinted distant mirages hovering over the desert.

I used to love Los Angeles and New York — they were exciting and full of energy — but I don't feel the same buzz now. They're too busy and noisy, and the traffic drives me crazy. I like to visit for a couple of weeks to see friends and catch some exhibitions and shows, but I certainly don't want to live there. I'm always glad to get back to Branson or La Quinta.

Branson has been transformed in the years that I've been here, and I'm proud to have played a part in that. It now calls itself, with some justification, "the live music capital of the world," but others, less kindly, call it "Las Vegas for people who don't like sex or gambling" or, as Bart Simpson described it, "Vegas if it was run by Ned Flanders." The whole town runs on entertainment; if the concept doesn't curdle your coffee, you can even be serenaded by singing waiters while you're eating your breakfast in a diner at seven o'clock in the morning.

Seven million people now visit the town every year to see one or more of the many shows. Of all American attractions, only Disneyland, Las Vegas, and Hawaii draw more visitors. In our first year there, 1992, the Branson season ran from only May 1 to November 1, and the town really didn't come alive again until the following May. I felt we could do well with a Christmas show, however, and now, sixteen years later, Christmas is the busiest time of the year, not just for the Moon River Theatre but for every theater in town. The season starts in April and runs until mid-December.

Not everybody does well in Branson. You have to know the audience and tailor your material to suit it. Wayne Newton opened a theater here; he's a big Vegas star and does everything in a grand way. He leased a farm about fifteen or twenty miles out of town, and a helicopter flew him to the theater every day and landed on its roof, Hollywood style. Right from the start he did his Vegas act, and what plays well in Vegas doesn't necessarily play well in Branson. He stayed about a year and then cut his losses and returned to Vegas, where he still is a big star.

There was a price to pay for my making the move to Branson, but it was one I was willing to pay. By going there I cut myself off from the mainstream media concentrated on the East and West coasts, and although the Moon River Theatre was packed every night, I began to fade from the wider public consciousness. Other singers, such as Tony Bennett, have continued to tour and have prolonged their careers that way, but it was not what I wanted to do. Even if the mainstream American media and some of the American public have forgotten me — some probably even think I died — I chose my own road and have never had a second's regret about doing so.

I had resigned myself to disappearing from the radar everywhere except Branson, but in 1998 something extraordinary happened. I had always done well in Britain; my television show had been very popular there, and in addition to worldwide hits such as "Can't Get Used to Losing You," "Happy Heart," and the theme from *Love Story,* I had had Top 10 singles in the United Kingdom with such tracks as "Almost There," "Can't Help Falling in Love," "Home Lovin' Man," and "Solitaire" that barely made the U.S. charts at all.

Neil Sedaka had originally written and recorded "Solitaire" but it hadn't done much for him. I loved the song but didn't like the part of the lyrics that compared love to a game of cards, which stirred uneasy memories in me of Wink Martindale's bizarre hit "Deck of Cards," and I really didn't feel comfortable singing them. So the album producer, Richard Perry, and I sat down and changed some of the words. The song was released as a single and, understandably, when Neil heard it, he wasn't happy.

His anger must have subsided a little when the rewritten song became a smash hit for me in the United Kingdom — the album also went gold — and his composer's royalty checks began rolling in. It was never a hit for me in the States, but when the Carpenters covered the song — also using the new lyrics, not Neil's originals — it became an even bigger smash there. And Neil never complained to me about the change of lyrics again.

Even after my record sales began to slip in the United States, my fans in Britain remained very loyal. I had another half-dozen U.K. Top 10 albums in the 1970s alone: *Can't Help Falling in Love, Home Lovin' Man, Solitaire, The Way We Were,* and *Reflections.* Then in 1998 a car company in the United Kingdom, Peugeot, used my record of "Can't Take My Eyes Off You," which I had recorded many years before, in a commercial on British television. Teenagers loved the commercial and asked radio stations to play the song. They had no idea who the hell I was — they were just kids and had probably never even heard of me — but they responded to the record. Sony re-released it, and it became an even bigger hit than the first time around.

It later had another new lease on life after someone got hold of a clip of my singing the song as the sound track to a commercial showing a very beautiful woman slowly and sensuously putting on her stockings. At the end of the song there's a knock on my hotel door, and there she is. We embrace, and the scene fades to black. Someone found it and posted it on YouTube, where it had well over a million hits.

The success of the commercial may have prompted other advertising agencies to have a look at my back catalog, because a year later "Music to Watch Girls By" was chosen as the sound track for a commercial, *Spirito di Punto,* for the Fiat Punto car. People loved the story line of a young woman getting increasingly angry as her boyfriend ogles a succession of beautiful women while they're driving down the street in her car. Finally, she pulls up, beckons to a passing hunk, and "kisses the face off him," as they say in England, just to teach her boyfriend a lesson. It was a very well done commercial and very charming.

I featured a reworked filmed version of it, *Spirito di Andy,* in my 2008 stage act. We filmed the new sections in Kansas City using a similar car and an American actress who was a near-double of the original, and it's so skillfully edited and montaged that you really can't see where the commercial ends and the unauthorized version begins. In the new version when the woman pulls up and beckons, I appear, give her a passionate kiss, pull away, and then come back and kiss her again, even more passionately. I just couldn't seem to get it right. We had to do take after take after take; I never knew making commercials could be so much fun.

I still didn't think we had done quite enough with it, so we reworked the final scene as well. In the original the car pulls up at a traffic light, and the boyfriend studiously ignores another very beautiful woman in the car alongside them. In the reworked version I now appear in an Alfa Romeo Spyder; the young woman jumps out of her car, abandoning her boyfriend, and drives off into the sunset with me. Now that's what I call a commercial! It still cracks me up when I see it, and audiences love it.

Just as had occurred a year earlier as soon as the commercial started airing, the switchboards at Fiat UK lit up with people calling to ask, "What's that song, who's that singing, and where can we buy it?" The song had charted in 1967 but now was hastily re-released as a single and became an even bigger hit than "Can't Take My Eyes Off You."

As a result of all this, a British tour was arranged that was completely sold out, but one night while performing in Branson before leaving for Britain, I developed a very bad case of laryngitis. There were two thousand people in the audience waiting for the show, and I thought, *I can't just cancel the show when many of these people have come a long way to see me.* So I went ahead with it. I had to strain a lot, and halfway through the show I knew that I'd damaged my throat. I told myself, *I'll be fine tomorrow,* but the next day I wasn't fine at all. I had no choice but to cancel a number of shows, and I was beginning to get really alarmed. My throat didn't hurt much, but if I talked or sang, it sounded as if I had been gargling with gravel.

I went to a throat specialist. He examined me, making the noncommittal noises doctors use on such occasions, and then sat me down in a chair and studied me for a minute over the top of his half-moon spectacles. "It's not good news, Mr. Williams," he said at last. "I've discovered a node, a swelling, on your vocal chords." He paused again and put the tips of his fingers together. "Now, it can be surgically removed, and that's the course of treatment I would recommend. I believe there is an excellent chance of success. However" — once more there was a long pause — "if the operation does not go as well as I hope, you may never sing again and possibly never even talk above a whisper."

He claimed that the risk of that happening was not great, but his assurances did not sound good enough for me. I decided that it was not a risk I was willing to take without exploring every other option first. I thanked him and said I needed some time to think about it, but as I drove away, I was absolutely horrified. What was I going to do if I couldn't sing or appear onstage, the thing I had hated for years but now loved? It was an integral part of my life, and now I might never do it again.

I remembered that Julie Andrews had had a similar problem with her throat, and I knew her well enough to call and ask her advice. Julie suggested that I speak to a specialist named Gerald Burke at UCLA. When I went to see him, he examined me and then asked, "Can you take the next three months off?" I replied, "Hey, I can do anything if I don't have to have surgery."

"Okay, why don't you just rest your throat and talk as little as possible. I'll take another look in three months' time."

So I went home, played golf, watched the sun come up and go down, and didn't sing a note for three months. I barely even spoke, so concerned was I about my voice. When I went back to see him, he examined my throat and said, "The node has gone down about half. Do you have to work at the moment?"

"Well, no, not really."

"Well, if you can keep resting your voice for another couple of months, we'll take another look then."

I cancelled every booking I had and continued to play golf. After another three months the node had disappeared completely. I rested my voice for a while longer just to be sure, and then gradually began testing it. I found that it was absolutely fine, as good as it had always been.

Once I was fully recovered, I flew to Britain for the postponed tour. I knew that "Can't Take My Eyes Off You" and "Music to Watch Girls By" had been big hits, but I was not expecting the reaction when I went onstage at the first concert in Belfast. It was unbelievable, like stepping back thirty years to when I had a number-one hit with "Butterfly," only this time half the audience was about sixteen years old and the other half sixty.

For a long time I'd had the image of being a wholesome, clean-cut, all-American boy; I was even described as "a farm boy in a tuxedo." I didn't feel that was me at all, but the label stuck, and in some ways I've never been able to shake it off. Now, suddenly, the wrong side of seventy, I had apparently become a sex symbol for the first time. It was weird: Andy Williams, seventy-year-old lounge lizard, and women even threw panties onstage! I had never had that kind of reaction before, though that might have been partly due to the material I sang. Andy Williams crooning "Danny Boy" didn't have quite the raunch factor of Tom Jones belting out "Sex Bomb."

I also made two tours to Asia, where I was likewise blown away by the crowds. There were lines for tickets stretching around the block at every theater where I appeared in Japan, Korea, Malaysia, Thailand, Singapore, Taipei, and the Philippines. I found that even though I had moved to Branson, I hadn't been forgotten after all.

The same enthusiasm greated me when I toured Britain again the following year; every concert, including London's Royal Albert Hall, was again sold out weeks in advance. It is amazing what a hit record can do for a sagging career! A couple of years later I had a hit for the third time when Marks & Spencer used "The Most Wonderful Time of the Year" as the theme music for its Christmas advertisements. Originally released in 1963, it promptly charted again.

18

During the years since the Williams Brothers broke up, I had performed with my brothers only on the Christmas specials of my television series. My brothers have all done very well in their own careers, and the only one who I feel may have some regrets, not about my success but that he didn't roll the dice once more himself, is Dick. He has had a great career as a studio singer and arranger, and he decided that he didn't want to pursue a solo career because he wanted to spend more time at home with his wife and children. I do wonder, however, if he doesn't sometimes ponder the "what might have been," though he's never told me as much, and I suspect he'd deny it if I asked him.

I have also pondered the consequences of the decisions I made all those years ago. Sometimes, seeing one or the other of my brothers at home with their families, I've felt a twinge of envy. I don't regret the path

I took in life, and have so much to be thankful for, but I'm also aware that the career I chose meant I missed out on many precious moments in my own children's young lives — Christmas Nativity plays, school concerts, softball games, and even birthdays — for which no amount of money or success can ever compensate.

We all lead separate lives and have settled in different places, so my brothers and I don't see as much of one another as we'd like. One reunion in 2002 was very special; it also brought my life full circle. I hadn't been back to Wall Lake, Iowa, since we left it when I was in the third grade. Then my brothers and I were invited back there to celebrate the restoration of our former house to its original condition. The townspeople did all the work themselves and put up a plaque commemorating it as THE BIRTHPLACE AND CHILDHOOD HOME OF ANDY WILLIAMS. When I arrived there for the ceremony, I found that my former schoolmates — all now in their seventies — were lined up wearing T-shirts printed with their names and photographs of themselves when they were kids.

Like most places, the house had been extended and altered over the years, but the townspeople had pulled down the additions and stripped off the newer materials, such

494

as aluminum siding and plastic drainpipes, replacing them with the traditional materials they had recycled from somewhere. The house looked identical to the way it was when we lived there. It has become a local tourist attraction, and I'm glad that indirectly I've helped put a little back into that small community where it all began for me.

Sadly, Bob's wife, Edna — the girlfriend from Wall Lake who had followed him to Des Moines and Chicago, married him, and shared his life — died in 1997, and then Bob, living alone, began to suffer from dementia. His house at his ranch had always been spotless, but now there was a thick layer of dust on the shelves and tables, and piles of unwashed dishes in the sink. We also suspected that he wasn't eating proper meals. He had bad days and good days, but on the bad ones he didn't even recognize us.

We were all concerned about him and wanted him to have some regular help, someone who would look in on him just to make sure he was all right, cook his meals, clean his house, and generally keep an eye on him. One day the three of us — Dick, Don, and I — went to see him to persuade him to do so. We knew it wouldn't be easy because Bob was a stubborn and fiercely independent man and would fight us tooth and nail, refusing to do anything we asked. He had a negative answer for every one of our arguments.

Don, the brother closest in age to Bob, went first. "Bob," he said, "we were thinking you could use a little help around the house."

"I don't need anyone," was the instant reply.

"We know that, but wouldn't it be good just to have someone come and make lunch and a good dinner for you?"

"No. I don't need anyone. I've always looked after myself."

"But, Bob, you're not eating properly. You're just eating chips and pretzels. Wouldn't you like to have some proper meals cooked for you?"

"No," he said. "I've always eaten chips and pretzels."

Don shrugged and turned to Dick, who took up the dialogue. "You could use a little help with the cleaning, couldn't you?"

Bob still wasn't giving an inch. "I don't need any help."

"But the place is getting awfully dirty."

"It's always been dirty," he said.

Finally, I came up with what I thought was the clincher: "Bob, you're pooping in your pants."

"I always did," he said.

Even though it was such a sad and serious situation, this was so funny that we all collapsed in fits of laughter, and even Bob joined in. We sat with him for the rest of the afternoon, talking and joking about the old days, and then we began singing some of the songs we used to do back in Iowa all those years before. Before long Bob was harmonizing with us. It was a wonderful moment. This man who couldn't remember the names of his brothers and his children was suddenly recalling every word of songs we hadn't sung for fifty years. We ran through every one we could remember, but when we finished, the spark in Bob's eyes began to fade again, and he retreated into his private world.

It was the last time we were all together. Bob died a few months later, but amid the sadness at losing a brother, I'm glad that I had as my last memory of him that laughter- and music-filled afternoon when for just a few hours we were the Williams Brothers again.

On Sunday, December 2, 2007, the day before my eightieth birthday, Debbie told me that some acts from Vegas were appearing in the ballroom at the Chateau on the Lake Resort in Branson. I was looking forward to a quiet night at home with a nice dinner and a glass of wine, but Debbie insisted we go. "It'll be a chance to see some acts that you might want in your show next year," she said. "We don't have to stay for dinner. We can just watch the acts and then come home."

When we got there, the hotel parking lot was full, and although the bar and restaurant seemed strangely quiet, I didn't think anything of it. We walked down the corridor to the ballroom, which was dark and apparently deserted. "Come on," I said, "it must have been cancelled. Let's go home." Then suddenly the lights went on, and 250 people waiting in the room all yelled, "Surprise!" I nearly didn't make it to my eightieth birthday because the shock almost killed me, but it turned out to be the most memorable night of my life. Debbie had spent months organizing the party — even our dogs were sworn to secrecy — and my family and friends had come from all over the world to be there. My son Christian and his wife, Cassie, and their children had flown up from Costa Rica. Noelle and her family, and Bobby and his new wife, Mystica, were all there, along with friends from every place I'd been and every era of my life; I don't think Branson had ever seen a lineup like it before!

Charo kicked things off by doing a breathy

Marilyn-Monroe-to-JFK-style "Happy Birthday, Mr. Williams." Ethel Kennedy never gives speeches — she hates doing so and turns down every request — but she made a speech that night that left me with tears in my eyes. She finished by saying, "That's my Ode to Joy and to Andy, which is basically the same thing." There were also filmed messages from many other friends, including John Glenn, who welcomed me to the "over-eighties group," and Arnold Palmer, who told me how nice it was to know there was still someone around even older than him.

There were birthday greetings, too, from Ann-Margret, the first President Bush and Barbara, the governor of Missouri, and Roy Blunt, a Republican member of the House of Representatives who had arranged to have a flag flown over the Capitol in Washington in my honor. A 140-strong choir from Texas, the Vocal Majority, sang "Happy Birthday," but even they were outnumbered by the entire Osmond extended family — 350 of them at the last count — who had come together and filmed themselves singing "Happy Birthday" to me. Finally, Debbie made a beautiful speech; she had had to record it because she was too shy to deliver it live in front of all those people. It really touched me, and I was in tears once more. She ended by saying, "And one more thing: May I have this dance?" The orchestra struck up "Moon River," and we did a slow waltz around the room. It was a wonderful night and one I'll never forget.

As I look back over my life, I realize more and more that one of the most important things about achieving success is that famous dictum of Winston Churchill's, "Never give up. Never give up," and, as Churchill also said, "When you're going through hell, keep going." You've got to be good enough, but while some of it is luck and timing, it is also being ready when opportunity comes along. Almost everybody gets at least one chance somewhere along the line, but many aren't ready to seize it and so miss their big opportunity. And even if you're not good enough the first time — like the Williams Brothers in our first audition at WHO in Des Moines — it doesn't mean you won't be good enough the next time.

The goal should never be to be successful so you can be rich and famous. It has to be about wanting to be the very best you can in whatever your chosen field might be. If you want to be a movie star rather than a good actor, then you're in the wrong business.

Likewise, talent isn't enough on its own — there are a lot of talented people on Skid Row. You must have grit and drive and determination to go with it. All that and a slice of luck, too. There may be times when you want to pack it all in, but as Kay Thompson told me all those years ago, you have to stick to it. You can't give up. Most "overnight sensations" have paid their dues with years on the road before they get their lucky break.

I have been very lucky in my life, and I've tried to give something back for those less fortunate. My father had very bad asthma, and having experienced his suffering firsthand, I was for many years closely involved with the Asthma Foundation — fund-raising, donating money, and becoming national chairman for a while. After Bobby Kennedy's death I was also involved in the Bobby Kennedy Foundation. I also support the Society of Singers, a charity that helps singers and their families who have fallen on hard times. Many, many very successful singers in their day were so screwed by agents, managers, or record companies, and sometimes all three, that they are virtually destitute.

Anytime I can help public libraries, I will, but the charity with which I'm now most closely involved is the Boys and Girls Club. They offer a place where kids can go to get off the street and use the Internet, learn things, take gym classes, and so on. I think the group does wonderful work, especially in deprived inner-city areas where often the only alternative is hanging out on the street. I support them any way I can.

Just as my dad predicted all those years ago when he told us that if we worked hard, one day our names would be immortalized outside Grauman's Chinese Theatre in Hollywood, my Walk of Fame star is now set in the sidewalk at 6667 Hollywood Boulevard, just a few blocks from Grauman's. I also helped restore an even more iconic Hollywood symbol to its former glory, paying for the replacement letter *W* in the 1987 restoration of the famous Hollywood sign. (Bob Newhart was also asked to buy a letter but said he would do it only if they changed the name to Hollynood!)

President Ronald Reagan was once kind enough to describe my voice as "a national treasure," and I've also had the accolade that every entertainer craves above all others: an appearance on *The Simpsons*. It turns out that the show's resident bully, Nelson Muntz, is an Andy Williams fan. In the episode "Bart on the Road," in which Bart obtains a credit card, hires a car, and hits the road with his friends, Nelson forces them to stop in Branson so that he can see me in concert. He then bursts into tears of joy when I sing "Moon River." To quote the tear-stained Nelson: "I didn't think he was going to sing 'Moon River,' and then BAM! Second encore!"

Perhaps my most cherished honor, however, because, uniquely, it is voted on only by my peers in the Society of Singers, is the Ella, the lifetime achievement award named in honor of the great Ella Fitzgerald. The award was presented to me in 2008 at a ceremony at the Beverly Hilton Hotel in Beverly Hills. The sixteen previous recipients, including Ella, of course, as well as Johnny Mathis, Tony Bennett, Elton John, Frank Sinatra, Barbra Streisand, and Barry Manilow, constitute a roll call of show business greats, and to be named alongside them was the ultimate accolade for me.

Debbie, my children, and my brothers and their families were all with me, sitting at a dais in the middle of the room, and there was quite a lineup of entertainment. Several singers did versions of some of my past hits. Petula Clark sang "Happy Heart," Glen Campbell did "Hawaiian Wedding Song," Henry Mancini's daughter, Monica, sang "Dear Heart," and Barry Manilow did "Born Free." Barry then made a movingly flattering speech, saying, "I wouldn't be here at all if it wasn't for Andy Williams. I used to copy absolutely everything he did — the key changes, the endings, everything. He was just the biggest influence I ever had."

Then I had to get up and sing, and faced with an audience of my peers, I was a little apprehensive before I started. Sometimes you can get away with a bum note or two in front of a normal audience, but not this one: They were all singers and musicians. They also showed a film of me back in the 1960s, singing "Do-Re-Mi" with Bobby Darin and Eddie Fisher. Eddie had one of the biggest voices I ever heard, and Bobby had impeccable timing and a great way with a song. He was huge fun to work with; we always laughed our way through rehearsals. It was a very complicated number to sing — it took us six days to rehearse it — and when the clip of our performance ended, people were standing up and cheering this number from forty years ago. As the Emmy award–winning producer and director George Schlatter said, "You just don't see stuff like that on television anymore; no one is willing to spend the time to learn how to do it."

It was a wonderful, memorable evening spent in the company of people I've known in some cases for fifty years and more, and if that was the curtain call for my career, then it was a great way to go . . . except that I'm not quite finished yet. And even more important than any success or awards I've been lucky enough to achieve, I've been blessed with a wonderful family and true friends who have been there through the bad times as well as the good.

I had great success in my career, but, more important, I found great personal contentment since moving to Branson with Debbie seventeen years ago. I've rediscovered the pure pleasure of being an entertainer that I had lost for a while, long ago. I haven't given any thought to retiring. As long as I'm singing well, I see no reason to stop. When my time is up, I'm expecting to leave the stage for the last time in a wooden box.

Those of us who perform and record or make movies and television shows are seen and heard by people over and over again. In a small way we become part of their lives, and the legacy of our work gives us some sort of immortality, if only in flickering black-and-white-films and television reruns on obscure cable channels. If I'm remembered at all, I hope to be thought of as a good man who brought much joy to many people, but above all I want to be remembered for my music. Whatever happens to me, I hope the music lives on. And finally, I'm beginning to accept the fact that maybe I really am as good as the others after all.

ACKNOWLEDGMENTS

First of all, I want to thank my son, Bobby, who introduced me to Mark Lucas and Alice Saunders at the Lucas Alexander Whitley literary agency in London. I thank Mark for introducing me to Neil Hanson, who worked on the book with me at my home in La Quinta, California, and Branson, Missouri. My thanks, too, to editor and publisher Alan Samson, Lisa Milton, Lucinda McNeile, Rebecca Gray, and the team at Weidenfeld and Nicolson at Orion Publishing in London for their encouragement and their decision to publish the book.

I also want to thank David Forrer and Kim Witherspoon at Inkwell Management in New York who, as my literary agents in the United States, connected me with Clare Ferraro, Rick Kot, and their colleagues at Viking in New York. I thank them for their belief in the book and for publishing it in the United States.

I also owe a debt of gratitude to my friend Keats Tyler, my former assistant, who was with me during the ten years of my television series, and the following ten years. He reminded me of some things that I had forgotten — his memory is sometimes better than mine. The book couldn't have been completed without the contribution of my current assistant, Judy Donohue. I also thank my Aunt Cornelia — many years ago I sat down with a tape recorder and asked her to tell me all about my mom and dad's early years — and my brothers Bob, Don, and Dick, who were responsible for much of the content of this book.

Thank you also to those who were important in my career: Kay Thompson, for guiding and teaching me so much; Steve Allen, for giving me the opportunity to be a regular on his nightly *Tonight Show;* Archie Bleyer, who started my recording career; and Goddard Lieberson, who brought me into Columbia Records.

Thank you to those friends who have become so important in my life over the years: Jerry Perenchio, Pierre Cossette, and Billy Pearson; and my lawyer Larry Kartiganer, who has been with me the past forty years.

I thank Claudine and my children, Noelle, Christian, and Bobby, who were such an important part of my life. And finally my love and gratitude to Debbie, my wife for the last eighteen years, who unselfishly made the move to Branson, Missouri, with me, and helped me build a life there that has been so fulfilling and wonderful. She is my "OAO."

The last chapter of my life is still to come.

ABOUT THE AUTHOR

Andy Williams has been one of the world's best-loved vocalists and entertainers since he began his professional career nearly seventy years ago. Known as the King of Hearts, the Emperor of Easy, and Mr. Moon River, he divides his time between La Quinta, California, and Branson, Missouri.

We hope you have enjoyed this Large Print book. Other Thorndike, Wheeler, Kennebec, and Chivers Press Large Print books are available at your library or directly from the publishers.

For information about current and upcoming titles, please call or write, without obligaton, to:

Publisher
Thorndike Press
295 Kennedy Memorial Drive
Waterville, ME 04901
Tel. (800) 223-1244

or visit our Web site at:

http://gale.cengage.com/thorndike

OR

Chivers Large Print
published by BBC Audiobooks Ltd
St. James House, The Square
Lower Bristol Road
Bath BA2 3SB
England
Tel. +44(0) 800 136919
email: bbcaudiobooksbbc.co.uk
www.bbcaudiobooks.co.uk

All our Large Print titles are designed for easy reading, and all our books are made to last.